D1520944

Culture and Customs
of the Choctaw Indians

Culture and Customs
of the Choctaw Indians

DONNA L. AKERS, PH.D.

Culture and Customs of Native Peoples in America

Tom Holm, Series Editor

 GREENWOOD

AN IMPRINT OF ABC-CLIO, LLC
Santa Barbara, California • Denver, Colorado • Oxford, England

Library of Congress Cataloging-in-Publication Data

Akers, Donna.
  Culture and customs of the Choctaw indians / Donna L. Akers.
      p. cm.
  Includes bibliographical references and index.
  ISBN 978-0-313-36401-3 (hardcopy : alk. paper) — ISBN 978-0-313-36402-0 (ebook)
1. Choctaw Indians—History.   2. Choctaw Indians—Social life and customs.   I. Title.
  E99.C8A42   2013
  976.004'97387—dc23   2012032912

ISBN: 978-0-313-36401-3
EISBN: 978-0-313-36402-0

17   16   15   14   13   1   2   3   4   5

This book is also available on the World Wide Web as an eBook.
Visit www.abc-clio.com for details.

Greenwood
An Imprint of ABC-CLIO, LLC

ABC-CLIO, LLC
130 Cremona Drive, P.O. Box 1911
Santa Barbara, California 93116-1911

This book is printed on acid-free paper ∞

Manufactured in the United States of America

Contents

Series Foreword   vii

Preface   xi

Introduction   xv

Chronology   xxiii

1   History of the Choctaws of the West   1

2   History of the Choctaws in the Deep South   51

3   Worldview and Spiritual Beliefs   61

4   Social Customs, Gender Roles, Family Life, and Children   73

5   Choctaw Oral Traditions   93

6   Choctaw Cuisine and Agriculture   115

7   Choctaw Arts, Ceremonies, and Festivals   129

8   Contemporary Issues   151

Selected Bibliography   169

Index   171

Series Foreword

SINCE THE 1960s, native and nonnative scholars have diligently sought to disassemble and understand the false and, frankly, harmful stereotypes and images of Native American peoples. Many Americans have recognized that stereotypes of indigenous people are not only often wrong, but have actually fostered adverse political and legal decisions and even sporadic and arbitrary attempts to have whole Native American communities eradicated. The steep and steady decline of the indigenous population, the dissolution of native governments, and the loss of culture and lands stem from an almost perverse lack of knowledge about Native American peoples.

Despite the dispossession of lands and many, many cultural features, Native American peoples have been astonishingly resilient. White Earth Anishinaabe author Gerald Vizenor, a word craftsman of no mean abilities and talents, coined the term "survivance" from the words "survival" and "resistance" to capture the twofold nature of why indigenous customs and cultures are still alive. The Greenwood Press series *Culture and Customs of Native Peoples in America* attempts not to cast aspersions on the motives, desires, and policies of the Europeans and Euro-Americans who colonized North America, but to highlight, especially to young people and a general audience, the beauty, knowledge, pride, and resiliency of the indigenous peoples of this land. "Survivance" is very real. Native Americans, as our authors show, are not extinct; nor have they become a single, relatively small U.S. ethnic group.

Rather, Native Americans are here today as members of many indigenous nation-states that have utterly unique relationships with the United States.

Today, the federal government recognizes 562 American Indian and Native Alaskan tribes and communities that are self-governing and hold certain sovereign rights and powers. More than 1 million people are citizens or members of these nation-states. Nearly 4.5 million people in the United States claim some degree of American Indian or Alaska Native racial heritage.

Most Americans do not quite understand that Native American sovereignty relates specifically to the survival of tribal cultures. When the Europeans came to North American shores, there were hundreds of indigenous peoples, each group with its own territorial boundaries, distinct language, religious customs, and ceremonial cycles attuned to the place in which they lived, and a unique and sacred history. All had developed governing bodies that maintained order within and could raise military forces to protect and defend their territories. Each was, therefore, sovereign, but each had different forms of governance, whether by council, kingship, or priesthood. Nearly all of the native nation-states based their social organization on kinship.

The European colonists came for land and human and natural resources. At first, they attempted to displace the indigenous nation-states or enter into largely unequal and oftentimes destructive trade relationships. Very many Native Americans perished as a result of new, pandemic diseases that were endemic to European populations. Native nations were also caught up in a series of colonial wars that led to further depopulation.

In an effort to end violence and bring about stability, native nations entered into a series of treaties with foreign powers. When the United States emerged from the stew of colonialism, it continued the treaty-making policies in order to expand its eminent domain from coast to coast. Of course, numerous terrible wars resulted from this policy, but for the most part, native nations and the United States maintained the relationships they created in the treaty-making process. Native nations lost territory, and many were displaced from their homelands, but 562 of them have maintained what has been called limited sovereignty. What this means is that although native nation-states have certainly lost some of their powers as sovereigns, they have maintained the rights of taxation, territorial integrity, determination of citizenship, and cultural sovereignty. Despite the fact that the U.S. government has violated nearly every one of their treaties with the native nations, the treaties established today's general guarantee that native peoples can continue as autonomous cultural entities with the ability to change or adapt on their own terms. This is only one of the reasons that native peoples assert their sovereignty rather than simply become assimilated into the general U.S. society.

Another indigenous people, the Native Hawaiians, were treated similarly. The descendants of Native Hawaiians number more than 4 million people. Their own nation-state, established over all the islands by King Kamehameha the Great in 1810, was undermined and finally usurped in 1893. Queen Lili'uokalani was actually imprisoned and replaced by a ruling cabal of businessmen and plantation owners. For a time, these men ruled the islands as "the Republic of Hawaii." In 1898, the United States annexed the islands, and the territory eventually became a state of the union in 1959. Since then, Native Hawaiians have adapted their customs and culture to ensure their survival. Cultural traditions have multiplied and the native language has been preserved in place names, ceremonies, and in a number of households.

The *Culture and Customs of Native Peoples in America* series hopes to serve as an exploration of the vibrant cultures and intriguing customs of several North American indigenous groups, from religious practice and folklore to traditional costumes and cuisine. It is an enjoyable and stimulating journey.

Tom Holm
Tucson, Arizona

Preface

THE HISTORY OF THE CHOCTAW PEOPLE is thousands of years old. Long
before Europeans crossed the Atlantic Ocean to North America, Choctaw
people had lived for hundreds of generations in their ancient homelands.
They passed down their ancient history from generation to generation, em-
phasizing the stories that taught about their belief system and the values they
held dear. Children learned about the importance of kinship and the values
of generosity and reciprocity and understood the place of humankind in the
greater world of plants and animals, rocks, and streams. Tens of thousands
of Choctaw people were born, came to adulthood, grew old, and died. Their
world was not a "New World," as the invading Europeans called it. It was a
wise and beautiful land that had sustained millions of indigenous peoples for
millennia.

In this book, the reader will come to understand that the story of the Choctaw
people is not a single story. Instead, it is made up of tens of thousands of
stories, reflecting the diversity of people who call themselves Choctaw. However, common bonds unite the Choctaw people, and a history in which the
United States infringed upon the autonomy and well-being of the Choctaw
Nation continues to be passed down in the oral traditions. Choctaw people
do not live in one geographical area. Originally, they all lived in what are
today the states of Mississippi and Alabama. However, during the 1830s,
under President Jackson, the Choctaw people were dispossessed, forced to
leave their homelands and go into permanent exile, and forced to give up

their homelands to invading white Americans. Some refused to leave and remained in hiding in Mississippi and Alabama, while the majority was forced upon the Trail Where We Cried, to what became the state of Oklahoma.

This book will show the results of this division of the Choctaw people into those who were driven out of their homelands, and those who remained behind. Of the latter, most were also forced off their land and out of their homes. They fled to nearby swamps and dense, rocky lands that incoming whites spurned. Continually harassed and often in fear for their lives for decades, these Choctaw had a starkly different experience from those who had traveled West into exile in Indian Territory.

The other major factor in the experiences of the Choctaw people lies in the degree to which they have adapted or rejected the belief systems and values of white America. Many Choctaws in Indian Territory were forced to assimilate after their lands were seized by the United States in the early 20th century. However, many of their relatives back in Mississippi rejected assimilation and strove mightily to remain apart from the white society. Although the racist views of many white Americans in the Deep South rejected the equality of Choctaw people and led them to commit many crimes and overt discrimination against Choctaw people that the federal and state governments tolerated, the Choctaws living in Mississippi and parts of other southern states maintained their distinctiveness as Choctaw people and passed their culture, heritage, and language down through each new generation.

This book begins with a Chronology, which lists the major events in Choctaw history from ancient times until the present. The Introduction follows with an overview of the Choctaw people. Chapter 1 gives a longer and more detailed history of the Choctaws. This chapter discusses how the Choctaw Nation and her people overcame enormous challenges perpetrated by Europeans and Euro-Americans, who wanted their lands, their wealth, and, eventually, simply wanted the Choctaws to vanish.

The Choctaws fought courageously to remain in their homelands. They even adopted a system of government and laws modeled on the values of the white society in an attempt to demonstrate that they should not be forced into exile on the basis of some sort of alleged savagery. Despite these efforts, President Andrew Jackson succeeded in passing the Indian Removal Act through Congress in 1830, and this bill resulted in about 18,000–20,000 Choctaws having to leave their homelands. An estimated 6,000–10,000 remained behind in the states of Mississippi and Alabama in hiding for many, many years.

The period of 1830 through the 1880s and the revival of self-sufficiency and even prosperity in the new Choctaw Nation in the West is presented, in the 50 years or so that the United States more or less left the Choctaws in relative peace. Chapter 2 tells of the persistence and determination of the thousands of Choctaw people who stayed in Mississippi and other areas in the South, who refused to go to the distant place of exile, yet who were made homeless and impoverished when whites took over their lands and farms and livestock. Left to gain sustenance from the swamps and other marginal land, these Choctaws courageously defied racism and bigotry for decades. Despite this suffering, and the many unnecessary hardships, the Choctaws who remained behind maintained their language, their traditional values, and triumphed over a shameful episode in American history.

Chapter 3 explores historical Choctaw belief systems and worldview and how these fundamental concepts have shaped the world of Choctaw people. The basis of this unique identity rests on several important concepts: first, that everything in the world—all people, plants, animals, and even inanimate objects—is interdependent on one another, in such a symbiosis that what affects one, affects all; second, that human beings are not privileged in these relationships, and are, indeed, dependent on them. Unlike white society's beliefs, mankind has no place at the top of a pyramid or hierarchy from which he can use or exploit the ecosystem and all other creatures and beings. Indeed, human beings are simply one of many entities that make up the great system of the world. Third are the concepts of harmony and balance, which, when achieved, form the basis of a world of order and predictability. Choctaw people traditionally believed that when harmony and balance are upset, the world will descend into a state of chaos and disaster. In traditional times, therefore, Choctaws strove to maintain balance between all things, and harmony in all relations.

The concept of spiritual power has always been important to traditional Choctaw people. Power, in this sense, refers to a belief that each person can tap into an unseen world of spiritual power, accessible through ritual and ceremony. In historical times, men tapped into this power when transforming themselves into warriors. Through dance, song, and ceremony, they transcended the roles of husband, son, and brother, and moved into the realm of the warrior. Today, Choctaw men continue to invoke power to prepare themselves for ball games.

Women, who were born with the spiritual power to create life, walked in power in their everyday lives. Nonetheless, they separated themselves from men during childbirth and menstruation, during which times their spiritual power was so strong that it did not mix well with that of men. Although beliefs in power have changed over time, many Choctaw men and woman continue to recognize the special strengths of men and women, and in many Choctaw homes today, women are still highly respected for their spiritual leadership, courage, and power. This chapter ends with a brief exploration of the effects of Christianity and the adaption of its teachings into the belief system of modern Choctaw people.

In Chapter 4, we examine family life in historical and contemporary Choctaw lives. We see how Choctaw kinship formed the bedrock of Choctaw life, and how Choctaws ordered their society around matrilineal clans. We view how Choctaws' family life changed during the 19th century, with the destruction of the clans and the imposition of the dominant society's system of patriarchy. We explore their ideas about what makes up a good woman and a good man and how children were taught the values and beliefs of Choctaw society.

In Chapter 5, we examine Choctaw oral traditions, the role of elders, and their beliefs in spirit beings, who were an important part of Choctaw lives, especially prior to the 20th century. Choctaw cuisine, along with dance, music, and art, are the subject of Chapter 6. Many delicious traditional recipes that brighten the meals of the Choctaw people are presented in this chapter. Modern Choctaw people do not eat the healthy, nutritious, and balanced diets of former days, leading to health concerns such as obesity and diabetes, among others.

In Chapter 7, we explore powwow dancing and traditional Choctaw dances performed today at exhibits and festivals. Last, we look at some modern Choctaw artists and their work. In Chapter 8, we explore contemporary issues affecting the Choctaw Nation, the Mississippi Band of Choctaw Indians, and other groups of Choctaws. The overarching concerns about self-determination, identity, and land that affect all tribes are briefly explained and followed by a few issues that Choctaw governmental entities have tried to resolve or address in recent years.

Finally, the reader will find a list of authoritative sources for further reading, listing both primary and secondary sources. This reading list includes books and articles on many aspects of Choctaw history and life, and is intended to provide assistance for further study.

Introduction

THE CHOCTAW PEOPLE are a Native American tribal people consisting of two major groups and several smaller ones. The Choctaw Nation of Oklahoma is the largest, with almost 200,000 citizens, and the Mississippi Band of Choctaw Indians numbers about 10,000 people. In addition, there are the MOWA Band of Choctaws in Alabama and several groups in Louisiana, including the Jena Band of Choctaw Indians; the Choctaw Apache Community of Ebarb, Louisiana; the Louisiana Choctaw Tribe; and the Clifton Choctaw Tribe. The original Choctaw Nation was broken up and scattered in the 1800s when the U.S. government dispossessed them from their ancient homelands.

Prior to American conquest, Choctaw homelands covered a vast amount of land in what today are the states of Mississippi, Alabama, and Louisiana. Between 1780 and 1835, all their lands in the southeast were taken by the U.S. government. The majority of Choctaws were forced into permanent exile in the land that is now the southern half of Oklahoma, which, at the time, was called the Choctaw Nation of Indian Territory. However, a large number of Choctaws remained in the swamps and backwoods near their old homelands, where they stayed and survived, and now are the Mississippi Band of Choctaw Indians.

After the Civil War, the U.S. government took away nearly half of the Choctaw lands in Indian Territory, until, at the turn of the 20th century, the United States took the remaining communal Choctaw lands, which were parceled out into private holdings.

In the traditional origin story of the Choctaw people, the Choctaws emerged in ancient times from a huge earthen mound, which is located in what is currently Winston County, Mississippi. They called the mound "Nanih Waiya," and they lived and prospered for many centuries in its shadow. The lands around the Great Mother Mound were given to the Choctaw people by the Creator. Nanih Waiya is still considered sacred and is visited today by the Choctaw people.

From ancient times, Choctaws have believed that all the creatures, beings, and things in the land have a living spirit, and that each has a consciousness and system of knowledge from which all others could learn. Everything within this Choctaw world is interrelated and interconnected, and human beings are simply one of many in this vast system of life. Unlike European and Euro-American beliefs, Choctaws did not believe that human beings were at the top of a pyramid in which they had the authority to exploit other creatures and the land for their own benefit. Instead, Choctaws believed that all creatures and even the rocks, trees, and water were sentient beings, aware of themselves and others, having spirits and thoughts and knowledge. Since all were closely related in this life system, Choctaws knew that if they mistreated other beings, terrible consequences might result. So they were careful to order their lives with respect and consideration for all living things and inert beings.

Choctaw women—the life givers—raised corn, beans, squash, and many other crops, while the men hunted, fished, and defended the people from enemies.[1] The Choctaw Nation grew strong and prosperous and traded surplus corn to its neighbors. Europeans invaded in the 16th century, introducing Choctaws and other Native Americans to violence, their unquenchable thirst for gold and other wealth, and diseases against which they had no immunity.

In the 1830s, the Choctaws were forcibly exiled from their homelands by the federal government, in response to demands from American citizens. The majority of the people walked hundreds of miles west under cruel conditions, resulting in thousands of deaths. Sent into permanent exile in what became the state of Oklahoma, the Choctaws tried to rebuild their nation and reform their institutions. But once again, in 1906, the U.S. government confiscated and divided the common landholdings of the Choctaw Nation into small parcels of land, which they forced individual Choctaws to own. This alien system of individuals owning certain pieces of the earth made no sense to most Choctaws. From time immemorial, Choctaws held their territory in common. They used as much as they needed, and no more, and everyone had equal access to the land. No one was subjugated by a system of private landownership, and anyone could open a little farm or build a cabin on any of the communal Choctaw lands that were not in use by someone else. This system worked for centuries, and no one was homeless or destitute. However, this system of landholding was deemed "uncivilized" by the Euro-American worldview, and in 1887, Congress passed a law abrogating the solemn treaty agreements that stated that the Choctaws would own this land communally as long as the rivers flowed and the grass grew. Soon, many Choctaws were landless and destitute, living in competition with whites in a society that denied them access to the United States legal system because they were not white.

In 1906, the United States unilaterally declared that the Choctaw Nation was dissolved, with the demand that Choctaw people assimilate completely into the American society. Under these unjust policies, the Choctaws and many other Native American nations were, once again, forced against their will to surrender vast territories that had been guaranteed to them forever. As a result, over the next 20 years following this seizure and redistribution of their lands, the Choctaws were pauperized, dispossessed, and exiled, and many were forced into subservient positions in the economy of the dominant society.

After decades of extreme poverty and lack of human and civil rights, Choctaws slowly began to organize, and with the Civil Rights Movement of the 1960s, leaders emerged to blaze a new path, reasserting Choctaw identity and demanding the restoration of Choctaw sovereignty. During the last decades of the 20th century, the Choctaw Nation of Oklahoma emerged strong and whole once again, with more than 100,000 tribal citizens.[2]

In the late 20th century, Mississippi Choctaws began to revive from more than a century of intense oppression and unremitting discrimination suffered at the hands of the white majority. Under the amazing leadership of *Mingo* (Chief) Phillip Martin, the Mississippi Band of Choctaw Indians regained their rightful recognition by the federal and state governments and emerged as an economic powerhouse. The opening years of the 21st century finds the Mississippi Band poised to take advantage of economic, educational, and social opportunities that they created themselves.

Other small communities of Choctaws continue their way of life in Louisiana, Tennessee, and Alabama. The Jena Band of Choctaw Indians has 240 citizens who live in communities around Jena, Louisiana. The people of the Jena Band chose to live in relative isolation from the dominant white society and preserved their ways of living, language, and social systems from the assimilation forced on Choctaws living in what is now called Oklahoma. In 1932, a small school welcomed children of the Jena Band; however, it was open only for a few years until its closure during the World War II. After World War II, Choctaw children from the Jena Band were allowed to attend

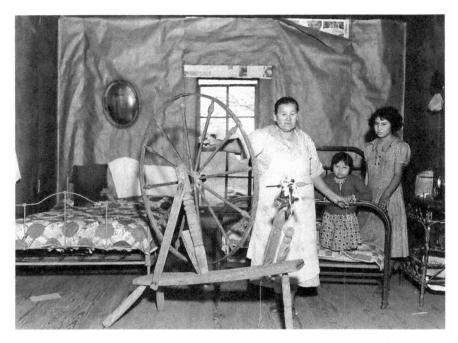

Miss Elies Winshin of the Choctaw tribe working at a wool wheel that has been in her family for more than 100 years, January 14, 1949. (AP Photo)

public schools. The Jena Band of Choctaw Indians is officially recognized by the state and federal governments and is a sovereign nation with nation-to-nation relations with the U.S. government.

The Choctaw Apache Community of Ebarb, Louisiana, has a fascinating history. Descended from Apache slaves who were sold at the slave markets in Spanish era Natchitoches and Los Adaes (present day Robeline, Louisiana), their ancestors mixed with Choctaws fleeing the European invasions of their homelands in Mississippi and Alabama. In addition, some of their ancestors include Adais Caddo people, thus giving the Choctaw Apache Community claim to residence back to as early as the 1720s. They are recognized by the state of Louisiana, but not by the U.S. government. Their headquarters is located in western Sabine Parish in Louisiana, and they have more than 2,000 enrolled citizens residing in Louisiana and elsewhere across the United States.

The Louisiana Choctaw Tribe and the Clifton Choctaw Tribe are also state recognized bands of Choctaw people. In addition to these, there are other small communities of Choctaws or Choctaw people who are of mixed Native American ancestry scattered around the state. Many of these communities were founded by Choctaws who refused to go to Indian Territory when the main body of Choctaws from Mississippi was forcibly exiled. Many of them have survived and maintained their culture and traditions through a cohesive identity as Choctaw people.

The MOWA Band of Choctaw Indians of far western Alabama has struggled for years to obtain federal recognition so that they can have access to the many federal programs used by the Oklahoma and Mississippi Choctaw people. In 2008, their lawsuit demanding federal recognition was rejected on a technicality. Today, nearly 6,000 people are citizens of the MOWA Choctaw Tribe, almost half of whom live in the vicinity of McIntosh, Alabama. In addition to Choctaw heritage, MOWA people have Cherokee, Creek, Lipan, and Mescalero ancestry. In 1979, they gained state recognition, and in 1983, they purchased 160 acres of land in Washington County, Alabama.

The Choctaw language is part of the Muskogee language family. Choctaw and Chickasaw are mutually intelligible and are classified as Western Muskogean languages. Many more than 100,000 Choctaws are living today, with approximately 10,000 who fluently speak the native language. Choctaw is taught in some of the school systems where large numbers of Choctaw children attend in order to try to maintain and strengthen the use of Choctaw by the younger generation. The Choctaw Nation of Oklahoma has used modern technology to make courses in Choctaw widely accessible, in addition to community-based language course offered throughout the Choctaw Nation. The University of Oklahoma pioneered a language program in Choctaw, which now has hundreds of alumni, and continues to teach Choctaw to native and nonnative students in Norman, Oklahoma.

In historical times, especially prior to the 20th century, Choctaw people had a unique identity and worldview. Their belief system, language, social and kinship systems, and values set them apart from Euro-Americans, and from many other Native American groups. Like all other societies, the Choctaw people have changed over time. Societies change in order to continue to exist as a distinct people. Oftentimes, pressures for change come from circumstances generated by peoples outside the group. For the Choctaws, Euro-Americans and their governments forced these changes upon them. Beginning in the late 18th century, conquest by the U.S. government and her people dramatically affected the traditional world of the Choctaw people and led to massive adaptations and changed living conditions that, in some cases, forced the Choctaws to give up traditional ways and adapt new ones.

Change did not destroy the Choctaw people. Choctaw society had changed slowly over time of its own accord. But some ancient values, ideals, and beliefs were more rapidly, adversely affected by outside contact. In the second decade of the 1800s, the United States became very aggressive toward Native Americans in the southeastern portion of the United States, in order to expel them from their homelands and take over their prime agricultural lands. White Americans did not believe Native Americans to be their equals; in fact, during this time, most white Americans did not believe any people of color should have the same rights and protection that they felt was only the birthright of white people. The Revolution Era's ideals that helped form the American government were abandoned when it came to "Indians" and "Negroes." That resulted in horrible suffering by Native Americans, who were forced into permanent exile and poverty so that white citizens could have their land.

The Choctaws have had a long and varied relationship with the United States, which has primarily served the interests of the dominant society. Between 1830 and 1930, the U.S. government expelled the Choctaws from their ancestral homelands and forced them into permanent exile. During this period, the American government implemented a policy of forced assimilation that devastated Choctaw lives. Their social, political, and economic systems were continually assaulted due to the dominant society's beliefs that Choctaws and other native people were "savages" who had to be forced to adopt a Euro-American worldview. After the dispossessions of the

Choctaw Indians Grady John with wife and daughter at Chucalissa Indian Town and Museum near Memphis, Tennessee. (Courtesy of the Library of Congress)

mid-19th century, the Choctaws in the West were again dispossessed. What little land they had left after the early 1900s was frequently taken by sheriff's sales for inflated taxes, or by scoundrels who cheated those who were uneducated and who spoke little or no English.

Despite this long history of oppression, the Choctaw people have survived through sheer courage and determination. Throughout their history, the Choctaw people found ways to survive and overcome adversity, and today the strength of their traditions and belief systems provides an inspiring success story.

Chronology

From the origin of the people until circa 1540 A.D.	The creation of the Choctaw people through the period unrecorded by written historical accounts.
1540–1543	Hernando de Soto's invasion and rampage through Choctaw homelands, resulting in a great number of casualties and the spread of European disease. De Soto died in 1542, and his men were chased out of the region by native warriors.
1543–early 1700s	Continued prosperity and traditional lifeways with occasional contact with European invaders, primarily the French along the Mississippi River.
Mid-1700s	Choctaws struggled to maintain sovereignty and independence while allying with various European nations—French, Spanish, and English—who were fighting each other over for hegemony in the Americas.
1748–1750	Civil war between two factions of Choctaws—those who allied with the French and those who favored the English.
1754–1763	The French and Indian War, or the Seven Years War, between France and England over hegemony in North America. Choctaws allied with the French who were defeated by the British in 1763.

1763–1776	Spain took over French Louisiana, moving into New Orleans, Mobile, and Biloxi, trying to influence the Choctaws, who remained aloof. The English colonial government also enjoyed little success with the Choctaws.
1776–1783	Most Choctaws allied themselves with the new Americans. Choctaw scouts served under Washington, Morgan, Wayne, and Sullivan.
1783	Treaty of Paris, 1783, ending the American Revolution. Britain withdrew from the former American colonies and also ceded Florida to Spain, placing the entire southern section of Choctaw lands under Spanish claims.
1784	Choctaw Treaty with Spain, who sought to protect its claims to Florida against the Americans by establishing a buffer state consisting of the Choctaws and other Native American nations.
1786	Treaty of Hopewell with the United States, establishing peace and friendship; it recognized that an American who resided on Choctaw lands would come under the jurisdiction of Choctaw law and gave the United States the right to construct three trading posts in the Choctaw Nation.
1792	Treaty of Nogales, establishing friendship between Spain and the Choctaw Nation.
1760s–1800	Continual dealings with European traders, travelers, and government officials led to huge changes in the Choctaw way of life. Imported European manufactured goods, warfare as allies on behalf of European nations, and the flood of cheap liquor into the Choctaw Nation corrupted the values and beliefs of the Choctaw people.
1800	In the secret Treaty of San Ildefonso, Spain ceded Louisiana back to France.
1801	Treaty of Fort Adams: Choctaw Nation ceded 2.6 million acres of land for $2,000. The United States would be allowed to open a road from Natchez to Nashville, Tennessee.
1802	Treaty of Fort Confederation: Choctaw Nation agreed to allow the United States to draw boundary lines to delineate the eastern and northern boundaries of the Choctaw Nation.
1803	Treaty of Hoe Buckintoopa: U.S. agents forced Choctaw Nation to cede 853,000 acres of land by redefining the boundary lines agreed to in the treaty of 1802.
1805	Treaty of Mount Dexter: Choctaw Nation ceded 4,142,720 acres of their southern lands to the United States in exchange for

payment of $48,000 in debts to a private trading company and $1,500 in cash, along with a yearly payment of $3,000.

1800–1815   Choctaw lifeways and tradition continually eroded by the influence of Americans. Scarcity of game and disruption in the agricultural economy led to widespread hunger and poverty. Alcohol flooded the nation, leading to widespread disruption of the economy and political institutions.

1811   Renowned Shawnee leader Tecumseh visited the Choctaws, asking them to join in his vast confederation of native people. *Mingo* Pushmataha dissuaded most Choctaws from joining this alliance.

1812–1815   War of 1812 between the United States and Britain. Choctaw warriors provided key assistance to their American allies in several major battles, and served with great distinction in the Battle of New Orleans. Choctaw leaders believed themselves to be the true friends of the American people. Chief Pushmataha achieved the rank of general, and led hundreds of Choctaw warriors against the British.

1816   Treaty of Fort St. Stephens: Vows of good will between the United States and Choctaw Nation marked this treaty, which adjusted boundaries in a small area on the Alabama–Mississippi border.

1817   Mississippi admitted as a state of the Union, a portent of coming disaster for the Choctaw Nation.

1820   Treaty of Doak's Stand with the United States: Choctaw Nation ceded more than 5 million acres in their Mississippi homelands in exchange for 13 million acres in southern Oklahoma.

1820–1825   White invaders in Choctaw homelands tried to force them into exile, while Choctaw people resisted. The U.S. government used bribery and dishonesty to try to wrest Choctaw agreement to their own dispossession.

1824   *Mingo* Pushmataha died in Washington, D.C., where he was given a hero's funeral and burial at Washington National Cemetery.

1825   Treaty of 1825: Choctaws received fulfillment of the terms of the 1820 treaty; U.S. payment of compensation owed to Choctaw warriors since the War of 1812, a few thousand dollars yearly; the United States to pay all trading debts owed by the Choctaws; and the Choctaws agreed to leave the lands the United States had ceded to them in Arkansas, which the United States now took back.

1825–1830   The United States deliberately broke its treaty promises to expel white invaders from Choctaw lands. Withdrew federal troops and stood by while thousands of whites poured into sovereign Choctaw territory. Conditions of anarchy reigned with whites forcing Choctaw people off their land and out of their homes. Western Indian haters were ecstatic when Andrew Jackson elected president.

1828   Andrew Jackson elected as president of the United States. His platform called for the expulsion of native peoples from their homelands, by force if necessary.

1829   State of Mississippi illegally took over Choctaw territory, extending their jurisdiction over it. Choctaws were forced to become second-class citizens of the United States, deprived of most of their civil rights, in white conspiracy to force them into permanent exile.

1830   Jackson got the Indian Removal Act passed by a few votes. This law authorized his administration to seek removal of all southern Indians.

1830   U.S. fraudulent Treaty of Dancing Rabbit Creek obtained and ratified by dishonest means.

1831   Choctaw were forced into exile. First of so-called removals began that winter: a death march, resulting in casualties of 20 percent of the people.

1837   Treaty between the Choctaw and Chickasaw nations allocating one section of Choctaw lands in Indian Territory for the residence of Chickasaw people.

1830s   Thousands of Choctaw people were forced into permanent exile from their homelands in Mississippi. They traveled the Trail of Tears to Indian Territory, the future state of Oklahoma. Several hundred Choctaws remained in Mississippi, refusing to leave their homelands and the bones of the dead. Today, their descendants are recognized as the Mississippi Band of Choctaw Indians.

1862–1865   Choctaw Nation of western Choctaw Nation allied with the Confederacy during the American Civil War.

1866   Treaty of 1866: Reestablishing a nation-to-nation relationship with the United States; required Choctaw Nation to cede a huge part of her territory to the United States, with $300,000 in compensation; forced Choctaw Nation to allow railroads to be built through her territory; the United States tried to force Choctaw

	Nation to give up communal landholdings for private property through allotments.
1865–1890s	Choctaw Nation overrun with white U.S. citizens who the United States failed to expel per treaty agreements.
1887	Dawes Act passed into law by the United States. Choctaw Nation and other subject native nations protested the abrogation of treaties inherent in Dawes Act provisions. All native nations unanimously opposed the blatant theft of their lands and dissolution of their governments.
1897	Choctaw leaders helped draft the Atoka Agreement, in which they tried to lessen the draconian measures the U.S. Congress desired to pass to extinguish the existence of the Choctaw Nation.
1906	With the U.S. passage of the Enabling Act, the Choctaw Nation was legislated out of existence.
1907	The state of Oklahoma was admitted to the Union.
1916–1918	Many native men volunteered to serve with the U.S. Armed Forces during World War I. Choctaw code talkers provided the United States with an unbreakable radio code in the Choctaw language.
1928	Meriam Report published: A government report that chronicled the abject pauperization of Native Americans as a result of U.S. policies and law. Population of native people hit an all-time low; disease was rampant and endemic on reservations and in the boarding schools; many native people were deprived of civil and legal rights.
1932	Election of Franklin Delano Roosevelt who appointed progressive John Collier as commissioner of Indian Affairs. Collier worked diligently to reverse oppressive U.S. policies that subjugated and oppressed Native Americans.
1934	Indian Reorganization (Wheeler-Howard) Act was passed by Congress, which imposed alien political institutions on native tribes, provided a small sum for purchase of land on behalf of nations who had been dispossessed by the United States, terminated the Dawes Act and allotment, established a court of Indian Affairs, and provided training and opened opportunities for employment with the Bureau of Indian Affairs.
1941–1945	Many native men volunteered for service in the U.S. Armed Forces during World War II. Choctaws and Navajos provided radio codes that were instrumental in winning the war.

1945	Mississippi Band of Choctaw Indians was recognized as a tribe and they organized a government structure approved by the United States.
1940s and 1950s	New U.S. policy of termination was instituted by Congress to end all U.S. governmental obligations to native tribes, with the goal of breaking up tribal communities, ending all vestiges of sovereignty, and forcing individual native people to relinquish their identity as tribal citizens.
	The new U.S. policy called relocation was used to entice individuals and nuclear families from their reservations and communities in order to force them to move to cities and assimilate.
	For most, relocation simply exchanged rural reservation homes for urban poverty, discrimination, and hopelessness.
1959	Choctaw Nation of Oklahoma Termination Act was passed by U.S. Congress, to be implemented in 1970. Lyndon B. Johnson repudiated and refused to implement termination of the Choctaw Nation.
1950–1975	Native Americans joined together in a Pan-Indian movement, Red Power, demanding civil rights, restoration of homelands, sovereignty, and an end to U.S. policies of oppression.
1968	Founding of American Indian Movement, a political activist organization that worked for equal rights and liberation from U.S. oppression.
1969	Indian activists seized Alcatraz Island, a dramatic social protest that riveted public and U.S. government attention on the shameful treatment of indigenous peoples and the need to rectify this wrongdoing.
1970	U.S. President Richard Nixon in a special message on Indian Affairs called for a new era of self-determination for native peoples and renounced U.S. policies of termination and paternalism.
1960s and 1970s	Demonstrations and protests such as the Trail of Broken Treaties and delivery of demands in the Twenty Points, the seizure of the Bureau of Indian Affairs building in Washington, D.C., and the standoff at Wounded Knee, South Dakota intensified pressure for equal rights for indigenous Native Americans.
1971	Alaska Native Claims Settlement Act of 1971 addressed land claims of native peoples after the invasion of their lands by U.S. oil companies. Imposition of alien political and financial institutions on Native Americans forced Alaska Natives to implement

	government structures that destroyed native traditions and political and legal institutions.
1972	Indian Education Act of 1972 was passed and promised to provide funding for the education of Indian children.
1980s– the present	The Choctaw Nation instituted a new constitution with legislative and executive branches with the goal of self-determination and enhanced self-government.
1982	The Supreme Court of the United States, in a series of decisions, weakened the sovereignty of native nations and strengthened the power of state and federal U.S. governments in their relations with tribal governments.
1990	Native American Grave Protection and Repatriation Act was passed, requiring all institutions receiving federal funds to inventory collections of Indian artifacts and human remains and return the items tribes request.
1996	John Echohawk of the Native Americans Rights Fund filed a class action suit against the U.S. Secretary of the Interior Bruce Babbit on behalf of half a million beneficiaries for misuse of billions of dollars held in trust by the Bureau of Indian Affairs. The U.S. District Court in the District of Columbia found in favor of Echohawk's suit.
2009	In December 2009, under the Obama administration, a settlement agreement was reached on the Indian Trust Settlement.
2010	President Obama signed legislation approving the settlement of the Indian Trust Settlement and authorizing $3.4 billion in funds. Two appeals have since been filed and final settlement awaits the outcome of these appeals.
2011	The Choctaw Nation of Oklahoma and the Chickasaw Nation filed a suit in federal court over water rights. The suit alleges that federal law grants the Choctaw Nation treaty rights regarding water dating back to the 1830 Treaty of Dancing Rabbit Creek.
2012	Choctaw Nation and Southeastern Oklahoma State University announced the launch of Choctaw University.

Notes

1. Devon Abbott Mihesuah, *Indigenous American Women: Decolonization, Empowerment, Activism* (Lincoln, NE: University of Nebraska Press, 2003), 42.

2. Devon Abbott Mihesuah, *Choctaw Crime and Punishment, 1884–1907* (Norman, OK: University of Oklahoma Press, 2009), 226.

1

History of the Choctaws of the West

ORIGINS

CHOCTAW ORAL TRADITIONS describe how the Choctaw people came to their ancient homelands long, long ago, past all human reckoning. These traditions tell of a great journey from the west or southwest, relating that the people crossed the enormous father river, the Mississippi, and came to the great Mother Mound, Nanih Waiya. Creator had brought them to the lands on which they were meant to live and prosper for all time. After a long period of time, a terrible epidemic disease attacked them, causing thousands and thousands of deaths, until eventually only one Choctaw was left alive. A cave opened up on top of Nanih Waiya, and the lone survivor entered the cave, which closed up after him. Much time passed, and again the cave opened, and two pairs of Choctaws emerged, two boys and two girls. Creator directed them to live on these lands, which He gave to them, for all time. He told them if they ever left these lands, the hunters would find no meat, and the entire nation would perish. Each couple left the great Mother Mound, traveling in opposite directions. From these couples, the Choctaw repopulated their lands, becoming strong and prosperous.

Some scholars say that all native peoples in North America are descendants of Asian prehistoric peoples who moved across the Bering Strait sometime in the Pleistocene epoch. According to this theory, during the last Ice Age, the water level of the Bering Strait dropped so much that a bridge of land provided a migration path from what is now Russia to Alaska. The great prehistoric beasts crossed this bridge into North America, followed by human emigrants, who eventually spread south and east, and populated the Western Hemisphere.

All Native American peoples have their own creation stories, and they do not match up to the Bering Strait theory. A few years ago, the late Lakota scholar Vine Deloria, Jr., questioned why this theory is so widely accepted, despite abundant evidence to the contrary. Aside from the fact that there is no proof of this theory, he suggests that Europeans and their descendants adhere to it because it would make Native Americans simply the first of many emigrants—not indigenous but simply early invaders. This also allows European descendants a way to justify their own invasions and conquest of Native America.[1]

Many Native Americans believe that they emerged from Mother Earth in the lands given to them by Creator. The Choctaw origin story tells how they came to be in the lands surrounding Nanih Waiya and their role as an indigenous people. Here is their origin oral tradition:

Long ago, in the misty swirls of ancient time, the People emerged from the place toward the setting sun, following a wise old man who was their leader. At night they camped under the stars, and the leader planted the tall staff he was carrying upright in the earth. Each morning, when he awoke, the staff would be leaning in the direction they were to travel. The People were carrying the sacred bones of their ancestors from their old home. The living had a sacred compact with the dead to care for and treat their bones with great respect and consideration. So when the People moved, the bones of the ancestors had to go with them.

After many, many years of travel, the number of bones grew, as more and more people died. The bundles of bones became so numerous that the people had to carry one load forward each day, then return to the starting point for another load. Thus, they slowly inched ahead, struggling to honor the compact with their deceased ancestors.

The long days of summer began to grow short and the temperature cooled, until one morning, frost covered the ground in every direction, and the leader knew they must stop to build winter shelters before it grew cold. Not far from this place was a great earthen mound called Nanih Waiya. It was a beautiful large hill made of earth. All the lands surrounding it had trees so tall they reached the sky. Under the fragrant pine needles that covered the floor of the forest, animals and birds were everywhere. Gurgling, clear streams abounded with fish, a tall oak trees let loose a bounty of acorns that Choctaw women used in recipes for delicious and filling stews and bread.

The next spring, the women gathered the seed corn which they had brought with them on the trail, and planted them in small hills, with seeds of bean and squash. That summer, the hunters were wildly successful, and the women were delighted to cook up tasty dishes of meat and corn, beans, squash. Fishing kept the young men busy, the wonderful array of plants provided food and medicines, and all the Choctaw people enjoyed their camp and dreaded the idea of leaving it.

At the end of the summer, the people gave thanks to Creator in a three day celebration they called the Green Corn Ceremony. They extinguished all the fires, cleaned and purified their living spaces and grounds, and bathed and washed everyone and everything. After purging themselves of any contamination, the People forgave past wrongs, and praised those who had done well and who had sacrificed for the community. In this symbolic rebirth, the Choctaws renewed the unity and close relationships of every Choctaw. A new central fire was lit and all the women took a burning twig from it to light their home fire. Soon, the aroma of delicious stews, banaha, and tom fullah drifted through the camp. When the dishes were done, the women laid them out on a long banquet table, and everyone ate and danced and sang.

At the end of their celebration, the clan elders and wise people knew the time drew near for them to leave, following the direction of the pole to their new homelands. Many dreaded leaving behind these bounteous lands and its mild and delightful climate to pick up the bundles of bones of the ancestors and set out once again across the land. They looked at their comfortable homes and fields, and cast their eyes down as they gathered at the council where they would decide their next move.

The leader stood up, and, speaking in his rich bass voice, began to talk in a gentle and calming tone, acknowledging the wonderful gifts Creator had bestowed on the Choctaws. He spoke quietly of the reasons the People had set out on their great journey to new homelands. He remembered the 43 winters that had passed on that trail. Throughout those many years, he said, the People had dutifully honored the bones of the dead, despite the great burden of carrying such huge bundles. The leader proposed they plant the pole in the ground again that night, and in the morning they would rise, and as they had for decades, would set out in the path the pole indicated.

That night many Choctaws prayed for courage and fortitude in taking up their journey once again. Children played out in the fields until the very last bit of daylight finally was extinguished, wanting to remember the good times and wonderful lands around Nanih Waiya. Young hunters recounted the great hunts and thought wistfully of the bounteous streams, teeming with fish, that they were about to leave. Old ones dreamed of the gentle summer breezes and mild weather they had enjoyed that year. Many of the women silently said goodbye to the rich lands which had yielded such plentiful harvests of corn and beans and squash. And everyone woke and rose with such reluctance, and silently began to pack up to start their new journey.

Before the sun rose on this beautiful late summer morning, the Leader and the clan elders met to see which way the pole leaned. As it gradually lightened, the council surrounded the pole, peering intently into the shadows to find out the direction of the morning's trek. The youngest among them, who could see best in the dark, suddenly exclaimed, "Look! The pole is straight! It does not lean! What could this mean?" The council members looked at the pole, then at each other. What could this possibly mean? The Leader and the wise men and women formed a circle around the pole and sat for hours, quietly contemplating what they should do.

After much thought, the eldest clan mother rose and spoke in her dignified, measured voice. "For forty-three winters, we have been on a great journey in which we followed the direction indicated by the lean of the sacred pole. During all this time, we have not faltered, nor questioned the wisdom of the hard road that we followed. But now, when we have come to a beautiful place, a place filled with game and fish, with fertile soil for our corn, and a mild and enjoyable climate, watered by lovely, gurgling, clear streams, our pole stands straight and tall, just like our young men and women. It means one thing—that we have arrived at the place that was promised; that this beautiful land that surrounds the great Mother Mound—this is our new home. We are to stay here and live happily, enjoying the great gifts of Aba, Creator. I have spoken."

As she sat down, the elders talked quietly, murmuring their agreement. Then everyone looked expectantly at the Leader, waiting for him to speak. The tall, dignified man rose and waited until they all looked up, giving him their complete attention. When all were quiet and looking up at him in expectation, he began: "The Clan Mother is right. If Creator wanted us to resume our journey and travel on, the pole would have leaned in the direction we were to follow. Yet it stands straight and upright. It is clear. Aba has given us this land. Its beauty and bounty are his gifts to us. We will begin our new lives here, in the shadow of the great Mother Mound, Nanih Waiya. We now call this place our home. And it shall be that when a man, at his hunting camp, is asked where is his home, he shall reply 'Nanih Waiya.' "

He paused as the people murmured their approval, and then one respected elder rose and asked, "What shall we do with the sacred bones of our ancestors, now contained in the bundles we have carried with us to this place?" After much discussion, one of the Clan Mothers rose, and she spoke with the unanimous consent of the People. "We will gather all the bones, and pile them up, closely and neatly, and then we will cover them with cypress bark. And then to honor the spirits of our ancestors, who watch over us always, each one of the People will gather dirt to build a mound over the bones of our relatives. All the People, old and young, great and small will show their respect through their careful and meticulous labor, and we will continued until every heart is satisfied."

The Leader then rose, and his voice carried far, asking, "What says the Nation?" Every Choctaw solemnly reflected. After several minutes of silence, an elder of about sixty winters rose in a dignified manner. He cleared his throat and then spoke in a strong and gentle voice, saying, "In my boyhood, one summer just as the Green Corn Ceremony ended, my much respected father died. All the members of his clan traveled to our village and mourned for a whole moon. Then the cry-poles were taken down, and when the death feast and dance had ended, my mother, having my younger brother to carry, asked me to carry the bones of my father, when the People first began this journey forty-three summers ago. I have carefully carried them over this long trail, through all our hardships and difficulties. From my beloved village on the little stream in the old homeland to this camp where we sit today, I faithfully and reverently carried the sacred remains of my father, and I would have sacrificed my life before I would have left them, or given them up to another. Now I grow old, and I know I will soon die. I ask myself, who in the coming generations will remember and honor the bones of my father? Will his bones be scattered and left to rot on the open plains? Who will be there to honor his spirit and all the spirits of our dead?

I have heard the proposal that we bury these sacred bones within a new mound. It stills my anxious heart, and relieves my worry that my father's spirit and his bones would be forgotten and be trampled under the feet of thoughtless living people. I am glad that we as a People are honoring our compact with the spirits who watch over us, and that they will rejoice with us when we build this great mound to house their sacred remnants, and fulfill our promises as a people."

The people then rose up and in one voice cried "Let us begin" and everyone left to bring tools and baskets for the great task before them. Some of the elders were appointed to select a good place for the great mound, and to direct the work of the People. They found a level plain of sandy land, not far from a nearby creek, and laid off an oblong square. The People worked diligently, from young to old, big and small, all gathering earth, carrying it to the mound, and raising the foundation until it was as high as a man's head and beaten down very hard. Then the People gathered cypress bark for the floor and when this was finished, they began bringing the sacks of bones and stacking them tightly together. This created a great high mound. On the top and sides, the People wrapped the structure in cypress bark, to keep the bones dry. Then, while some of the skilled workers finished the bark, the remainder of the women and children and men, (except for the hunters) laboriously carried basket after basket of soil to cover the bark. When they finished, the mound reached half the height of the tallest forest tree.

The Leader kindled a new council fire, and calling an assembly of all the people, told them their work had been done in a skilled and wonderful manner. Now that the bones were respectfully laid and covered in the great mound, they rested for a season, so that the acorns could be gathered and the winter hunt go on. The next spring, as always, the women went to the fields and there grew bounteous amounts of corn, beans, and squash, and soon, it was time again for the Green Corn Ceremony. Then the People went back to work on the mound, and they followed this cycle year after year until the celebration of the eighth Green Corn Ceremony, when the great mound reached the height of the tallest tree in the forest. On its level top they planted with acorns, nuts, and seeds. When it was finished, it was sixty steps in length and thirty steps in width. At last, the People left the new mound and went into the forest to prepare for winter.

They found fruit in great quantities, and brought back acorns, hickory nut, and best of all, chestnuts, which they preserved by drying and smoking them, and then encasing them in airtight mud cells, in the same manner as the mud daubers (lukchuk chanuskik). The hunters were very successful that year, and in midwinter, when everyone returned to their camps, they found themselves rich in food and supplies. They decided to hold a celebration to express their gratitude to Aba. They feasted and danced for five days, with joy and gladness in their hearts. They planted the pole that directed their long journey from the west, on the top of the mound, and all rejoiced.

The Leader then directed the people to plant an ornamental pole representing each of the iksas, or clans. To show their respect for the spirits and bones of the dead, now interred in the beautiful and great mound, each clan held a month-long cry to remember and celebrate the ancestors. Each of the clans crafted a pole from a very tall pine tree, peeled it and bleached it white; then each sacred pole was draped with garlands of evergreens and flowers. Three times every day, for an entire month, each clan met for the cry at their pole on the top of the great mound. Then at the end of the cries, all the People gathered for the pole pulling, where they ceremoniously took down the poles, and all the People rejoiced and had a great feast, putting their grief behind them. The Choctaw People lived in great prosperity and joy in the shadow of the great Mother Mound, Nanih Waiya.

After many years of happiness and prosperity, a great and terrible disease epidemic raced through the People, killing thousands. Finally, all the Choctaw People had died, except for the bearer of the book, who could not die. An entrance down into the earth opened upon Nanih Waiya, and this lone Choctaw entered this cave and disappeared. After many, many winters, the Great Spirit created four infants out of the ashes of the dead at the foot of Nanih Waiya. They were suckled by a panther. When they had grown strong and were able to take care of themselves, they were given bows and arrows and an earthen pot. The prophet stretched forth his arms and, in a great, resounding voice, said, "I give you these hunting grounds for your homes. When you leave them you die." Then he stamped his foot, and the cave entrance opened up on the top of Nanih Waiya, and he disappeared forever. The four children of Nanih Waiya separated into pairs, two going to the left, and two to the right. Their descendants maintained these traditional divisions which form the two great moieties.[2] All of today's Choctaw People descend from these four infants, who repopulated the nation after the massive epidemic.[3]

THE INVASION OF HERNANDO DE SOTO

For many centuries, the Choctaw people lived in the lands of what is today called Mississippi and parts of Alabama and Louisiana. They supported themselves by hunting, fishing, farming, and gathering foods such as berries and roots, and they themselves made everything they needed for all aspects of their life. Their highly developed systems of knowledge included expertise in the production of weapons and tools and in the creation of beautiful basketry and clothing that was both utilitarian and aesthetically pleasing, while complex spiritual beliefs acquired over a lifetime provided a path for their lives and understanding of their world.

The Choctaw Nation lived in relative peace and prosperity until the invasion in 1540 of the Spaniard, Hernando de Soto, and his army of 600 men. They brought with them more than 200 horses, trained in warfare, and savage Irish wolfhounds, which they trained to track and kill Indians. De Soto rampaged through Native American homelands, greeting villagers with senseless killing and wanton cruelty. His quest was to obtain riches and to discover and plunder native civilizations. De Soto learned his techniques from Pizarro's conquest of the Incas. Under Pizarro, de Soto had gained a notorious reputation for devising ways to extort native leaders and he then used these techniques when he led the expedition to what is now the southeastern United States. Everywhere he went, he and his men attacked and killed native people, trying to force them to reveal the whereabouts of the gold and silver he sought. He seized men and forced them to be porter and guides, and threw them to the wolfhounds to be ripped apart and devoured when they displeased him. He kidnapped women and girls for his men to rape and dismember.

De Soto's marauders met their match when they entered the province of the great Choctaw *mingo,* Tuscaloosa, who was a giant of a man. *Mingo* Tuscaloosa awaited the invaders seated on the top of a high hill, surrounded by his men. De Soto and his men tried to intimidate the Choctaws, jousting and racing their horses, but Tuscaloosa and his people maintained their composure. The Spaniards demanded that porters and women be provided as slaves, but *Mingo* Tuscaloosa cleverly put them off by telling de Soto that he could give them what they asked, but that first they would have to go to his town of Mabila (present day Mobile). The *mingo* secretly sent messengers throughout the area, requesting all warriors to assemble in Mabila, and ready themselves to repel the Spanish invaders.

Tuscaloosa traveled with the Spanish until on October 18, 1540, they arrived at the town of Mabila. However, before they reached their destination, as they passed through other towns, the Spanish soldiers could not resist pillaging them. So when de Soto arrived at Mabila, many of his soldiers were left behind.

One of the accounts written by the Spanish relates that

> Having entered within, we were walking with the Indians, chatting, as if we had them in peace, because only three hundred or so appeared there . . . they began to do their dances and songs . . . fifteen or twenty women in front of us . . . Chief Tuscalusa arose and entered one of those houses . . . the guard entered to bring him out, and he (the guard) saw so many people within . . . that he told the Governor that those houses were full of Indians, all with bows and arrows. . . . The governor called to another Indian who was passing by there, who likewise refused to come. A Nobleman . . . seized him by the arm in order to bring him, and then the Indian gave a pull that set himself free. The Nobleman put hand to his sword and gave him a slash that cut off an arm. Upon wounding this Indian, all began to shoot arrows at us . . . we suffered so much damage that we were forced to leave, fleeing from the town. . . . When the Indians saw us outside, they closed the gates of the town and began to beat there drums and to raise banners with a great yell, and to open our trunks and bundles and display from the top of the wall all that we had brought.[4]

The Choctaws killed many of the Spaniards, shooting arrows from the town, and the fighting lasted for hours. At last, the horses and war dogs of the Spaniards turned the tide in their favor. Once the Spaniards gained entrance to the fortified town, they systematically slaughtered everyone they could find and then burned the town to the ground.

De Soto and his men continued their rampage in a northwesterly direction, under continual sniper fire by native warriors. They were attacked day and night by Choctaw defenders, and they failed to find the kind of riches they were seeking. After months of harassment, when the futility of his search for riches became apparent, de Soto became despondent. He fell ill with fever and died in May 1542, near present day McArthur, Arkansas, on the western bank of the Mississippi River. His lieutenant, Luis de Moscoso Alvarado took over, and the next year the Spanish were expelled from the region and chased down the Mississippi River by thousands of native warriors who attacked them with six-foot spears fired from spear-throwers. The survivors of the de Soto-expedition limped back to Mexico City in late 1543. Although the Choctaws' valor and prowess as warriors could repel the invading Europeans, they could not even see a much greater foe that entered the region along with the Spanish: European disease microbes.

Choctaws, like other Native Americans, were terribly vulnerable to European diseases, since none of the peoples of the Americas had ever been exposed to these microbes. Europeans had had centuries to develop some immunity to most of the diseases that decimated the people of the Americas. But with no immunity to diseases such as smallpox, cholera, influenza, and measles, Native Americans suffered astronomical mortality rates. In many cases, every person in an entire village would die. Death rates of up to 95 percent were common. Scientists refer to these epidemics as "virgin soil epidemics," in which the "virgin soil" is the human body that has never before been exposed to these diseases and thus has had no time to build up any immunity or defenses from the microbes that cause the disease.[5]

With such enormous numbers of deaths, whole societies collapsed, unable to perform even the most basic functions. Crops were not planted, and hunters did not hunt, so the few survivors often died of starvation. Even before the arrival of the first European invaders in the region, huge numbers of native people were wiped out by diseases. The elaborate system of trade routes throughout the Americas provided routes into the interior for people fleeing the epidemics, who unknowingly carried these pestilences to fresh populations. De Soto's chronicler related that in many villages, no one was alive, but the grim evidence of massive epidemics remained in the form of human skeletons.[6]

The terrible European disease epidemics continued to decimate Choctaws and other Native Americans throughout the period from 1500 until the early 20th century. Literally, millions of Native Americans were wiped out from the greatest demographic disaster the world has ever known.[7]

EUROPEAN COLONIALISM

By the 17th century, large areas of North America were claimed by European nations, but these were only paper claims. They sought to attain dominance and territorial rights over these lands, and the only other claims they recognized were those of rival European nations. With few variations, they viewed the entire world outside of Europe as available for military conquest, with themselves as the rightful owners of the land, minerals, and other wealth possessed by indigenous peoples anywhere. Europeans often believed that if they were the first Europeans to see land, they had a God-given "right" to claim the entire territory for their king. Native peoples had no rights; in fact, if they did not submit immediately to having Europeans take over their lives, their lands, and their freedom, they were, according to the European viewpoint, "hostile." This ideology of violent theft and domination came to be called "colonialism" and was a system implemented most successfully in North America by Europeans from England, France, and Spain.[8]

Colonialism was a system created by Europeans that created an ideology that justified the confiscation of the lands, wealth, and power of indigenous peoples. Indians and other non-Christian peoples were labeled "savages" who were to be forced to convert to Christianity. In AD 1240, Pope Innocent declared that the entire world was subject to his authority and that the Pope, as God's vicar on earth, could intervene in the affairs of all nations. If infidels, including Native Americans, violated what Europeans called natural law (defined by European culture), Christian nations could wage what Europeans called a "just" war of conquest and subjugation against native peoples. This belief or ideology was used by Europeans to wage unprovoked and unexpected wars against native peoples throughout the Western Hemisphere. In addition, this ideology spurred the European nations to compete with each other to discover new lands, which led to the invasions of the Americas, Australia, New Zealand, the South Pacific, and many other regions around the globe. The indigenous populations of these lands were ruthlessly slaughtered and subjugated over the course of five centuries. Implementation of this ideology by the Spanish, English, and French reshaped the world known by indigenous North Americans into one of an unrelenting European invasions and conquest.[9]

Native American nations were strong and successful societies that were highly advanced, but they had not developed the war technology used by Europeans. Guns, ammunition, cannonry, and the human institutions that supported warfare—strict, hierarchical systems of administration, centralized decision-making, and undemocratic governance—formed the foundation of European societies and belief systems. The deadliness of European warfare astonished Native American warriors, because death was not the ultimate goal of warfare in their societies. In indigenous societies, war captains and leaders were selected on how well they avoided casualties and how many live captives they obtained, not on the infliction of death. Indigenous peoples were repulsed by the wanton slaughters that to the Europeans indicated victory. For example, during the conquest against the Pequot Nation, the English surrounded one of their villages on Mystic River, which was full of women and children and old people. The English soldiers forced the entire population into the houses, and set fire to them, guarding the exits and killing those who tried to escape the fires. The Narragansetts, who were allies of the English, were horrified by what they believed were barbaric tactics of slaughter, and they left the village in disgust after registering their dismay at the killing of women and children.[10]

De Soto introduced these tactics to the Choctaws and other native southeasterners, many of whom never adjusted to the ruthless and brutal system of warfare practiced by European countries. To Native Americans of the plains, for example, counting coup, or touching the enemy during battle, was considered much braver than killing one's enemy, since it took great courage and skill to do so and live to tell about it.

CHOCTAW DIPLOMACY AND RESISTANCE

From 1700 until the end of the Seven Years' War (also called the French and Indian War), the English and French fought each other to a standstill for dominance in North America. War after war, battle upon battle, they were both nearly bankrupted in their quest for ascendency and possession of the wealth and lands of Native Americans. In order to accomplish their goals, they not only fought Native nations, but they also manipulated them to try to recruit allies and then deploy them to fight against other native nations on behalf of the English, French, or Spanish.

In self-defense against these tactics, Choctaw leaders became adept at playing off rival European powers against each other. European nations sought alliances with the Choctaws, since they were a strong and formidable presence in the Southeast. The proximity of the French in New Orleans, Natchez, and Mobile gave them easier access to Choctaw leaders than that of the English, whose nearest locations were in the Carolinas. The English—represented by government agents, traders, and settlers along the Atlantic coast—nevertheless, continually sought to influence and bribe the Choctaw Nation and its leaders. Spanish influences were also ever present because they claimed the lands along the Gulf Coast and the whole of what today is the state of Florida, in addition to points far west of Choctaw lands.

Geography was the key to European relations with the Choctaw people. In 1700, Spain claimed the land along the Gulf of Mexico and all of Florida, placing them in close proximity of the Choctaws. France held the Mississippi River valley against all European comers, establishing the towns of Natchez and New Orleans, and constantly treating with the Choctaws for their favor and alliance. The English's closest town of any significance was Charlestown, Carolina (Charleston, South Carolina today), but they sent traders and government agents to meet with the Choctaws and try to gain their allegiance. For most of the 18th century, these three European powers schemed, cajoled, bribed, and manipulated Choctaw leaders in every possible way imaginable, trying to turn them against their enemies, or against other native peoples who were allied with their enemies.

This constant intrigue kept the Choctaws in a situation of constant change and political turmoil. During the first half of the 18th century, France and England each tried to stir up trouble between the Choctaw Nation and her indigenous neighbors, especially the Chickasaws. These European nations were obsessed with defeating each other, and found the Native Americans nations to be extremely valuable allies, or terrible foes, in their fight for dominance in North America. They both became intimately involved in the political affairs of the native nations, through bribes, gifts, gossip, and slander, inciting their own allies to attack the allies of the other European nation. In the early part of the century, the Chickasaw Nation allied with English slave-traders in Charlestown and constantly raided Choctaw territory to kidnap women and children, who they sold to the English slavers in Charlestown. Meanwhile, the French in New Orleans tried to get their Choctaw allies to exterminate the Chickasaws.

The Natchez Nation, centered geographically near the present day city of Natchez, Mississippi, opposed French conquest of their territory, and in 1729, tried to expel them entirely. They attacked the French colony at Natchez, and killed about 200 men, taking probably 300 women and children captive. The French retaliated, but without much success. However, they prevailed upon their Choctaw allies for help, and a great victory against the Natchez followed. The French continued their attempts to exterminate the Natchez. In 1731, in a final battle, the Great Sun of the Natchez and other key leaders were captured, and all were sold into slavery in the French Caribbean. Some Natchez escaped and found shelter with the Chickasaws, who then became the target of French and Choctaw warriors.

One of the major consequences of European manipulation and political intrigue was factions that split the Choctaw Nation into divided and hostile segments. In 1748, these antagonisms resulted in a bloody civil war. In the 1740s, a great peace chief or *mingo,* Shulush Homa, or Red Shoes, tried to

bring peace to the warring factions within the tribe, and between the Chickasaws and Choctaws. He almost succeeded, but the French governor defeated
his efforts, and hostilities again broke out. The French hoped to see the
Chickasaws completely exterminated, and then they planned to subjugate
their Choctaw allies. In 1750, the French faction of Choctaws defeated the
English faction, which resulted in the Grandpre Treaty with the French. In
this treaty, the French allies among the Choctaws betrayed the nation's interests, agreeing to become subjects of the French. [11]

In 1754, the final war erupted between the French and English in North
America, in Europe, and in other colonies around the world. This war became a world war, involving many thousands of people around the world.
In North America, the French and Indian War pitted the French and their
Native American allies against the English. The Choctaw Nation sided with
their long-standing French allies. The war ended with the English defeat of
the French, and in the peace treaty called the Peace of Paris of 1763, France
relinquished all its claims in North America to Britain, who then claimed the
French-allied Native American nations as defeated enemies.

The ideology that caused European nations to view only other European
nations as equals resulted in assertions of dominance over native nations that
the Choctaws found quite strange. Although they had become accustomed
to European trade goods and had incorporated them into their lives, the
Choctaws were not dependent on European nations, and continued to be an
important power in the Southeast. In the years leading up to the American
Revolution, the Spanish, to whom the French had relinquished its claims to
Louisiana Territory, wooed the Choctaw Nation, trying to take the place of
the French in Choctaw politics.

In 1784, Spain and the Choctaw Nation made a treaty of friendship. This
was quickly countered by Americans, who in 1786 obtained the Hopewell
Treaty, which declared friendship between the United States and the Choctaw
Nation. Among several other important provisions, the treaty recognized
the sovereignty of the Choctaw Nation by declaring that any American citizen who invaded in the Choctaw Nation would forfeit U.S. protections and
would be subject to Choctaw law. The Choctaws also allowed the Americans
the opportunity to open three trading posts in the future, and defined the
eastern boundary of the Choctaw Nation at the line agreed to in an old British treaty signed in 1765. [12]

The Spanish kept up their intrigues and influence peddling with the
Choctaws in opposition to the Americans for the remainder of the 1700s.
In October 1800, under pressure from Napoleon, Spain ceded Louisiana
Territory back to France in a secret treaty called the Third Treaty of San
Ildefonso. In 1803, European claims to the Louisiana Territory were sold by

France to the United States, thus ending claims by European powers near any of the lands of the Choctaws. But the danger to the Choctaw Nation from external aggression did not end with the expulsion of European powers. The United States launched an unrelenting campaign of conquest and colonization that ultimately resulted in the dispossession of the Choctaw people from their homelands. With rival Europeans out of the picture, the United States could now deal with the Choctaw Nation without fear of interference or competition.

U.S. COLONIALISM: TAKING CHOCTAW LANDS

During the years after the French and Indian War, several British and French adventurers and traders came into the Choctaw Nation, and married Choctaw women—often women from families of great influence. Several prominent families from this era still have descendants living in Oklahoma today, including the Pitchlynn, Folsom, Perry, Harris, Durant, Harkins, LeFlore, Nail, and Cravat families. These men brought the first cattle into the nation, introducing stock raising as a new economic sector, which many Choctaws adopted. They also provided Choctaws with greater knowledge about Americans and they often worked as interpreters for important negotiations and meetings with U.S. government agents. Their children and grandchildren became prominent and influential in the tribe; their bicultural, bilingual upbringing helped facilitate communication and understanding across the social and political boundaries between the United States and the Choctaw Nation. But their strong influence also led some to doubt their loyalty to the Choctaw Nation and others to wonder if they truly acted in the best interests of the Choctaw people or to their own personal advantage. Were the descendants of these Choctaw–American unions Choctaw or American at heart? Were their loyalties divided? When they interpreted for the Choctaws, did they polish American communications to persuade Choctaws to agree with the Americans or did they use their bicultural abilities to truly look after Choctaw interests and to uncover American duplicity or unfair dealings?

Whether for good or evil, the children of Choctaw–American marriages figured prominently in almost all important national debates and decisions over the next century. Besides cultural, social, and linguistic expertise and knowledge, they introduced the American ideology of progress, and assisted the spread of Christian religion, along with the dominant society's belief in private property and quest for individual wealth. These concepts ran counter to Choctaw beliefs, and the resulting dissension caused factions to develop, which disrupted Choctaw unity and caused great confusion, anger, and disharmony.[13]

The lands of the Choctaw Nation gradually became surrounded by white American invaders, who were squatting on land, building houses and barns, and clearing fields to plant crops. Many of these intruders caused constant problems among the Choctaws, bringing the worst vices of American society with them. Some imported whiskey in enormous quantities, selling it to the Choctaws. The importation and sale of liquor into the Choctaw Nation was against American and Choctaw law, as was their intrusion on Choctaw lands. However, the United States refused to enforce these laws and to expel white intruders, so the problem grew to huge dimensions over the first quarter of the 19th century. The most enterprising of the intruders would bring barrels of cheap whiskey into the nation, then wait for the return of hunters coming back from the long winter hunts, when they were tired and susceptible, and offer them free drinks. Within an hour or so, when the Choctaw men were drunk, the traders would then offer them more whiskey, but at the cost of the bales of pelts and hides they had obtained after months of hunting. Often intoxicated and unable to resist, many men lost all they had, arriving back in their towns with nothing to trade for needed goods, and no way to pay off the debts accrued over the past year. Cheap liquor flooded the nation, and eroded not only the economy, but also the social, cultural, and political functioning of Choctaw daily lives. The devastating effects of the scourge of alcohol included impoverishment, violence within the community, neglect of family and clan responsibilities, and disruption of the traditional rhythms of daily life.[14]

WHITE INVASION AND THE TREATY PROCESS

After the War of 1812 ended in 1815, thousands upon thousands of white invaders came into the region of the Choctaw lands, squatting, clearing land, and intending to fight to stay. These invaders put tremendous pressure on game populations, and before long, the deer and bear became quite scarce. Although the Choctaws had a mixed economy in which hunting was only one part, it formed an important part of their food supply, and furs and pelts to sell to the traders. As the game receded, hunters had to travel longer and longer distances away from the traditional Choctaw hunting grounds to find game. Many went to the present state of Oklahoma, where game was still plentiful. The long absences of most of the men from the towns of the nation further disrupted traditional life. New fields could not be cleared in the absence of the men, training and education of the young boys suffered, and invading whites became more and more audacious. The economy worsened significantly, and many of the old ways were disrupted.[15]

At the same time, white Americans, who viewed Indians as less than human, clamored for the U.S. government to force the Choctaw Nation to give up vast quantities of territory through so-called treaty negotiations, which were often more akin to criminal acts than to international diplomatic relations. American negotiators routinely bribed and suborned susceptible captains and *mingos* (chiefs). Whenever there was a treaty negotiation, whiskey traders arrived several days early to hand out free whiskey at the behest of the U.S. treaty commissioners. Excessive drinking and drunkenness weakened the ability of Choctaw leaders to effectively represent the interests of their nation.

The U.S. government wrested their homelands from native people across the country through a century of fraud, bribery, and dishonest tactics. U.S. treaty commissioners routinely used threats of military annihilation if indigenous leaders refused to agree to their peoples' dispossession, exile, and pauperization. The U.S. government set up a special treaty system that it used only with Native Americans. It differed from the treaty system used with European countries in important respects. For example, it was standard in international treaty negotiations for each nation to appoint its legitimate representatives, who then met with the opposing nation's authorized representatives. Both groups of representatives would then exchange credentials, which were documentary proof of their authorization to conduct negotiations on behalf of their nation. The two delegations would meet and negotiate the terms of a treaty. Then each delegation would return to their own nation to present the terms that had been negotiated. The national government of each nation would consider whether or not to ratify the treaty, and after due deliberation and within a time frame agreed upon by both parties, each nation would then convey by official message, whether or not the treaty had been ratified by the national legislature or official authority. Each step in this process conformed to international rules of diplomacy, which legitimated the process and made it above manipulation by either of the parties. This process was devised over centuries to prevent war.

However, with Native Americans, the United States conducted sham negotiations in which acts of bribery, fraud, threats of violence, actual violence, and all sorts of unethical behavior were repeatedly utilized by U.S. negotiators, usually under the explicit instructions of the American government. The United States frequently dealt with people from tribes who were not the appointed negotiators of the native nation, and who had no legitimate authority to meet or conclude any agreement with U.S. treaty negotiators. Time after time, the United States would obtain a treaty in this manner, and would proclaim it to be legitimate, insisting that this agreement was the legitimate will of the native nation with whom they were dealing. Hundreds of treaties were obtained in this manner, every one of them fraudulent, but claimed by the U.S. government to be legitimate. The U.S. Senate would then ratify the so-called treaty and it would become law, despite thousands of protests from the citizens and friends of the native nation in question.

At other times, the U.S. government would find a minor leader from a tribe whom they would bribe, proclaim him to be the official head chief, and then get him to sign a treaty ceding enormous regions of the tribe's territory, claiming that this person was authorized to act for the native nation. To make this dishonest transaction appear more legitimate, the United States would give a few cheap presents or a tiny payment in goods or cash to the nation, allegedly in compliance with the treaty. These treaties were presented as valid legal agreements, even though they were clearly not obtained by honest means.

As mentioned above, the treaty system that the United States used with native nations also differed from the international treaty system with European governments in another crucial way. In the legitimate process used with European nations, the treaty negotiations conducted between teams of negotiators for each nation were only a tentative agreement. This agreement was then taken back to the respective nations for consideration. Each nation then took time to review and ratify or reject the agreement before it became bound by its terms. However, with Native American nations, the United States insisted that the treaty terms agreed to by the negotiators during negotiations were absolutely binding on the native nation without any chance for them to review or ratify the terms. This allowed the United States to successfully use nefarious and dishonest tactics to get someone's signature on a treaty and to proclaim the native nation to be bound by whatever that person had agreed to. For example, in the Treaty of Dancing Rabbit Creek of 1830, U.S. negotiators declared the treaty negotiations to be at an end when the Choctaw leaders refused to agree to their own dispossession. U.S. Secretary of War John Eaton then waited for all the people to leave the treaty grounds, and met secretly with Greenwood LeFlore, a Choctaw who was on the U.S. payroll. Although he had no authority to do so, he signed a treaty agreeing to the dispossession and permanent exile of the entire Choctaw Nation. Eaton immediately rushed back to Washington with this fraudulent document, and the U.S. Senate ratified it and it became U.S. law.[16]

These dishonest tactics began with President Thomas Jefferson, whose instructions to U.S. Indian agents and treaty negotiators set the tone of American policy for years to come. He instructed U.S. traders and agents to extend credit at the trading posts to any Choctaw who wanted it, and to be very liberal with this policy when dealing with Choctaw headmen or chiefs. His scheme was to draw unsophisticated native people into debt, and then have the traders demand payment. At that point, he instructed the U.S. Indian agents to suggest that the debts could easily be paid off by giving up a portion of Choctaw lands to the United States, who would then pay off their debts.[17]

Many of the treaties for land cessions between the United States and native nations contained terms that were so one-sided that they hardly made sense. For example, in December 1801, the United States sent treaty negotiators to the Choctaw Nation and met the Choctaws at Fort Adams, which was about 120 miles south of present day Natchez. Fort Adams was the port of entry for the United States in 1801, and remained so until America bought France's claims to the Louisiana Territory (and the city of New Orleans) in 1803. Choctaw leaders erroneously believed that if they ceded this region contiguous to the Mississippi River, the Americans would be appeased and would leave them in peace. A famine was underway, and many Choctaw people were suffering in want. The game in the territory had been chased away by thousands of white intruders on Choctaw lands. Under these circumstances, the United States procured the Treaty of Fort Adams, in which the Choctaw Nation handed over 2.6 million acres of prime river fronting land that lined the Mississippi River, from the mouth of the Yazoo River to the southern Gulf Coast. The Choctaws also affirmed the eastern boundary fixed by the old treaty of 1765 with the British and allowed the United States to build a wagon road from Natchez to Nashville across the heart of the Choctaw Nation. In exchange, the Choctaw Nation received $2,000 and some blacksmith tools, or $0.00076 per acre. Most people would call this transaction theft.[18]

The Choctaw leadership resented the one-sided deal demanded by the Americans, but they tried to comfort themselves that this magnificent cession of valuable land would surely appease the Americans and would be the last territory they Choctaws would cede. However, within six months, U.S. negotiators were back, and the Choctaw leadership refused to receive them. However, the Choctaws were finally persuaded to meet with American negotiators when they were assured that the United States simply wanted to confirm the boundary between the United States and Choctaw Nation so that it could expel white American intruders squatting on Choctaw lands. The Treaty of Fort Confederation was concluded in 1802. When the Choctaw leaders signed this treaty, they made their anger plain, and told the Americans that they would not negotiate any further agreements with the United States. However, in 1803, the Americans were back, goaded to seek more land by the Euro-American invaders who squatted on lands around the Choctaw Nation.[19]

President Jefferson instructed the American negotiators to force a concession from the Choctaw Nation for debts incurred by individual members that were owed to the private French trading house of Panton, Leslie & Company. When the Choctaw leaders refused to cooperate, U.S. negotiators demanded immediate payment on behalf of Panton, Leslie & Company. This is like the United States going to Canada and insisting that the Canadian government give up a huge amount of land in exchange for the United States paying off the debts of private individuals owed to private American companies. This would certainly be unthinkable. The federal government has never had constitutional authority to act as a debt collector for a private company, and it has no legal authority to threaten a sovereign nation in the collection of such a debt. However, despite the illegal and unconstitutional nature of these actions, U.S. negotiators even threatened the Choctaws with war if the Choctaw Nation refused to give up a huge area of land. By these actions, the United States made it clear that these debts were simply a pretext for a land grab, one that the United States intended to have even if it meant war. In August 1803, Choctaw leaders were forced to sign the Treaty of Hoe Buckintoopa, so that the United States could keep up a fiction of a diplomatic agreement to which both parties agreed. Thus, the United States obtained 853,760 acres of Choctaw land north of Mobile.[20]

The Choctaw national government could not control the indebtedness of its individual citizens. Just as in Euro-American society, each person was free to go to the trading posts and incur debts that they would intend to pay off from the sale of furs and pelts they obtained through the winter hunt. With President Jefferson instructing all the traders to give the native people easy credit, and encouraging them to run up debts they could never hope to repay, the American government then replayed the Treaty of Hoe Buckintoopa. In 1805, U.S. treaty negotiators again showed up in the Choctaw Nation to force the Choctaws to cede a huge area of land in exchange for the United States paying off the debts incurred by private individuals to a private trading company, the Panton, Leslie & Company. The debt owed by individual Choctaws amounted to $46,000. At Mount Dexter, near present day Macon, the furious Choctaw *mingos* were again forced to sign a treaty ceding more than four million acres of excellent farmland in what is today the state of Mississippi. In exchange, the United States paid them only $50,500, of which $48,000 went to Panton, Leslie & Company for their debts, while $2,500 was paid to their white interpreter, John Pitchlynn. Thus, the U.S. government obtained 4.1 million acres of land for a penny an acre, and all the money went to pay the debts of individuals. Not one cent went to the Choctaw people, except the bribe of $500 each, which was paid to the three chiefs of the nation. Each chief also received a sum of $150 every year as an annuity.

In addition, the United States agreed to pay the Choctaws a payment of $3,000 every year in goods. Thus, the United States procured another crooked treaty in which they received four million acres of the best farmland in the country for about one penny an acre, plus a few trade goods yearly. This land was rich Mississippi delta lands, which became the heart of the agricultural wonderland of King Cotton that made hundreds of millionaire plantation owners in later years. Even President Jefferson was evidently embarrassed by the unfair terms of the Treaty of Mount Dexter. He actually refused to send the treaty to the Senate until 1808, when to appease the white settlers invading Choctaw lands, he finally submitted it for ratification, without changing the terms.[21]

LAND SPECULATION AND OTHER SCHEMES TO OBTAIN INDIAN LANDS

During the first decade of the 19th century, the people of the United States engaged in rampant land speculation on territory belonging to Native American nations. A process to obtain these lands developed as a result of influence on the American government that was exerted by these wealthy speculators. First, agents of rich land speculators would travel to interior lands west of American settlements and identify areas that they would recommend as prime lands for speculation. They would survey the lands and then return to the East. The speculators formed huge land companies and offered shares to the fellow rich citizens. The whole purpose was to make enormous profits by buying land very, very cheaply from native nations, then selling it to individual Euro-American farmers. After the lands had been located and surveyed, these wealthy conglomerates would lobby the state or territorial government, where many of them either had great influence or were, in fact, elected officials. In exchange for favorable decisions, the land companies often gave government officials shares in the land speculation company. The entire upper class of American citizenry was involved, and a list of their names includes the Founding Fathers and their families and friends. Benjamin Franklin, Patrick Henry, George Washington, Thomas Jefferson, and many others speculated in lands that were owned and occupied by native nations.[22]

Many speculators formed small armies of men whom they sent to the land they wanted to try to provoke hostilities with the native owners. Once the native nations tried to expel these intruders or defend their homelands and people against these invaders, the armies would withdraw to the nearest white settlement, clamoring for protection from the "savages." They would claim that the Indians were on "the warpath" and that they were attacked for no reason. In response, the state or federal government often sent military forces into these nations to punish the Indians and to force them to give up the land wanted by the speculators in exchange for peace. Millions of acres of native lands were obtained through these tactics.

In the early 1800s, a great Shawnee leader formed a Pan-Indian alliance to stop the Americans and their ruthless and insatiable conquest of native lands. His name was Tecumseh, and he saw and understood the tactics and methods that were being used by the American government to trick, bribe, or force native nations to give up their land, and how it was leading to the their impoverishment and destruction. He believed that native people must unite across traditional tribal boundaries and identities, to become one unified Indian nation. If all native people were united, the United States would be less able to manipulate them. This was the only chance to survive the ruthless aggression of the United States. Tecumseh's brother, Tenskwatawa, was a prophet whose followers believed had been shown the path native people must take to maintain their freedom and sovereignty. In a dream, Creator showed him how all native peoples should put away European trade goods and return to the ways of their ancestors. They should expel all whites from their lands, and refuse all the ways of the whites. No one should drink alcohol, and the old ceremonies and native beliefs should be invigorated. They must call on Creator for the power to do all these things, and when native people had revived the traditional ways of living, the whites would disappear into the sea.

Tecumseh and Tenskwatawa attracted thousands of followers, especially among the Delawares, Shawnees, and Kickapoos. Native people came from across the land to hear him speak, and many joined his movement. In 1811, Tecumseh traveled to the South to speak to the great southern native nations: Choctaws, Chickasaws, Creeks, and Cherokees. He was a mesmerizing speaker and was tall and strong: one of those people whose presence is always noticed. He spoke to a gathering of hundreds of Choctaws and was very well received. At the end of his statement, the most prominent *Mingo* Pushmataha rose to answer him. All eyes were riveted on Pushmataha, who waited several minutes until he had the attention of everyone. He told the people that the Americans had never harmed the Choctaws, and that he believed they should continue to be their allies and friends. He believed it would be a huge mistake to antagonize the United States by joining a native alliance to oppose them, and even said that if any Choctaw decided to side with Tecumseh against the Americans, he would personally kill them. The Nation was stunned at this threat, since Choctaws had always been free to individually decide their own path, and coercion in decisions such as this was unheard of.[23]

The influence of Pushmataha was so great that only a few young men joined Tecumseh, and the vast majority of the Nation remained at peace with the United States. While Tecumseh was away, William Henry Harrison and his American troops attacked Prophetstown (near present day Lafayette, Indiana), and in the fighting some of his followers were injured or died, thus shattering Tenskwatawa's promises that the white man's bullets could not hurt them. Disillusioned, many men who had joined the alliance left the Shawnee town and returned to their homes. Tecumseh rushed back, only to find many of his followers had departed. Still, many remained, but without the southern tribes, his alliance could not stop the American invasions.

The Choctaws continued to serve as allies of the Americans. Pushmataha brought hundreds of his warriors to fight against the Red Sticks Creeks at the Battle of Horseshoe Bend. Andrew Jackson led the U.S. troops and was almost defeated in a disastrous frontal assault, but his native allies surprised the Red Sticks from the rear, thus winning the battle for the Americans. Jackson asked *Mingo* Pushmataha to continue to fight for him, and he promoted the *mingo* to the rank of brigadier general in the U.S. Army. Pushmataha and his troops served at the Battle of New Orleans, and were praised for their efforts by General Jackson, who continued to portray himself as a true friend to the Choctaw Nation. Jackson promised U.S. pay to the Choctaw and other native allies, but it was years and years before even part of it was paid.[24]

Jackson's victories over the Red Sticks and at the Battle of New Orleans during the War of 1812 made him a household name. The defeat of the British culminated in the Treaty of Ghent, in which no concessions were made by either side. Many historians believe that the war was more of a draw than a defeat by the United States of Great Britain, and the treaty terms seem to bear evidence for that interpretation.

American invaders poured into the South after the peace with Britain. They simply overran many portions of the Indian nations, and the United States disregarded its treaty promises to expel them. Instead, with war hero Andrew Jackson leading the way, the United States sent negotiators to dozens of native nations insisting on further land cessions to accommodate the illegal squatters.

All native nations were terribly alarmed at the terms Andrew Jackson dictated to the Creek (Muskogee) Nation at the end of the American war against the Red Sticks. Instead of punishing only those who fought against the United States, Jackson punished the whole nation, many of whom had fought with great distinction and valor on the side of the Americans. These allies could not believe they were to be forced to sacrifice their lands, but Jackson would not reason with them. He and his family and friends speculated in lands held by the Creeks (Muskogees) and they stood to make huge profits once these lands were taken away from native owners. Jackson, like many Americans of the era, considered Native Americans to be inferior to whites, who should be forced to give up their homelands because whites wanted them.[25]

After the defeat of the Muskogee Creek Nation in 1814, native leaders began to realize that since the United States had grown in size and population to great military strength, the American government began to treat native nations quite differently than it had in earlier times. In addition, with the defeat of Great Britain, all foreign threats of interference vanished in American plans for expansion over the continent. After 1815, thousands of Americans poured over the mountains and rivers into Indian lands. This full-scale invasion was led by men such as Jackson, and he was anxious for a more visible role so that he could increase his political prospects. Jackson used his popularity to demand that President Monroe appoint him to negotiate treaties with all the southern Indigenous nations that he claimed he had defeated, conveniently forgetting the fact that without thousands of Cherokees, Choctaws, and other southern Indigenous soldiers, he could not have won. Nonetheless, he quickly demonstrated his ruthless determination to wrest these lands from their rightful owners, resorting to threats of annihilation, widespread bribery, and boundless fraud to force native people off their homelands.

The Choctaws naively assumed that Jackson and the American government would recognize and honor their alliance and joint military forces, and expected the United States to demonstrate their gratitude by payment of the amounts owed to Choctaw warriors for their service during the War of 1812. However, the United States was only interested in procuring more Choctaw land. Ignoring the payments owed to Choctaw warriors for their military services, the United States instead once again sent treaty negotiators to try to obtain more of the Choctaw homelands. The negotiations at Fort Stephens began on a pleasant note: Choctaw leaders and the U.S. commissioners sat together reminiscing and exchanging stories about the recent war. Soon, however, the U.S. negotiators changed the tone of the meeting entirely. First, they sought clarification of the boundary changes resulting from the treaty forced on the Muskogee Nation, for which they requested Choctaw acquiescence in a survey of the lands. Surprisingly, the United States sought only a small cession of Choctaw land in exchange for a $6,000 annuity lasting for 20 years, and a gift of merchandise worth $10,000.[26] Choctaw leaders very reluctantly agreed. The U.S. treaty commissioners had brought wagonloads of merchandise to Ft. Stephens, in order to tempt the poverty stricken native people. While the negotiations were proceeding, the commissioners would have the nicest articles displayed in front of the chiefs and headmen. Guns, ammunition, clothing, knives, hatchets, and other highly desired trade goods would prove so tempting to impoverished indigenous peoples that it was almost a foregone conclusion that the United States would procure a treaty. Second, the U.S. government had long experience in dealing unfairly with indigenous peoples, and knew that it would be almost impossible for the leaders of the nation to reject the merchandise and have it roll away in wagons while the people watched. In addition, the United States frequently simply cheated indigenous peoples on the value of the merchandise. It was rarely worth what the U.S. commissioners stated, but this would only be discovered after the treaty was signed, and after the commissioners had left the territory.[27]

In 1817, Mississippi was admitted to the Union as a state; having obtained much of the homelands of the Choctaws, Chickasaws, and Muskogee nations, the lands now owned by the whites used the American legal system to establish themselves as states. Once established, they began demanding that Washington confiscate all the remaining lands owned by the southern Indians, claiming that the native people constituted an obstacle to development of the state, and that the indigenous nations had sprung up in their midst and were withholding valuable lands that should be in the hands of white citizens. In addition, each of the southern states characterized the Indian nations as being "nations within a nation," which, they argued, was unconstitutional. Therefore, they argued that the United States had an obligation to obtain their lands and force them off the lands that white men wanted.[28]

President James Monroe was elected in 1816, and he appointed John C. Calhoun of South Carolina as secretary of war. Calhoun proposed a new Indian policy informed by three doctrines. First, the United States would stop treating native nations as sovereign nations. Native nations should be dissolved and the laws of the United States should be extended over them. Second, the United States would confiscate their lands, and allow them to live on small plots of land west of the Mississippi River. And last, the United States would teach them to desire private property and individual ownership of land. Calhoun called his plan the "removal" of the Indigenous Nations, which does not convey the tremendous suffering caused by the forced dispossessions that followed.[29]

DEATH, DESTRUCTION, AND DISPOSSESSION

In October 1818, and again in August 1819, to implement his program of dispossession of native peoples, Secretary Calhoun sent U.S. commissioners to the Choctaw Nation. When the Choctaw leaders understood that the American wanted to discuss their expulsion to the West, they broke off the meetings and refused to meet again. White Mississippians were outraged, and insisted that the U.S. government take military action to force the Choctaws to move West. In August 1820, under intense pressure from Mississippi and other southern states, Calhoun sent another team of commissioners to the Choctaw Nation including the famous hero of the Battle of New Orleans, Andrew Jackson; a more aggressively ambitious and ruthless man could not have been found. Jackson not only wanted the remaining lands of the Choctaws and all other southern nations of indigenous peoples, he also intended to use whatever means necessary to force them west of the Mississippi River. Jackson longed to be president of the United States and was building his name by obtaining cheap indigenous land, a policy which was wildly popular with American citizens in the South and areas west of the Appalachian Mountains. This constituency fondly called him "Old Hickory," creating all kinds of legends and myths that contributed to his fame. By 1820, Jackson planned to run for president in 1824, and he was determined to build up his fortunes politically by seizing the homelands of indigenous nations.[30]

The treaty that Jackson sought was completely different from the ones that the Choctaws had signed previously. The United States not only wanted their remaining lands in Mississippi and Alabama, but it also insisted that the Choctaw Nation agree to move their entire nation west of the Mississippi to the so-called Great American Desert—a wilderness that U.S. explorers had declared to be worthless for farming.[31] Jackson threatened the Choctaws with the U.S. military force if they refused to agree to give up their homelands. He told them that if they did not go into exile west of the Mississippi River very soon, the United States would give away all the best land in Indian Territory to other tribes, and the Choctaws would be left homeless to wander the western plains. Jackson threatened the Choctaw leaders and people with military force, until finally *Mingo* Pushmataha, a great hero to the Choctaw people, rose to answer him.

Pushmataha informed Jackson and the other commissioners that he and many of the Choctaw warriors were very familiar with the lands in the West that the United States had designated as their place of permanent exile. He said that he was disappointed with the misrepresentations of those lands by Jackson. Since he and his men had spent much time hunting and fighting the Osage and Comanche there, he knew that "a vast amount of it [the lands] were poor and sterile, trackless and sandy deserts," and that there were few trees over much of it, and that in the summer the rivers and springs dried up, making it unfit for agriculture. He also informed Jackson that there were thousands of white squatters already living in this region, and innocently asked him exactly what the Choctaws were supposed to do with them. Jackson replied that he would make them leave; he would bring an American army and drive them into the Mississippi, but Pushmataha was not convinced.[32]

Despite very deep misgivings, the three *mingos* approved the Treaty of Doak's Stand, in which the Choctaws agreed to exchange roughly 5 million acres of land in Mississippi for 13 million acres in Indian Territory. Evidently, they did so primarily because Jackson threatened them with extermination by the United States. The old *mingo* Pushmataha used his enormous influence to convince the other leaders of the nation to sign the treaty. He believed that white Americans led by Jackson would not hesitate to murder all the Choctaw people to get their lands.[33]

Mingo Pushmataha was right on all counts. The lands west were far more arid than the Choctaw homelands, unsuitable for the agriculturally based economy practiced by Choctaw people. Whites occupied much of the eastern section of the proposed exchange, which had an ecosystem and topography much more like that of the Choctaw's Mississippi and Alabama homelands.

PUSH-MA-TA-HA,
A CHOCTAW WARRIOR.

Nº22.   RICE, RUTTER&CO. Publishers.

Portrait of Pushmataha, a Choctaw warrior, by 19th-century American painter Charles Bird King, from *The Indian Tribes of North America*. (Thomas L. McKenney and James Hall, *The Indian Tribes of North America,* 1836–1844)

However, many of the white people living there had been there long enough to build sturdy homes and to clear and plant fields, and they had no intention of moving so that the Native Americans could be accommodated. Within weeks of signing this treaty, the U.S. negotiators returned, requesting that the Choctaws agree to an adjustment of the boundaries of their new lands in the West. *Mingo* Pushmataha was correct—there were hundreds of white settlers illegally squatting on the eastern section of the lands the United States ceded to the Choctaws. Instead of making these people move, they wanted the Choctaws to give up part of the lands they were to receive, before they even received them.

White Mississippians were overjoyed at the news of the Treaty of Doak's Stand, and thousands of them poured onto the Choctaw Nation in Mississippi to stake claims. However, this news enraged American citizens in what is now the eastern area of the Oklahoma–Arkansas border who were illegally squatting out west on the new lands promised to the Choctaws. These Americans fought tooth and nail to defeat ratification of the treaty, to no avail. However, their bitterness remained. As the *Arkansas Gazette* editor wrote, "Never, since the union of these states, has there been a treaty concluded with any Indian Nation so disadvantageous to the United States, or so injurious to any section of country, as this will be to the Territory of Arkansas."[34] They asserted that it was "no doubt good policy" for the more easterly states to "get rid of all the Indians within their limits," but that by sending them to the Arkansas Territory, a "thinly populated area," the Arkansans would "not be able to resist the aggressions of a fierce and savage enemy, whose resentment has already been raised to the highest pitch, and who, probably, in making the exchange, calculates on glutting his vengeance on a weak and defenseless people, for unjuries [*sic*] which he has sustained in his native country."[35] Although their message was obviously calculated to express the utmost outrage and was unrealistic in their description of the Choctaw people, they were certainly correct in asserting that the Choctaws could rightfully feel great resentment and anger for the injustices perpetrated by the United States.

Despite the treaty, very, very few Choctaws chose to move to the new lands in the West. Secretary of State Calhoun cajoled, pleaded, increased the offers, and begged them to go, but almost none would listen. Meanwhile, the outcry of the white squatters in the new western Choctaw lands was taken up by their representatives in Congress, who demanded that the United States renegotiate the boundaries of the new Choctaw lands in the West to exclude the land that these people had illegally occupied. Unfortunately, this ploy always worked with the federal government. In June 1824, Secretary of War Calhoun, desperate to solve this crisis, invited the Choctaws to send a delegation to Washington, D.C. to discuss the issue. Among them were *mingos* Pushmataha, Apukshunnubbee, and Moshulatubbee. Two of the great leaders died on this trip, a terrible calamity that weakened the ability of the Choctaw Nation to meet the challenges they faced. Apukshunnubbee fell off an embankment one evening on October 1824 in Maysville, Kentucky en route to Washington, while *Mingo* Pushmataha became ill one night in the Capitol and died on Christmas Eve. He was buried in the Congressional Cemetery with full military honors as a brigadier general of the United States, the only Native American leader entombed there.[36]

After the funeral, the remaining Choctaw delegates met with Secretary Calhoun, who tried to persuade them to give up more territory in Mississippi and move West. He asserted that nothing short of giving up all their remaining homelands and moving into permanent exile in the West would satisfy the U.S. government. Thinking to persuade them, Calhoun offered them $5,000 cash when they had complied with this request, with $6,000 annually for 10 years. Highly insulted by this offer, the Choctaw leaders abruptly cancelled the talks and began preparations to return home. Calhoun desperately tried to persuade them to stay, floating several ideas, offering various sums. Finally, he suggested that the Choctaw delegation present a list of demands to the war department, to clarify their position. They were ready with a long list that demanded the United States comply completely with the provision in the Treaty of 1820 that allowed any Choctaw who so desired to stay in Mississippi and retain one square mile of land. In addition, they demanded $30,000 worth of goods over 2 years, $9,000 for 20 years to support a Choctaw college in Mississippi, and $3,000 for 20 years for education of the Choctaws who went to live in the West.[37]

After weeks of debate and compromise, the Choctaw leaders and Secretary Calhoun agreed upon terms. The United States promised to pay $6,000 per year to support education forever; pay $6,000 for 16 years, as agreed in the 1820 treaty; cancel the debts of individual Choctaws to the American trading post; and to pay the compensation still owing warriors from the War of 1812. For these considerations, the Choctaw Nation would agree to cede the most eastern portion of their lands in the West back to the United States, which gave the United States the lands on which white squatters had located. Choctaw leaders succeeded in getting out of Washington, D.C., without ceding any more of their homelands east of the Mississippi, while reaffirming the debts owed to the nation by the United States. However, Calhoun's frequent assertions that nothing short of complete surrender of the remaining Choctaw homelands east of the Mississippi River and that their movement into permanent exile would appease the United States gave Choctaw leadership notice of the battle ahead of them.

PRESIDENT JACKSON AND CHOCTAW DISPOSSESSION AND EXILE

In 1828, Andrew Jackson was elected president of the United States. The Choctaws knew that Jackson's election ushered in a new and ruthless era of American aggression. In the eyes of many native leaders, Jackson was recognized as a man of weak character, a consummate politician who courted popularity at the expense of justice. Campaigning on a platform of Indian removal and expansionism, Jackson appealed to the basest instincts of Americans. Strong racism against all people not of European heritage imbued Americans with race hatred and justified monstrous injustices against native people. Jackson's speeches were filled with dishonest stereotypes of southern native peoples—for example, Jackson stated that the Choctaws and other southern Indians were nomads, who roamed over the land, and had no permanent dwellings. He characterized them as unable to adapt "civilized" ways,

This anonymous political cartoon entitled "Andrew Jackson as Great Father" appeared as a satirical comment shortly after the Indian Removal Act was passed. (Clements Library, University of Michigan)

thus playing into the jingoism and racism that was used to justify American wrongdoing against native peoples.[38] Jackson knew better than this. He had spent months with Choctaws, Chickasaws, Cherokees, and Muskogee peoples. He had visited in their homes, eaten with them, and observed their fields of corn, beans, squash, and other crops. But white Americans did not want to hear that indigenous nations were farmers who lived in villages in peace; they wanted their land. The best way to justify the wrongful seizure of native homelands was to falsely paint them as "savages." Jackson provided white Americans with a stereotype to help them think of Indians not as people, but as part of the wilderness; "savages" who had no homes, no civilization, and, in the eyes of white people, no human or civil rights.

"Might makes right" sums up Jackson's attitude and policies toward native people. The end justified the means in his eyes, and expelling Native Americans by force from their homelands became, for him, a patriotic endeavor. Critics of this injustice were vilified by Jackson and his followers, who viewed native peoples as simply an obstacle standing between them and the wealth that they felt that only whites deserved—wealth in land and resources. Not one native nation truly voluntarily agreed to give up their homelands and go into permanent exile. The Choctaws, Cherokees, Chickasaws, Creeks (Muskogees), and Seminoles fought the confiscation of their homelands with every means available to them. Unfortunately, the U.S. legal system was deliberately rigged against them. Under American law, Native Americans had no rights.[39]

As soon as Jackson was elected, powerful southern state legislators and key politicians in both federal and state governments began implementing their final solution to the Indian problem. The deadly weapon they used was the law. The goal of southern states was to finally force all native nations out of their homelands. All of the southern Indian nations had treaties with the federal government, and the U.S. Constitution reserved the right to deal with Indians to only the federal, not state, government. But now that the states had an ally in the White House—President Jackson—they devised a plan, with his cooperation, that would be unconstitutional, but that would almost certainly achieve their goal.

Mississippi, Alabama, and Georgia, one by one, each passed a law outlawing tribal government and declared the native peoples to be second-class citizens of the state, subject to the laws of the state without the full protection of the law enjoyed by white Americans. They made it a crime for native people to meet to discuss anything, and arrested anyone who claimed to speak as a tribal representative. No Indian could testify in a court of law against a white man and Indians could not serve on juries. In effect, this meant that any white person could make a claim against a native person—for example, that the native person owed them money—and, when it went to court, the native person could not testify. If a white man forced a family of Choctaw people out of their home and off their land at gunpoint, the Choctaws could not press charges or testify against the person who stole their property.[40]

In effect, each state legislature declared open season on the property and legal rights of native people. They made them subject to the law, but withheld the rights that white people had. If a white man saw a Choctaw homestead that he wanted, he simply had to swear that the Choctaw had sold him his land (or lost it in a game of cards, or traded it for whiskey, etc.). The Choctaw had no standing in court, so he could not defend himself or his property. The white man could then call upon the sheriff to dispossess the Choctaw family, and could simply move in and take over. This scenario occurred throughout the South, and was used by both the state and federal governments to unfairly force native nations to agree to their own dispossession.[41]

In 1830, Jackson proposed the Indian Removal Act. This act would give the president the right to engage in negotiations with indigenous nations for their homelands, and, in exchange, the president was authorized to designate U.S. land west of the Mississippi to be conveyed to the nation for their new homeland. Under this bill, the U.S. government would make arrangements to transport the native people to their new lands, and would compensate them for the improvements (barns, cleared fields, etc.) that they had to leave behind. In addition, any native person who refused to move and go west could remain on their land in Mississippi, if they became subject to the laws of the state. The act required the government to obtain the voluntary consent of the native nation. No coercion or force was allowed.[42]

The opposition to this bill was fierce. Some U.S. citizens, especially those living on the East Coast, clearly understood that Jackson and his followers in the South wanted the native peoples forced off their lands, if necessary. The opposition argued that this bill was a blot on the honor of the United States and that the United States had no right to force native nations to give up their homelands against their will. They pointed out that the Indians were the original owners, and if white Americans moved in and surrounded them, it was not right for the Americans to then claim that the indigenous nation had no right to be there. To their dismay, the Indian Removal Act passed by the slimmest of margins, and Jackson then disregarded the limitations included in the bill and implemented his plans to forcibly expel the Choctaws from their homelands and into permanent exile in the West.

Jackson almost immediately sent U.S. treaty negotiators to the Choctaw Nation to try to wrest the remainder of their homelands from them. However, the Choctaw people were almost unanimously opposed to giving up their homelands and being forced into exile. They refused to seriously consider ceding even another foot of their lands. One of the U.S. commissioners was the secretary of war, John Eaton. When the Choctaws refused to consider agreeing to their own dispossession, he became enraged, telling the stunned Choctaw leaders that the United States would send its army to annihilate them and would exterminate them all, if they did not agree to U.S. terms. Many of the Choctaws still adamantly refused to cede any more land to the United States, and they left the treaty grounds, being told the negotiations were over.[43]

But Secretary of War John Eaton had other tricks up his sleeve. After all those opposed to the treaty left the grounds, his secret ally, *Mingo* Greenwood LeFlore, and his men remained behind. Without the authorization of the Choctaw Nation, they signed the treaty and received their bribes. Secretary Eaton hurried back to Washington, D.C., claiming that the Choctaw Nation voluntarily agreed to removal. Immediately, the Choctaw National Council, clan leaders, and others sent petitions signed by hundreds of Choctaws, all asserting that the treaty was procured fraudulently, declaring that the vast majority of Choctaws did not agree, and that Eaton had tricked them by stating that the negotiations were over. However, Eaton proclaimed to the Senate that the authorized Choctaw leaders willingly signed the treaty, and that "no secret meetings were held, no bribes were offered, no promises made."[44] In fact, the president himself had held secret meetings with LeFlore, bribes were paid to LeFlore and his followers, and the United States promised him that he would be recognized as chief of the entire nation, as soon as the Choctaws moved to the West. In addition, LeFlore received large gifts of land in the old Choctaw Nation. He never went west to the new lands that he had forced on the other Choctaw people. Instead, he remained in Mississippi, a rich cotton planter, eventually being elected to the Mississippi legislature.

Back in Washington, President Jackson ignored all the protests and petitions, and the U.S. Senate eagerly ratified the Treaty of Dancing Rabbit Creek on February 25, 1831. The treaty devastated the Choctaw people. According to one of the missionaries who witnessed the aftermath, the entire nation went into mourning. The women wailed and cried for days, and the men stared, unmoving, out into the forest. Missionary Cyrus Kingsbury reported that the consequences of the treaty "almost beggars description. Loud exclamations are heard against the treaty in almost every part of the nation. . . . The nation is literally in mourning. . . . Multitudes are so distressed with their prospects as to sit down in a kind of sullen despair. They know not what to do."[45]

Instead of waiting for Choctaw lands to be put up for sale by the government, whites flooded their homelands, trying to claim the best land. Small groups of armed men stormed into clearings of isolated farms, forcing

Choctaw families out of their homes, dispossessing thousands of them. The state authorities refused to help these Choctaws and often participated in these crimes.[46]

The Treaty of Dancing Rabbit Creek contained a provision, in Article XIV, which allowed any Choctaw who wanted to stay in Mississippi the right to select 640 acres and to become a citizen. Jackson and his allies touted this provision to argue that the United States was providing the opportunity for Choctaws who wanted to remain in Mississippi to do so. This looked good on paper, but it never happened. U.S. Indian Agent William Ward was supposed to register those who wanted to remain in Mississippi, but he personally decided that no Indians should be allowed to remain, especially none who were "full blood." Yet thousands wished to do so, and they traveled to the U.S. Choctaw agency, sometimes on journeys that took days to complete. Nonetheless, Ward turned them away, proud that he was complying with the real intentions of his superiors, and certainly of whites who lived in the South. Despite their letters to Washington, D.C., the U.S. government did not intervene, so many of those who stayed behind were not able to secure the land guaranteed them under the Treaty of Dancing Rabbit Creek. Ten years later the U.S. government looked into the allegations that Ward had refused to register them for the land to which they were entitled, and it was confirmed by government investigators. However, these Choctaws were never recompensed for their loss, and they never obtained the land due to them. By the time the U.S. government decided to investigate, their lands had long ago been claimed by white men.[47]

THE TRAIL WHERE WE CRIED

In 1831, hundreds of Choctaw people were rounded up in staging areas to begin the march west. The U.S. government failed to provide the goods and services promised to the Choctaws, causing the death of thousands of people. The United States decided to begin the move in the early autumn, which meant that the Choctaw people were out in the wilderness, on foot, with little extra clothing, and only one blanket per family. The conditions on the trail were terrible. For example, one party traveled through sleet and snow for 24 hours, most of them barefoot and nearly naked, in order to reach Vicksburg without exhausting their inadequate supplies. The disgusted U.S. Army captain, who was their official escort, reported that "If I could have done it with propriety I would have given them shoes. I distributed all the tents and this party are entirely without." He complained about the inadequate provisions made for the Choctaws and said that the "sight of these people and their suffering would convince anyone of the need for an additional allowance for transportation."[48] That this scene so touched a hardened military man shows how truly awful it must have been. The evidence also shows that the main concern of the United States was to keep the expense of the forced dispossession of the Choctaws down to the lowest possible cost, even if it caused the deaths of thousands, despite the fact that the Choctaws themselves were forced to pay the costs of their own expulsion out of the proceeds from the sale of their homelands.[49] Some scholars compare this U.S. policy to the infamous Bataan Death March, where hundreds of U.S. soldiers died on a trek under similar conditions in World War II.[50]

A large majority of the Choctaw Nation went West over the Choctaw "Trail Where We Cried," or Trail of Tears. More than 3,000 of them died on the trail, and many more died shortly after they arrived in Indian Territory from exposure, exhaustion, starvation, malnutrition, or heartbreak. With their immune systems weakened, many succumbed to illnesses that, had they remained in their homelands, would not have killed them. Many Choctaw families still pass down oral histories of their families and friends' experiences during this dreadful time.[51]

After arriving in the new Choctaw Nation in the West, the people found that the other promises by the United States that food and shelter would be provided for everyone for the first year after they arrived, also went unfulfilled. Then in 1833, when the so-called removal was still going on, the Arkansas River and its tributaries flooded in the worst flood in its history. The new houses the Choctaw people had built and their cleared fields were all washed away, as though they had never been there. With their crops gone, thousands of Choctaws began to starve, and since the U.S. government storage buildings had also been flooded or destroyed, there was no one to help them. The carcasses of dead animals floated through the area's lakes and streams, rendering the water unfit for human consumption. Disease broke out all throughout the nation. As this disaster unfolded, the U.S. agent wrote that many of the people were starving. He reported many came to him begging for food, having had nothing to eat "for 10, 12, 15 days." The children cried continuously from hunger, and many died. "Within the hearing of a gun from this spot," he wrote, "one hundred Choctaws had died within the past week."[52]

Of the reduced number of Choctaws who reached the new nation, another one-fifth of them died during the floods, disease, and starvation during their first two years in the West. The provisioning officer of a nearby U.S. Army unit responded to the appeals of their U.S. Indian agent by remarking that he was sending the 50 barrels of spoiled pork that the Choctaws had refused to take the year before the floods. "But now," the officer reported to his superior that he was happy to inform General Gibson that "since they were reduced to starvation, they would doubtless be glad to get it."[53]

These terrible physical problems of starvation, death from exposure to the elements, and deaths from diseases caused great suffering. However, physical suffering was only a part of the effects of the dispossession and exile. To the Choctaw people, expulsion from their ancient homelands was far greater than a simple physical relocation. In their origin tradition, confirmed by the testament of the elders of the tribe, the Choctaws were given the specific lands in the Southeast by *Aba,* Creator, who told them they were to live there forever. The existence of the nation depended upon it. According to the prophecy, if the Choctaw people ever left their homelands, the hunters would find no meat, and the nation would die. The Choctaws also believed that they had a sacred compact with the spirits of the dead to take care of their remains, and to see that they were treated with reverence. Their origin story related that they traveled from the West for 43 years, carrying with them the bones of their dead. Even in modern times, when the Choctaws moved, they also moved the special houses they built to hold the sacred remains of those who had gone before them. During the Trail Where We Cried, U.S. officials refused to allow them to transport the remains of their ancestors to the West, which caused much psychological trauma and suffering. Many Choctaws, who stayed in the South and refused to go to the new lands, did so because they did not want to leave the bones of their dead ancestors.[54]

Thousands of Choctaws refused to leave their homelands even after all their homes were taken over by white invaders. Many of them were forced to live in hiding, deep in the swamps or back hills on the lands unwanted by white farmers. For decades, they worked as day laborers on farms, picking cotton and performing other backbreaking labor and paid a pittance for working on the lands that had once been their own. They suffered from poverty, malnutrition, and disease, and had to move frequently to stay away from whites, who claimed the Choctaw people had no right to be there. Racially, the Choctaws were considered not white. The biracial South had no place in its racial hierarchy for native people.[55]

In Alabama, the remaining Choctaws were called Cajuns, even though they were not Cajuns at all.[56] This label provided a convenient category for these native people, distinct from the only other racial identities of black or white that the white majority recognized. Choctaws were also sometimes classified as Mulattos, by the federal government. As a result, Choctaws in Louisiana, Mississippi, and Alabama suffered from nearly a century of racial discrimination, finding it hard, if not impossible, to find work, educate their children, or exercise any civil, legal, or political rights. They suffered horribly from being hunted down and hauled off to prison, being declared black and enslaved, and from a shocking assortment of atrocities committed against them by whites. Many hate crimes were perpetrated against the Choctaws as late as the 1970s.[57]

THE CHOCTAW NATION OF THE WEST

The Choctaws who were now living in Indian Territory continued their own government. During the 1840s, many Choctaws succeeded in building new homes, businesses, and farms. Some engaged in the market economy, selling cotton to factories in New Orleans, but most simply got by. They grew or made everything they needed and did without those things that required money to purchase. When they needed something that they themselves could not make, they bartered for it—trading labor or goods in exchange for what they needed. Many of the Choctaws did reasonably well, and most had plenty to eat and a comfortable home.[58]

The Choctaws in the West duplicated their traditional communal land-holding system in the West that had always been practiced from time immemorial in their ancient homelands. No one owned any particular piece of land, it was all owned in common. There were no land titles or deeds. The Choctaws, like most indigenous peoples, believed that land could not be sold like a commodity. They believed everyone owned the land in common. Each person could use as much land as he or she needed. If land was vacant and unused, a Choctaw family could use the land, build a house, and raise crops, and no one could encroach on his home. If a person moved, he was entitled to be paid for any improvements that he had made—for example, if he built a barn or a new house she or he could request the people moving in to pay for those. In this manner, there were very few conflicts over land, and everyone had plenty. No one was ever homeless among the Choctaws.

A growing problem in the Choctaw Nation of the West was the increasing numbers of white intruders. The U.S. government, under the Treaty of Dancing Rabbit Creek, was supposed to eject white intruders from the Choctaw Nation in the West, and occasionally they did so. However, each year, especially after the Civil War ended, more and more whites came into the nation and squatted on Choctaw lands. The Choctaw National Council repeatedly requested the United States to live up to its treaty obligations and expel these people, but this invasion was the method the Americans had used since 1776 to obtain indigenous lands. The difference this time, or so the Choctaw Nation hoped, was that the nation had received a patent from the United States that was a valid legal instrument verifying their right to this property. Unfortunately, in the years to come, the United States would abrogate its solemn treaty promises, and would invalidate the legal ownership of the Choctaw Nation against their will.

THE AMERICAN CIVIL WAR

During the American Civil War, the Choctaw Nation tried to remain neutral. They wanted no part of this fight. Unfortunately, their location next to Arkansas and Texas made it impossible not to choose sides. At the very beginning of the war, the federal government withdrew all the troops who were stationed in Indian Territory. As the war heated up, Texans formed large groups of armed men and crossed over into the Choctaw Nation to terrify the citizens and try to force them to join the Confederacy. Without federal troops for defense, Choctaw civilians were at their mercy.[59]

After awhile, Chief Peter Pitchlynn and the other leaders of the nation realized that they could not remain neutral without the support of federal troops. Some people believe that the Choctaws joined the Confederacy because some of the wealthy Choctaws owned African American slaves. But only a small minority of the Choctaws were slaveholders. More importantly, the Confederacy lobbied the native nations of Indian Territory to join them. They sent Albert Pike, who had been the U.S. Indian agent to the Choctaw Nation, to

Peter Pitchlynn was a Choctaw leader and diplomat who served as chief during the U.S. Civil War, and who represented Choctaw interests to the U.S. government for many years. (Courtesy of the Library of Congress)

try to persuade them to ally with the South. He presented several very persuasive arguments, including that the Confederate government would honor all the treaties and fulfill the annuities owed by the United States. But most importantly, the Confederates offered official representation in the Confederate legislature, a tempting visions of equality unlike anything they had in previous policies with the United States. Choctaw leaders understood that the raids from Texas would continue and escalate, and with the southern offer to treat the Choctaw people as equals, they were persuaded to throw in their lot with the South.

Terrible warfare, mainly internecine (civil) war, raged through Indian Territory between the tribes and factions of tribes that were on opposite sides of the fight. Native southern partisans attacked and fought other members of their tribe, who sided with the Union. Widespread destruction swept over the lands of Cherokees, Seminoles, and Muskogees (Creeks), and thousands of refugees fled their homes for the borders. The Choctaw and Chickasaw nations suffered less destruction than other Indian Territory nations, but they were inundated with Cherokee refugees. Everyone suffered, and the economy of Indian Territory was devastated.

When the war finally ended, no help was forthcoming for Indian Territory, despite the fact that many of the nations who lived there had sent hundreds of troops to fight with the Union. Instead, the United States viewed them as defeated enemies. The U.S. government sent representatives to meet with the native nations to dictate the terms on which they could reestablish relationships with the United States. The Choctaws came out fairly well, led by the old *mingo* Peter Pitchlynn. The United States wanted to confiscate much of the land held by the Choctaws and other nations in Indian Territory in order to continue with the forced relocation of native peoples from the Great Plains and Far West, against whom the United States was waging a terrible, genocidal war. Determined to clear a space on which to incarcerate the Great Plains and Far West peoples, the United States insisted that the native nations of Indian Territory give up this huge expanse of land. In exchange for a small payment, the Choctaws had to relinquish nearly half their land base in Indian Territory. This wasn't quite the blow it could have been to the Choctaws because the western part of their lands were sparsely settled. The land was arid and unsuitable for farming without irrigation, so most Choctaws made their homes in the eastern half of the Choctaw Nation. Nonetheless, these western lands were enormously valuable, and the United States paid them next to nothing for them, in order to complete the conquest of native lands.

Every year, beginning just after the Civil War, members of Congress, especially those from the West, tried to pass legislation that would incorporate

Indian Territory as an official U.S. territory. This action would have been a repudiation of the solemn treaty promises the United States had made with each of the native nations in the territory. Forming a territory was the first step in the process of creating a state. The native nations knew that once a territory was established, the U.S. cycle of eviction and confiscation of native lands would once again be set in motion. This was the beginning of the campaign to seize Choctaw lands, following the same system of eviction and confiscation that had taken place in Mississippi in the 1830s. Of course, all the native leaders understood clearly that once this process began they would again be dispossessed. All the Indian nations vehemently objected, every one of them sending lobbyists to represent native interests in the U.S. Congress. But since Indians had no rights under the U.S. law and no representation in Congress, white lawmakers could dismiss them without fear of losing reelection.

THE NOTORIOUS DAWES ACT

In 1887, Senator Henry Dawes of Massachusetts introduced a bill called the General Allotment Act, or Dawes Act, that would end up devastating the native nations throughout the United States. This law would force all the Indian nations to divide up their lands into 140-acre plots, one to each family. Then the United States would declare all the rest of their land to be surplus and it would be offered for sale to white Americans, against the will of the native people who had legal title to this land. All the nations of Indian Territory held title to their lands communally. All the land belonged to all the people—it was not divided into individual plots owned by individuals. Instead, in accord with native tradition, every person in a tribe had an ownership stake in every acre of tribal territory. Individuals were free to establish homes and farms or other businesses on any land that was not being used by someone else. If an individual decided to leave, they could sell their improvements—houses, barns, cleared fields, etc.—but could not sell the land itself, because that did not belong to any one individual. The advantage of this system of landholding was that no one was ever homeless or without access to a piece of land. Second, native peoples had learned that if the United States succeeded in forcing them to own their land as individuals, it was much easier for the Americans to cheat native landholders out of their land. If all the tribal lands were owned by all the nations' people, it was much more difficult for the United States to get their land.

The U.S. government leaders, determined to wrest these lands away from the native owners, claimed that they were doing this for the benefit of native people, and went through amazing intellectual contortions trying to come up with reasons why destroying the way native peoples lived would be good for them. The bottom line, however, was that since native peoples were outside the system of U.S. law—in other words, they had no rights under the law or U.S. Constitution—this status allowed U.S. leaders to do anything that they pleased. They simply passed a law that made it legal.

In 1903, in the decision on Lone Wolf v. Hitchcock, the Supreme Court even declared that Congress could change or repeal any treaty with native people whenever it wanted to do so.[60] This left the native people with no legal position—the United States could simply make up laws as it went to suit their own needs and desires. The only grounds left to native leaders to fight the Dawes Act and the confiscation of their lands was to appeal on moral and ethical grounds; that it was simply wrong to break all the treaty promises and take their land against their wishes, which did not slow the greed that drove confiscation of their lands at all. These new policies went largely unopposed. The proponents couched the motives of the United States in propaganda, asserting that the United States was confiscating native lands in order to benefit the native people, and to help them become civilized. Tens of thousands of protests from native people and nations were sent to Washington, to no avail.

Aside from the fact that the United States was treating native people with gross injustice and forcing them to give up their lands to which they held legal title, the plain facts of the matter were that individual native people did not understand buying and selling and leasing land as private property.[61] Many of them spoke no English and had little, if any, education, not to mention the fact that they were not U.S. citizens and had no protection under U.S. law. Under these circumstances, they became the target of every crook and con man in the country. The Choctaw people had never owned individual plots of land. They had always believed that Creator meant for all members of the tribe to share their territory, and anyone who wanted to claim a portion that no one else was using at the time, could do so. Under this system, every single person in the nation had as much land as they wanted to use. There was plenty for all. The land was protected from white confiscation only so long as the nation held the lands in common, because then it took a treaty to take away their land. However, once the Dawes bill and private property was forced on them, they no longer had any protection from the tribal government, which the U.S. government simply dissolved. This left every single Choctaw family alone, and at the mercy of whites who took advantage of every dishonest and unethical means of obtaining their property. For example, a common ploy was to simply bring a piece of paper with English writing to a native family that spoke little or no English and could not read, and told they had to sign the paper to register their land, the unwitting native person would sign what was actually a deed of sale, which the crook would then take to the land office, transferring the native family's land to his name. He would then have the sheriff dispossess the native family, and would move right in, having legally acquired the land. Fraud and all kinds of dishonest dealings prevailed throughout the old Choctaw Nation, transferring millions of acres of land out of the hands of the rightful Choctaw owners.

Over the continuous protests of all native nations, the Dawes Act was passed and resulted in a frenzy of corruption and fraud, with white citizens frantically trying to obtain, by fair means or foul, the land that the United States had seized. Native peoples and their nations fought the redistribution of their lands in every way possible, but the political and economic might of the United States was overwhelming. Forcing the redistribution of the lands of the Choctaws and other native nations inflicted the final blow to many native people. By 1930, more than 90 million acres of land had moved from native hands to white ones. Thousands of native people were now homeless and most lived in dire poverty. Stripped of their land and resources, the Choctaw people, along with all other Native Americans, had no way to support themselves. With the Dawes Act and the resulting breakup of the native reservation lands, the United States had set up a system of grinding poverty and despair as the norm for Indian peoples, and from which almost none could escape. The United States thus solved what it called the Indian problem by seizing all their wealth and forcing them into abject dependence on government rations, medical care, and shelter. In 1906, the U.S. government unilaterally terminated the government of the Choctaw Nation.[62]

THE LOWEST POINT IN THE HISTORY OF THE CHOCTAW NATION

The effects of the Dawes Act and other colonial U.S. legislation and the resulting impoverishment of native peoples in Indian Territory were reflected in the Meriam Report, which was released by the U.S. government in 1928. The U.S. Department of Interior had commissioned an investigation into the economic and social conditions of Native Americans after 150 years of U.S. colonialism. The results shocked the world. It graphically described the abject poverty of almost all native peoples, the rampant diseases endemic in Indian boarding schools, malnutrition, substandard housing, and almost nonexistent medical care. Tuberculosis was extremely prevalent, and trachoma, a highly contagious disease that causes blindness, affected thousands upon thousands of Indian children in boarding schools that the U.S. government forced them to attend. Most children in these schools did not receive proper nutrition, and had an insufficient quantity of food. The food that they did have was very poor, and consisted almost exclusively of meat and starches. There was great overcrowding in the schools, where dormitories full of native children lay in row upon row of cots, often in unheated buildings. The housing was often dilapidated or poorly built, and the crowding made it impossible to isolate children with contagious diseases. In many instances, the health of native children was sacrificed because school officials had to keep the schools completely full to comply with the requirements dictated from Washington.[63]

Housing on reservation lands was basically unheated shacks, into which sometimes dozens of people crowded. There were no bathrooms or running water in native houses, and they had to get their water from streams or rivers located at a distance. Often, their water supply was entirely insufficient or of poor quality, which contributed to ill health. On reservations throughout the Midwest and northern states, native people died from the cold because their housing was so poor. For thousands of years, great indigenous nations like the Sioux and the Northern Cheyenne, among many others, had developed and utilized technology to build warm houses, supplying themselves with all the necessities of life. In one short century, however, the United States was able to beggar them, stripping them of basic human rights and their dignity, making them completely dependent on government programs that were grossly inadequate.[64]

The declared goal of the policies of the Dawes era were to force Native Americans to assimilate and become part of the dominant white society, but in many ways the realities imposed on native peoples were little better than imprisonment and were clearly a form of subjugation. For example, if a native person received a payment resulting from the lands confiscated by the U.S. government, it was not given to the native person, but was held by the U.S. Indian agent in trust for the native person. If this person wanted to purchase something with his money, he had to go to the agency and ask the agent to allow him to do so. The agent had complete authority. He could deny permission, if he chose to do so. The level of control asserted over adult Native Americans was all pervasive, a constant form of punishment for being Indian. For the Choctaw people, the main problems during this period resulted from their lack of land, from being cheated by whites, and from not having equal rights under U.S. law with whites. Thousands of Choctaws lost all their land in this period. Having no place to go, they bunched up with relatives who still had some land, or drifted homelessly from place to place. Employment was almost nonexistent, and the timber companies had arrived and were clear-cutting their lands, creating a hideously devastated landscape.[65]

WORLD WAR I AND CHOCTAW CODE TALKERS

In 2002, a new movie, *Windtalkers,* was released that heralded the story of the Navajo code talkers, who during World War II, serving in the U.S. Marine Corps, created and used a code for communication that was never broken by the enemy.[66] However, the Navajos were not the first Native Americans to develop a top secret code to assist U.S. military efforts. In World War I, 14 Choctaw men served in the U.S. Expeditionary Force that defeated the Germans in the final Allied campaign to force the Germans to end the war. In one of the major battles, the American 142nd Infantry was pinned down by German artillery at St. Etienne. Communications were regularly intercepted and translated by Germans, so some officers asked Choctaw soldiers to speak the messages over the field radios in the Choctaw language. They did so, completely baffling the listening enemy, and the tide was turned in favor of the Allied forces shortly thereafter. The 14 Choctaw men who were able to fool the enemy and save their units were recognized by the Choctaw Nation of Oklahoma at their annual festival in 1986, where they were awarded the

The Choctaw code talkers, originally called the Choctaw Telephone Squad, June 7, 1919, Camp Merritt, New Jersey: Mitchell Bobbs, James Davenport, James Edwards, E. H. Horner, Taylor Lewis, and Calvin Wilson. (Mathers Museum of World Cultures, Indiana University)

Choctaw Nation Medal of Valor.[67] On November 3, 1989, the French government awarded these Choctaw heroes the Chevalier de L'Ordre National du Merite (the Knight of the National Order of Merit), which was the highest medal the French can bestow.[68]

WORLD WAR II AND THE POST-WAR YEARS

Years passed, and finally, World War II offered an opportunity to leave extreme conditions of poverty, so many Choctaw men enlisted when the war broke out. Choctaws had served with distinction in World War I, creating an unbreakable code that was never deciphered by the enemy. Called Choctaw code talkers, they were used in the last campaign of World War I, and set a precedent for the use of Native American languages as codes in other conflicts. In World War II, Choctaws distinguished themselves in many theaters, mixed in with white units. Van Barfoot, a Mississippi Choctaw, received the Medal of Honor for his actions in the breakout from Anzio to Rome. "He

Many Choctaw men and women have distinguished themselves in the armed forces of the United States. (Courtesy of Choctaw Nation of Oklahoma)

knocked out two machine gun nests and captured seventeen Germans. Later that same day, he repelled a German tank assault, destroyed a Nazi fieldpiece, and, while returning to camp, carried two comrades to safety."[69] Many other Choctaw men and women served in the Armed Forces during World War II.

When Choctaw men returned home from World War II, many of the women they left behind had gone to Dallas, Ft. Worth, Kansas City, and many to California, to work in the war industries.[70] They were given opportunities formerly unknown to most, and they were paid good wages. They took pride in their work, especially in making a contribution to the war effort, and when the men came home, they were pushed out of these good jobs and told to go home. For some, going home meant returning to rural Oklahoma or Mississippi, and returning to a life of poverty. Choctaw veterans, accustomed to working side by side with whites, were disillusioned with the prospect of returning to rural economies where there were few opportunities or prospects. However, other opportunities resulted from military service.

The GI Bill changed the lives of many of these men and women. It paid enough that they could attend college or university, and would help them support a family. Cheap housing sprung up near college campuses and in suburbs, and many Native Americans became the first generation to attain a college education.

TERMINATION AND RELOCATION

Along with new opportunities, however, came another U.S. government attempt to destroy tribal communities. After World War II, Congressional leaders decided to terminate native nations by ending their special relationship with the federal government, which was mandated by the Constitution and many treaties. The Choctaw Nation had been officially terminated by the U.S. government in 1906, in keeping with Dawes era legislation that also seized their lands. In 1934, the Choctaw people had been allowed by the U.S. government to organize a tribal government. However, shortly after World War II ended in 1945, an extremely conservative American government decided to proceed with a new round of terminations, adding another program of relocating people from reservations and moving them to big cities. Once again, the justification used was the alleged best interest of native people, whether native people agreed or not. White proponents argued that Native Americans had been held back from full assimilation into the mainstream community by tribalism. If the government dissolved the tribe and tribal relations, individual Native Americans could be freed from the close communal relations of tribal communities. To facilitate the dissolution of tribal communities and help individual Native Americans and their nuclear families assimilate, another program called Relocation was instituted to remove native people from their rural or reservation homes and send them to big cities. Once off the reservations, Native Americans would be able to find work and they would act in their own individual interest, instead of that of the community. In reality, however, Termination and Relocation destroyed the lives of many native people, pushing them deeper and deeper into abject poverty.[71]

The Choctaws in Oklahoma had been divested of their land base and terminated in 1906 during the Dawes era. Now, they were targeted for the new program of Termination. Congress passed the legislation empowering government officials to end federal relations with the Choctaw Nation of Oklahoma. Chief Harry Belvin, an ardent assimilationist, favored termination, and persuaded tribal leaders to sign an agreement for termination. However, the vast majority of Choctaws opposed this plan, and their protests delayed Congressional implementation twice during the 1960s. Chief Belvin obscured the true nature of the agreement he had signed, presenting it as a great opportunity for individual Choctaws to receive a large amount of money from the distribution of assets held in trust by the federal government. The termination of the Choctaw Nation was presented to the Choctaw people not as termination but as Belvin's "law." In the late 1960s, Choctaw protests grew steadily and in August 1970, Congress repealed the law. All across the United States, the Termination and Relocation policies were, to many native people, the last straw. After a century and a half of domination and subjugation, of being strangers within their own country, of having their lands and wealth seized, and their lives sacrificed, Choctaws and other indigenous peoples in America began to fight back.

CHOCTAW RESURGENCE

Among the Choctaws, opposition to termination created an activist movement leading to a Choctaw national resurgence in the 1970s. Choctaw youth blazed a new path of nation building for the future, envisioning a strong, viable tribal community, infused with pride in being Choctaw. With this resurgence of Choctaw nationalism, a new constitution was adopted in 1983. Thousands of Choctaws reestablished ties with the Choctaw Nation. Tribal programs and services expanded, and their administration was assumed by the Choctaw national government. Urban Choctaws, many from Oklahoma City who had been transplanted from rural areas during the Relocation era, played prominent roles in Choctaw resurgence. Economic development became a priority, and annual Choctaw events were reinstated that fueled the trajectory of activism and provided cultural and social opportunities for renewal of Choctaw traditions, especially among those Choctaws whose ties to the nation had weakened over time.

In 1975, the Choctaws elected a new chief, David Gardner. Gardner's progressive vision for the Choctaws included a revival of the Choctaw language and traditional arts and crafts. Tragically, Gardner was diagnosed with lymphatic cancer and he died only two and a half years into his first term. Shocked and distressed that Gardner's vision for the nation was to be left incomplete, Choctaws elected another young chief, Hollis Roberts, shortly after Gardner's death. Roberts, 35 years old, was an able and charismatic professional politician. He ran against the very popular Charles Brown, an older man, who had led the fight against termination in the 1960s. Defeating Brown by only 339 votes, Roberts retained his position until 1997, when he was convicted of sexual assault and aggravated sexual abuse and sentenced to 11 years in federal prison, he was forced to resign as chief.

In 1983, the Choctaws voted in favor of a new constitution, which restructured Choctaw government. The new leaders worked to accomplish three goals that were identified as most important issues to the Choctaw people. First, they wanted to expand their land base; second, to expand the Choctaw newspaper and community centers; and third, to define and implement a new tribal roll of membership.

In the 1970s, the Choctaw land base consisted of only 10,746 acres. By 1997, after two decades of land acquisition by the Choctaw government, lands belonging to the nation were increased sevenfold, totaling only 75,000 acres. Although this was an improvement, many Choctaws reflected that in the 1870s, the nation's lands consisted of 7.5 million acres. In addition to land losses, more than a century of U.S. oppression and forced assimilation resulted in Choctaws constituting of only 10 percent of the people living within tribal boundaries. More than 80 percent of enrolled members of the Choctaw Nation lived outside these boundaries.

Under Chief Gregory Pyle, who was elected in 1997, the Choctaw Nation of Oklahoma continues striving to improve its citizen's lives and to expand opportunities in education. Medical care, community and cultural activities, economic development, job creation, and social services constitute important aspects of the nation's agenda. The number of citizen members of the Choctaw Nation of Oklahoma now exceeds 120,000 people.

Notes

1. Vine Deloria, Jr., *Red Earth, White Lies: Native Americans and the Myth of Scientific Fact* (New York: Scribner, 1995), 82, 84.

2. A moiety is one half of a community.

3. John W. Swanton, *Source Material for the Social and Ceremonial Life of the Choctaw Indians* (Birmingham, AL: Birmingham Public Library Press, 1993, reprinted from the original), 10–36; Alfred Wright, "Choctaws: Religious Opinions, Traditions, etc.," *Missionary Herald* 24 (June 1828): 215–16; Gideon Lincecum, "Choctaw Traditions about Their Settlement in Mississippi and the Origin of Their Mounds," *Publications of the Mississippi Historical Society* 8 (1904): 521–42; and interview, Charlie Wilson, 1977, notes in possession of author.

4. Luys Hernandez de Biedma, "Relation of the Island of Florida," *Biedma's Original DeSoto Writings,* http://www.floridahistory.com/biedma.html.

5. David E. Stannard, *American Holocaust: The Conquest of the New World* (New York: Oxford University Press, 1992), x.

6. G. S. Garcilaso de la Vega, *The Florida of the Inca,* translated and edited by J. G. Varner and J. J. Varner (Austin, TX: University of Texas Press, 1951), 316.

7. Stannard, *American Holocaust,* x.

8. Robert J. Miller, *Native America, Discovered and Conquered: Thomas Jefferson, Lewis and Clark, and Manifest Destiny* (Lincoln, NE: Bison Books, 2008), 10, 25; Reginald Horsman, *Race and Manifest Destiny: The Origins of American Racial Anglo-Saxonism* (Cambridge, MA: Harvard University Press, 1993); and John Wunder, *Retained by the People: A History of American Indians and the Bill of Rights* (New York: Oxford University Press, 1994), 18, 21, 33.

9. Stannard, *American Holocaust,* iv–xv; Walter R. Echo-Hawk, *In the Courts of the Conqueror: The 10 Worst Indian Law Cases Ever Decided,* (Golden, CO: 2010), 14–22.

10. Stannard, *American Holocaust,* 114–15.

11. Greg O'Brien, *Choctaws in a Revolutionary Age* (Lincoln, NE: University of Nebraska Press, 2005), 10.

12. Charles J. Kappler, *Indian Affairs and Treaties* (Stillwater, OK: Oklahoma State University Library, 2003), http://digital.library.okstate.edu/Kappler/.

13. O'Brien, *Choctaws in a Revolutionary Age,* 89.

14. Ibid., 83–84 and Michelene E. Pesantubbee, *Choctaw Women in a Chaotic World: The Clash of Cultures in the Colonial Southeast* (Albuquerque, NM: University of New Mexico Press, 2005), 140.

15. James Taylor Carson, *Searching for the Bright Path: The Mississippi Choctaws from Prehistory to Removal* (Lincoln, NE: University of Nebraska Press, 2003), 64.

16. Donna L. Akers, *Living in the Land of Death: The Choctaw Nation, 1830–1860* (Lansing, MI: Michigan State University Press, 2004), 89–92.

17. Ibid., 11–16.

18. Kappler, *Indian Affairs and Treaties,* 13–14.

19. Arthur H. DeRosier, Jr., *The Removal of the Choctaw Indians* (Knoxville, TN: University of Tennessee Press, 1970), 30.

20. Ibid., 31.

21. Akers, *Living in the Land of Death,* 14–15.

22. Daniel M. Freidenberg, *Life, Liberty and the Pursuit of Land: The Plunder of Early America* (Buffalo, NY: Prometheus Books, 1992), 43, 150, 154, 161, 168.

23. Akers, *Living in the Land of Death*, 70–71.

24. Rogin, *Fathers and Children*, 154, 156, 161.

25. Rogin, 157–8, 170, 191,195, 197.

26. Kappler, *Indian Affairs and Treaties,* 137.

27. David Wishart, *An Unspeakable Sadness: The Dispossession of the Nebraska Indians* (Lincoln, NE: University of Nebraska Press, 1994), 175.

28. Echohawk, *In the Courts of the Conqueror*, 94.

29. Report of Calhoun, January 28, 1825, cited in Francis Paul Prucha, *American Indian Policy in the Formative Years: The Indian Trade and Intercourse Acts, 1790-1834* (Lincoln: University of Nebraska Press, 1962), 229.

30. DeRosier, *The Removal of the Choctaw Indians,* 65–67 and Michael Paul Rogin, *Fathers and Children: Andrew Jackson and the Subjugation of the American Indian* (New York: Transaction Publishers, 1992), 175–78, 197, 202, 254.

31. "Stephen H. Long's 1822 Geographical, Statistical and Historical Map of Arkansas Territory (from the Carey and Lea Atlas of 1822)," *McFarlin Library,* http://www.lib.utulsa.edu/speccoll/collections/maps/long/index.htm.

32. H. B. Cushman, *History of the Choctaw, Chickasaw and Natchez Indians* (Greenville, TX: Headlight Printing House, 1899), 64–69.

33. DeRosier, *The Removal of the Choctaw Indians,* 66.

34. *Arkansas Gazette,* January 6, 1821.

35. DeRosier, *The Removal of the Choctaw Indians,* 71.

36. Cushman, *History of the Choctaw, Chickasaw, and Natchez Indians*, 70, 270–71.

37. Ibid., 81.

38. Rogin, *Fathers and Children,* 216–17.

39. Ibid., 218.

40. Ibid., 212, 213, 219–21, 226, 228–29, 242.

41. Ibid., 215.

42. "A Century of Lawmaking for a New Nation: U.S. Congressional Documents and Debates, 1774–1875," *Library of Congress,* http://memory.loc.gov/cgi-bin/ampage?collId=llsl&fileName=004/llsl004.db&recNum=458.

43. Rogin, *Fathers and Children,* 223–25; Akers, *Living in the Land of Death,* 89–91; and DeRosier, *The Removal of the Choctaw Indians,* 116–28.

44. DeRosier, *The Removal of the Choctaw Indians,* 127–28.

45. Letters from Cyrus Kingsbury to Jeremiah Evarts, October 16, 1830, File 6, Number 24, Cyrus Kingsbury Collection, Western History Collection, University of Oklahoma, Norman, OK.

46. Rogin, *Fathers and Children,* 220.

47. Ibid., 228–29 and Mary Elizabeth Young, *Redskins, Ruffleshirts, and Rednecks: Indian Allotments in Alabama and Mississippi, 1830–1860* (Norman, OK: University of Oklahoma Press, 1961), 51–58.

48. Donna L. Akers, "Removing the Heart of the Choctaw People: Indian Removal from a Native Perspective," in *Medicine Ways: Disease, Health, and Survival Among Native Americans* (Walnut Creek, CA: Alta Mira Press, 2001), 10.

49. Rogin, *Fathers and Children,* 244, 247 and Grant Foreman, *Indian Removal: The Emigration of the Five Civilized Tribes of Indians* (Norman, OK: University of Oklahoma Press, 1932), 81–92.

50. Rogin, *Fathers and Children,* 123.

51. Akers, "Removing the Heart," 11.

52. Letters from Armstrong to Herring, September 17, 1833, Office of Indian Affairs, "Choctaw Agency," quoted in Foreman, *Indian Removal,* 97 and Akers, "Removing the Heart," 11–13.

53. Akers, "Removing the Heart," 12.

54. Ibid., 5–9.

55. Young, *Redskins, Ruffleshirts, and Rednecks,* 51–53 and Ronald N. Satz, "The Mississippi Choctaw: From the Removal Treaty to the Federal Agency," in *After Removal: The Choctaw in Mississippi,* eds. Samuel H. Wells and Roseanna Tubby (Jackson, MS: University Press of Mississippi, 1986), 7–9.

56. Cajuns were French-speaking Arcadians from Canada who moved en masse to Louisiana.

57. Jacqueline Anderson Matte, "Extinction by Reclassification: The MOWA Choctaws of South Alabama and Their Struggle for Federal Recognition," *The Alabama Review* 59 (July 2006): 177.

58. Angie Debo, *The Rise and Fall of the Choctaw Republic* (Norman, OK: University of Oklahoma Press, 1934; 2nd edition, 3rd printing, 1972), 78–79.

59. Ibid., 81–84.

60. Blue Clark, *Lone Wolf v Hitchcock: Treaty Rights & Indian Law at the End of the Nineteenth Century* (Lincoln, NE: University of Nebraska Press, 1999), 3–4.

61. Devon Abbott Mihesuah, *Choctaw Crime and Punishment, 1884–1907* (Norman, OK: University of Oklahoma Press, 2009), 213, 217.

62. Sandra Faiman-Silva, *Choctaws at the Crossroads: The Political Economy of Class and Culture in the Oklahoma Timber Region* (Lincoln, NE: University of Nebraska Press, 2000), 205.

63. "Meriam Report: The Problem of Indian Administration," Meriam, Lewis. *The Problem of Indian Administration: Report of a Survey made at the Request of Honorable Hubert Work, Secretary of the Interior, and Submitted to Him, February 21, 1928/ Survey Staff: Lewis Meriam . . . [et al.].* Baltimore, MD: Johns Hopkins Press, 1928, accessed on the website of the *Native American Rights Fund,* http://www.narf.org/nill/resources/meriam.htm/.

64. Ibid.

65. Ruth Fowler Dodd, interview notes in possession of author, December 28, 1992 and Faiman-Silva, *Choctaws at the Crossroads,* 74–75, 90–95.

66. John Woo, *Windtalkers* (United States: MGM Home Entertainment, 2002), http://www.imdb.com/title/tt0245562/maindetails.

67. Bruce L. Brager, "The Battle of St. Etienne: The 36th Division in World War One," *Military History Online,* http://www.militaryhistoryonline.com/wwi/articles/stetienne.aspx.

68. Russell Lawrence Barsh, "American Indians in the Great War," *Ethnohistory* 38, no. 3 (Summer 1991): 91 and Brager, "The Battle of St. Etienne."

69. *Naval History and Heritage Command,* http://www.history.navy.mil/faqs/faq61-3.htm.

70. Charles Roberts, "A Choctaw Odyssey: The Life of Lesa Phillip Roberts," *American Indian Quarterly* 14, no. 3 (1990): 269–70.

71. Charles Wilkerson, *Blood Struggle: The Rise of Modern Indian Nations* (New York: W. W. Norton & Co, 2005), 57–58, 64–65.

2

History of the Choctaws
in the Deep South

IN 1830, THE U.S. CONGRESS passed the Indian Removal Act, which authorized the president of the United States to negotiate so-called removal treaties with indigenous nations. Under this law, no force, fraud, or coercion was to be used in obtaining such a treaty. The homelands of the native nations that were coveted by the United States were to be exchanged for new lands west of the Mississippi River, and the government was authorized to pay the expenses of those who moved and to give them food and assistance as needed during their first year of residence in the western lands. Any Choctaw who wanted to remain in Mississippi was supposed to be allowed to do so, according to Article 14 of the Treaty of Dancing Rabbit Creek, as long as they agreed to become a citizen. That was never a realistic option. First, William Ward, the Choctaw agent, refused to allow the Choctaws to formally sign up to stay in Mississippi, simply because he felt they should go. Second, the Choctaws who remained behind would not have had the same rights as white citizens.

In 1830, Jackson bribed a few Choctaw leaders to sign a fraudulent treaty, and, despite the dishonesty used to procure this document, the Senate ratified it, forcing thousands of Choctaws off their homelands. But in the midst of all this trouble and chaos, many Choctaws refused to travel to the lands designated by the United States in the West. Regardless of the threats of the U.S. and state governments to use military force, they would not abandon the sacred compact with the spirits of the ancestors and their agreement to honor the bones of the dead. Instead of leaving, they hid out in the swamps and backwoods. Forced into hiding, they abandoned everything, but were true to their spiritual beliefs.

At least 4,000 Choctaws remained behind as group after group of Choctaws left for the West. Forced to endure unbelievable hardships and impoverishment for more than a century, they lived for decades outside the society built by whites that excluded nonwhite people from civil and human rights. Despite all this adversity, the Mississippi Choctaws and other pockets of Choctaw survivors in Louisiana, Tennessee, and Alabama maintained their indigenous identity, preserved their language and customs, and finally, in the 20th century, obtained some of the opportunities formerly denied them.[1]

These Choctaw survivors remained as close to their homelands as possible, experiencing great deprivations and intense poverty. For years, they avoided all white contact. White southerners treated the Choctaws similarly to blacks—believing intensely in their own superiority, using the legal and political system in the South to exploit and harass Choctaws, and whom they considered to be nonwhite.

White invaders took over their homes and their fields, oftentimes using African slave labor to prosper on the land unjustifiably seized from the Choctaw people. Whites went out of their way to try to capture Choctaws—women and children were seized and held to force the men to surrender. Some of them were forced to work for the white people that had taken over their lands and homes. Others were deported West to join the other Choctaws in permanent exile. Those who successfully avoided these fates eked out a miserable existence, constantly on the lookout for attacks.

During the 19th century, Choctaws were sometimes kidnapped, tortured, or hung by whites, without provocation or any wrongdoing on their part. People of color, especially after the U.S. Civil War, were preyed upon by racists. Some were lynched, while others were simply assaulted. Wealthy slave owner and planter, Joseph Beckham Cobb, in his book *Mississippi Scenes,* reported that the "lot and condition of the Indians" was "far more deplorable" than that of the African American slaves[2]. The Ku Klux Klan actively terrorized Choctaws along with African Americans, while law enforcement looked the other way. Many Choctaws moved their little camps frequently trying to avoid the notice of the Klan and other white people.

The unrelenting hatred of the people of the dominant society in the South continued unabated. Avaricious merchants preyed upon them, selling them goods at grossly inflated prices. Congressmen John F. H. Claiborne reported in 1844 that "the plight of the Indians was 'worse than the subjection of slaves.' "[3] One of the Mississippi Choctaws confided in a trusted white friend that "Our tribe has been woefully imposed upon of late. We have had our habitations torn down and burned; our fences destroyed, cattle turned up into our fields and we ourselves have been scourged, manacled, fettered and otherwise personally abused."[4]

Over the following decades, Mississippians continually demanded that the United States expel the remaining Choctaws. Jefferson Davis, the future president of the Confederacy, a U.S. senator, informed the government that it was "a matter of great importance" to the white citizens of Mississippi that the federal government round up and expel that remaining Native Americans and that they "be prevented from returning." Outraged at the Choctaws who had the audacity to remain in Mississippi, whites were even further angered when some of the Choctaws who were forced into exile returned to their old homelands.[5] Those who did so certainly received no welcome from the dominant society. U.S. Indian Agent Douglas H. Cooper visited Mississippi in 1856 and reported that although the state of Mississippi had been mandated to extend citizenship to the Choctaws, they were only "nominally" citizens, and all lived in "a very hopeless and degraded condition."[6]

The terrible poverty and marginal existence of the Native Americans continued throughout the century, and several groups of Choctaws traveled to the new nation in Indian Territory, with contractors hired to remove natives from Mississippi. In the mid-1840s, for example, 1786 Choctaws moved West. At least 2,262 Choctaws remained behind in Mississippi and Louisiana, according to a census taken by Special Indian Agent Douglas Cooper in 1853. One can assume that there were many more Choctaws that were not counted, since many of them would have feared that the government was counting them to begin another forced exodus.

With the outbreak of the Civil War in 1861, Choctaw men were impressed into the Confederacy as soldiers. Their unit was called the First Mississippi Choctaw Infantry Battalion, and was trained and officered by whites. While in training in Louisiana in 1863, the entire unit was captured during the Vicksburg campaign. Historian Ronald Satz claims that none of them returned to Mississippi and that they were assumed to have been sent into permanent exile in the West.[7]

Nevertheless, when the Civil War ended, whites demanded that the federal government expel the remaining Choctaws and force them to go to Indian Territory. In compliance with these demands, the United States tried to lure the Mississippi Choctaws to move West by promising them a share in the allotment of the land of the Choctaws. But first, the government had to come up with a plan to force the Choctaws in Indian Territory to give up communal land holding and agree to hold their land in individually owned plots. The idea was for the government to seize the communal land holdings of the Choctaws in Indian Territory and divide the lands into individually owned 140 plots. All the land that was left over after each Choctaw received land was then to be put up on the market for sale to whites. This scheme was the first step in taking over the region and creating states out of the indigenous peoples' last remaining lands. But time after time, the Western Choctaws rejected allotment of their lands and so this government plan failed.

For the next three decades, whites sought even the marginal lands in Mississippi and other southern states, to which the Choctaws had retreated. Thousands of African Americans left the South, determined to find a place to live that was less racist, where they might have an opportunity to support themselves and their families. This exodus created a shortage of cheap, exploitable labor. As a result, the dominant society began to hire Choctaws to fill the labor shortage. Sharecropping arrangements began to be common, where Choctaws traded their labor in return for goods, supplies, seed, and other necessities. Although this system kept the Choctaws locked into a state of debt peonage, they still managed to build schools near their small communities. In the meantime, the state of Mississippi drew up and adopted two constitutions, both of which excluded Native Americans from equality under the law and continued their disenfranchisement.[8] In the 1880s and 1890s, the United States finally succeeded in confiscating all the remaining lands of the Choctaw people in the West, breaking the Treaty of Dancing Rabbit Creek and refusing to allow Choctaw people a say in their own future. The Dawes Act was designed to legitimate the seizure of native lands, stating that taking Choctaw lands was beneficial to the tribe. This was the second betrayal of the Choctaw Nation by the United States.

The Choctaws and several other indigenous nations in Indian Territory fought the U.S. government over the Dawes Act, arguing that forcing them to own their lands in severalty (individually) and dissolving the tribes broke the solemn treaty promises, which had guaranteed that the native peoples' lands in Indian Territory would never become a part of a U.S. territory or state. Every tribe held a legal title to their lands, the same as white Americans. But the United States decided that it would break all the treaties and force the nations to give up their lands, knowing that it would lead to millions of native lands becoming available to whites.

Between 1900 and 1930, two-thirds of all Choctaw lands in Indian Territory moved from Choctaw to white hands. Many so-called full-bloods were targeted by thieves and con men who rushed to Indian Territory to take advantage of native people who did not speak or read English, and who, because of their unfamiliarity with the marketplace, were easy prey to whites whose sole concern was personal profit. During this period, more Choctaws from Mississippi were forced to travel to the West, to add to the number of potential victims. White speculators and criminals went to Mississippi to persuade gullible Choctaws to travel West with them so that they could get a share of the Choctaw lands being seized from the Western Choctaws and turn it over to these criminals.

The myriad of injustices perpetrated by the United States continued until 1917, when a congressional team traveled to Mississippi at the request of Congressman William Venable of Meridian. The investigators found that the Mississippi Choctaws lived in terrible conditions, suffering from all kinds of diseases. They lived in shacks on the worst land in a constant state of indebtedness to white merchants who cheated them, charging them exorbitant prices for everything they were forced to buy. Subjected to constant violence and without protection from the law, most Choctaws could neither read nor write, spoke little English, and lived in extreme poverty, suffering from malnutrition. One in every five Choctaws in Mississippi died during the 1918 influenza epidemic. In that year, the federal government finally opened an agency in the town of Philadelphia, Mississippi, in Neshoba County, which offered a few minimal services. A little land was purchased for them by the federal government. After 85 years of trying to forcibly evict the Choctaws from their homelands, the U.S. government finally recognized their right to exist.

The state of Mississippi in 1882 passed a law that established schools for Native Americans in East Mississippi. However, these schools served just two counties, Neshoba and Leake. In all areas of the state, Choctaw children were not allowed to attend the white schools, and they refused to attend those that served African American children. The state schools were closed during the first decade of the 20th century, when officials once again tried to evict the remaining Choctaws and forced them to join their relatives in the West. Despite these measures, many remained in Mississippi.

In 1916, a federal investigator for the Indian Service reported that the Choctaws had little opportunity to obtain education, and that all were unimaginably poor, many without sufficient clothing, food, or shelter. Their main source of income was occasional day labor, cotton picking, or woodcutting. He stated that many of them were in danger of starvation. As a result of the shocking conditions in this report, the U.S. Congress passed a bill recognizing the Mississippi Choctaw as an Indian tribe and creating the agency in Philadelphia.[9]

By 1930, seven schools for Choctaw children had been created and the federal government opened an Indian hospital in Philadelphia. In 1944, a reservation was created and the next year, the Mississippi Band of Choctaw Indians formed a tribal council and adopted a constitution and bylaws that conformed to the requirements of the U.S. government.

Although the 20th century saw some improvements in the standard of living for Choctaw people in Mississippi, the U.S. government continued a dizzying path of changing policies, some of which were very harmful for native peoples. In 1934, the Indian Reorganization Act was passed, which allowed native governments to be formed, but only as prescribed by strict rules of the federal government. Each tribe could draw up a constitution, which had to be approved, and it had to conform to meet the requirements of the United States. Traditionally, Choctaw people had established their own laws and decision-making processes, and these were always based on the fundamental recognition of the value and worth of each individual in the tribe. When important decisions were to be made, villages and clans came together for discussions that sometimes lasted for days. Everyone who wished to speak was allowed to do so and was listened to with respect and consideration, until they had completely finished. No one was allowed to interrupt. Talking out the different sides of the decision and considering everyone's views was normal for Choctaw people, who would then come to a decision that was consensual—in other words, a decision that all agreed upon. No chief or headman was allowed to dictate or decide for anyone else, and every person had an equal say. Unfortunately, with the 1934 Indian Reorganization Act, the United States dictated the form of government they would allow the Indian tribes to have, including that their government install a hierarchy of power, as in a pyramid. At the top, the tribal council was to make important decisions by majority vote, which was completely unlike traditional Choctaw government and policy-making. Traditionally, Choctaw people decided important tribal issues and plans by consensus, with each tribal member having an important say in every action. Decisions could take days or even weeks, because all people spoke, and many compromises were made, until a consensus of opinion was reached. But under the U.S.-enforced reorganization, traditional forms of native government were forbidden. Instead, the Choctaws and other tribal nations had to install a form of government modeled after U.S. state governments. These U.S.-dictated governments still exist, and have contributed greatly to factionalism, coercion, and, especially, the further disintegration of traditional native ways of life.[10]

A variety of other U.S. government policies that had deleterious effects on the Choctaws were passed during the 1940s–1960s. In the late 1940s, the federal government and many Congressmen sought ways to terminate the special relationship between the U.S. government and native nations, to end tribal sovereignty, and to destroy traditional beliefs and ways of life. In the early 1950s, schools for native children, clinics, and hospitals were targeted for closure. On August 1, 1953, Congress passed the Termination Act, with the goal of freeing Native Americans from federal supervision and to abolish the Bureau of Indian Affairs. Unfortunately, the Choctaws and most other Native Americans existed in a terrible state of poverty and want, plagued by excessive rates of unemployment, and subjected to rampant racial discrimination. Despite this reality, Congress wanted to simply terminate all federal programs for native peoples and nations, and shut down the reservations.

Fortunately, President John F. Kennedy decided that Native Americans needed the federal government to foster their development, rather than abandon them. A succession of programs were passed into law in the 1960s that began to address some of the long-term problems experienced by the Choctaws and other Native Americans as a result of U.S. colonialism over the past century and a half.

In the 1950s, the federal government's policy of termination emphasized the removal of Mississippi Choctaws from their small towns and encouraged them to move to big cities, specifically Chicago, Cleveland, Dallas, Denver, Los Angeles, Oakland, San Jose, and San Francisco. The General Employment Assistance Program required participants to leave the reservation for job training. Although some individuals did find work, this program did little or nothing to address the economic problems on the reservations, and tended to break up families and alienate young people. In fact, in 1961, Tribal Chairman Phillip Martin reported that the average family income was $600 per year. Most Choctaws worked as farm laborers for $2.50 per day from sunup to sundown.

Chairman Martin began an economic development program for the reservation that resulted in what many termed an "economic miracle." In the early 1960s, the tribe purchased a cabinet company and a lumber business. Over the next 20–30 years, Choctaw leaders emphasized vocational training and education programs. The Choctaw Housing Authority was established in 1965, and more than 400 homes were built on the reservation by the Chata Development Corporation. In addition, the Choctaws built an industrial park and filled it with going concerns. As a result of the entrepreneurial spirit of Choctaw leaders and citizens, the Choctaw people have raised their standard of living considerably, and established a number of social programs to benefit anyone who needs them.

In 1994, the Silver Star Casino opened for business in Philadelphia, and in 2000, a second casino, the Pearl River Resort complex—which included a new casino, the Golden Moon—was launched. Today, big name acts play in this beautiful venue, and people from around the world visit the Choctaw Nation during the annual fair.

In 2007, Phillip Martin retired and Beasley Denson was elected tribal chairman. The Denson administration has continued to pursue economic prosperity for all Choctaws. Today, the Mississippi Band of Choctaw Indians provides more than 6,000 full-time jobs for tribal members in a variety of manufacturing, service, and retail businesses. Its annual payroll is $100 million, which makes the tribe one of the 10 largest employers in the state. Tribal

The modern architecture of this beautiful building stands out in the Mississippi night and illustrates the economic progress of the Mississippi Band of Choctaw Indians. (AP Photo/Dave Martin)

membership is 9,660 people, all of whom are required to have a minimum of 50 percent Choctaw blood. Half of the population is under the age of 25.

The Mississippi Choctaws hold about 35,000 acres of land in 10 counties, 1 in Benning, Tennessee, and the other 9 including Malmaison, Attala, Crystal Ridge, Red Water, Pearl River, Bogue Chitto, Standing Pine, Tucker, Conehatta, Bogue Homa, and Ocean Springs. After many long years of struggle and deprivation, the Mississippi Choctaws have established a remarkable presence in the state of Mississippi, where they continue to preserve their language and traditions, and their distinct identity as Choctaw people.

Notes

1. Ronald N. Satz, "The Mississippi Choctaw: From the Removal Treaty to the Federal Agency," in *After Removal: The Choctaw in Mississippi,* eds. Samuel J. Wells and Roseanna Tubby (Jackson, MS: University Press of Mississippi, 1986), 15.

2. Ibid., 16.

3. Ibid.

4. Ibid.

5. Ibid., 14.

6. Ibid., 17.

7. Ibid., 18.

8. Ibid., 19.

9. U.S. Congress, House, Committee on Investigation of the Indian Service, *Condition of the Mississippi Choctaws, Hearings,* Vol. 2 (Washington, D.C.: Government Printing Office, 1917), 150–53.

10. Carole Goldberg-Ambrose, "Of Native Americans and Tribal Members: The Impact of Law on Indian Group Life," *Law and Society Review* 28, no. 5 (1994): 1123–48.

3

Worldview and Spiritual Beliefs

RELIGION AND SPIRITUAL BELIEFS have always been an important part of Choctaw lives. However, just as with all other societies, their beliefs have changed over time. All societies change in response to external and internal stimuli and conditions. As conditions change, the society must be flexible enough to accommodate to these changes, or the society will soon pass away. One of the great strengths of the Choctaw people has been their ability to adapt to changing conditions, and new ways of doing things, while maintaining their own cultural integrity. They have not only accommodated the huge changes brought by the invasion of the colonists, but also retained distinctive beliefs and values that provide cohesion and a unique identity. As a viable people, they have accepted some ideas, rejected many others, and incorporated or blended the old with the new. Today the Choctaws display a range of spiritual beliefs, drawing from both traditional and Christian beliefs.

Today, Choctaw spiritual beliefs have been heavily influenced by Christianity. In some places and among some Choctaws, a syncretic or blending of both traditional and Christian spirituality is practiced. Among other Choctaws, Christianity has replaced many of the former traditional beliefs almost entirely. However, many Choctaw people value and appreciate the beliefs that make them a distinct group of people, and they continue to participate in society without succumbing to complete absorption or assimilation.

In traditional times, Choctaw spiritual beliefs and worldview (way of seeing the world) permeated their everyday lives. Before the 19th century, there were no church buildings or Sunday schools, but nonetheless, they were very religious. Their spiritual ceremonies were integrated into their daily lives, rather than performed on a particular day or in a particular building. When Europeans first came into contact with Native North Americans, they mistakenly thought that Native Americans were people without religion because there were no churches, no Bible, no preachers, and no pews. Europeans thought that since they did not have these things, they must have no religion. Of course they had religious and spiritual beliefs, but since they were expressed differently from European practices, the latter simply assumed that they had none.

Unique Worldview

Traditional Choctaw spiritual beliefs were based on a way of seeing the world that differed tremendously from Europeans. Spiritual beliefs guided every activity and every decision of their lives, and ritual and ceremony were incorporated into the process of daily living. Choctaws believed that spirits surrounded them and were a part of the world they lived in. Choctaws, Cherokees, and other southeastern Native Americans believed in supernatural beings who communicated with humans through signs, visions, and dreams.

The creation stories of the Choctaw people explain the origins of the nation and the original gift from the Creator of the homelands in present-day Mississippi (see Chapter 1). Emerging from the great Mother Mound, Nanih Waiya, the Choctaw people were given a beautiful Eden-like territory in which they thrived for countless generations. The creation story relates how the people promised to never leave their homelands and how they would never know hunger or want while they stayed in these lands. The Creator admonished them to never forget this promise for if they did, the nation would perish from hunger and disease. In the migration story believed by many Choctaws and related in newspapers and magazines of the 19th century to avidly interested white audiences, one of the sacred duties of the tribe was to treat the bones of the dead with great care and deference. If they ever moved, the bones of their ancestors were to be taken with them and accorded a special place in the new location. This reverent tradition was part of the compact the Choctaw people had with the spirits of their ancestors, who promised to watch over them and to communicate warnings and advice to the living people.

Over the centuries, Choctaws faithfully carried out the pact with the spirits of their ancestors. Every village had a special bone house, where the physical remains of the deceased were kept and faithfully tended. In the 1830s, when the U.S. government forced the Choctaws from their homelands on the Trail

Where We Cried, the Choctaws were coerced by the military to abandon the bones of the ancestors, breaking their sacred pact with the dead. Thousands of Choctaws fully expected the death that awaited them on the trail and shortly after arrival in Indian Territory in the West. Every year, the Choctaw Nation of Oklahoma reenacts the Trail Where We Cried and honors the memories and sacrifices that accompanied those terrible times.

Other unique beliefs of Choctaws include the Little People, who lived in the woods and were usually invisible, but could appear at will. Children were warned not to wander off alone into the woods because they might be kidnapped by the Little People. In some Choctaw homes today, one still hears stories of the Little People and their abilities. The Irish who occasionally visit the Oklahoma Choctaw in recognition of the contribution collected and sent to help alleviate suffering during the Potato Famine, hear the interesting stories of the Little People and share those of the Irish leprechaun. Other stories say that healers were taught their medicinal knowledge by *Bohpoli,* a little forest dwelling man who was rarely seen, but who had wondrous abilities to cure illness.[1]

The world of the Choctaws in older times also included supernatural beings that could manifest themselves as human, but were, in fact, creatures that were not human. They plotted to make people sick and to make bad things happen to the people. Disasters were caused by witches, and witchcraft was blamed for all sorts of adverse events, accidents, or illnesses. The Choctaw clan system was a kinship system that provided identity and belonging. Each person, at birth, automatically became a member of the clan of his or her mother. As nonhuman beings, witches were not part of this clan system, and as outsiders, they did not have the safety, security, and belonging that birth into a clan afforded every Choctaw. They were not part of the bear people, or the spiritual beings of the rivers and streams, nor did they fit into any defined group that the Choctaws recognized. They were an abomination, outside the ordered world of relationships, and, therefore were outside the law of the clans and Choctaw Nation. If a witch was identified, he or she was often killed. Choctaws believed that the sole aim of a witch was to bring chaos, disorder, and destruction on a community, and they were thought to have supernatural powers. At night, they often turned themselves into owls or other night creatures, and perpetrated terrible crimes against the innocent—bringing illness or death.

INTERCONNECTEDNESS

Several fundamental concepts, shared by most Native Americans, form the essential foundation of the traditional Choctaw worldview. The most basic and fundamental Native American belief about the world is that everything within the world is connected. Every rock, tree, stream, deer, insect, and human is interdependent on every other object or being in the world. Native people believe these objects and beings are sentient, alive—having perception and consciousness. The Choctaw world is filled with these beings and with an unseen world of spirits. The interconnectedness of the world means that everything that affected one—a stream, the forest, the deer, the Choctaws—affected all. If man overhunts the deer, they will disappear, leading to mankind's starvation. If the river is polluted, every creature and being that depended on that river is likewise adversely affected.

Interrelatedness is not random connections or mixing of different beings. It has a systematic orderliness that is extremely important. Order has always been tremendously important in the Choctaw cosmology, because the result of disorder is chaos, a state of random unpredictability that can be disastrous. Choctaws, even today, classify like objects or beings in one category, which is reflected in the Choctaw language.

ORDER AND PURITY

The order at the heart of Choctaw cosmology provides humans with categories of like objects that have fundamental similarities. For example, logs and fingers belong to a category of cylindrical objects. Intermixing of objects from different categories has always been avoided and Choctaws believe this sort of intermixing causes each category to become polluted. Ceremonies are the answer—in the past, there were ceremonies that could restore purity and balance. Most objects or beings that belonged to two different categories were regarded as abominations and formed the basis of many taboos. For example, flesh-eating birds, such as crows, eagles, and buzzards, were not eaten and were considered anomalies because "normal" birds ate only vegetation. Likewise, when hogs were first introduced among the Choctaws, many of them would not eat hog meat since they are cloven hoofed and, thus, defy categorization. Bears also could be classified in either of two categories, but, unlike hogs, they were seen as supernatural creatures rather than abominations. Choctaws believed them to be both two legged (or human) and four legged (belonging to the animal world). Among the native peoples of the American Southeast, many believe the bear to be sacred and to have special powers.[2]

Thus, purity from contamination has played a large role in Choctaw beliefs, and many rituals and ceremonies that restored purity were very important in Choctaw lives. The most important of these ceremonies by far is the Green Corn Ceremony.

Green Corn Ceremony

Usually held at the time of the ripening of the crop of late corn, the Green Corn Ceremony takes place in late August or early September. In ancient times, it was, in part, a celebration of thanksgiving, an expression of gratitude for corn. It also was about purification—a ritual cleansing of the whole world of the Choctaws. All the fires were put out, including the main village fire. The men would fast and drink the black drink, which was a tea made from the leaves of the yaupon shrub. It made them vomit, thus purging the body of impurities. This tea is still used by traditionalists to purify the body.

It was also a time for accounting and recognition. Each clan met and reviewed each person's record for the year. Some were complimented and recognized by the group, while others were called to account, to make right any wrongdoing and hard feelings with others. Serious problems were resolved. Any problem or crime settled at the Green Corn Ceremony was considered closed for all time.

The most important part of the ceremony was the lighting of the new fire. With great ceremony, everyone would gather in the square and the ranking spiritual leader would ritually light the new village fire. Each woman then took an ember home to light her own fire. All the women then prepared a great feast—huge quantities of corn and other vegetables were set out on tables beside venison, squirrel, rabbit, and other meats. The men then danced in three concentric circles around the new year's fire, later joined by the women, who were dressed in their best finery. At the end of the dancing, a spiritual leader would announce the ceremony to be ended, that everyone had been purified and old grudges resolved. Then everyone would cover themselves in white paint and go to water, immersing themselves. After that came more dancing, and after some hours, all the people would leave the square and go home. In this manner, the Choctaws spiritually renewed themselves, forgave each other, resolved all conflicts, and then were ready to begin a new year.

Today, the Green Corn Ceremony is celebrated through an annual festival that includes many events attuned to modern times. Oral traditions and history form a part of this event, and many of the traditional beliefs in the importance of renewal and purification and restoration are in evidence during these festivals.

HISTORICAL BELIEFS IN HARMONY AND BALANCE

Traditional Choctaws believe that balance is a basic need in relationships between all creatures. The world is composed of parts that are opposites, which strive against each other. Misfortune and chaos result when one part gains ascendancy over another. For example, if mankind overhunts game, they seriously impair the balance of the relationship between man and other creatures. Traditionally, the only route to restore balance was to ceremonially repair the damage, with the participation of both groups. One of the ways to restore purity, and thus, harmony and balance to one's world, was by going to water. Every morning, winter or summer, Choctaws bathed in nearby creeks or rivers.

Choctaws understand that human beings can have a negative impact on the earth and must curb their wants and desires in consideration of the well-being of other creatures and parts of creation. Choctaws have traditionally always taken great care to have a minimal impact on their environment. Wanton destruction of the environment was unknown among native peoples, since everything in the world had a spirit and belonged to a community like that of humans. Native people restrained their impact on other beings, plants, or inanimate objects, and tried to refrain from having any adverse impact on any part of the world. Not only did they fear retaliation from other beings, but they also strove to maintain harmony and balance, which were fundamental precepts.

The Choctaw belief in the centrality of balance stands opposite to Western society's belief that everything in the world has been placed here for the benefit of man, and for his use, or even exploitation. Western thought draws its fundamental beliefs from Christianity, which is reflected in biblical assertion that God placed everything on earth to be at the disposal of man: "God said, 'Let us make man in our image, after our likeness: and let them have dominion over the fish of the sea, and over the fowl of the air, and over the cattle and over all the earth, and over every creeping thing that creepeth upon the earth.' "[3] The belief that mankind stands at the apex of a great pyramid of life contrasts vividly with native beliefs that man is simply one part of a living world of interconnected beings. Native people believe that the well-being of all creatures is so tightly interwoven that deleterious events that happen to one kind negatively affects all creatures, including mankind.

In the native worldview, harmony between the creatures of the world and balancing the interests of each are of paramount importance. Maintaining the harmony and balance of the natural world is the most important concern of mankind. Therefore, native peoples who adhere to this traditional worldview do not exploit other creatures or wantonly consume natural resources for personal profit and desire.

In ancient times, Choctaws believed that the Sun (hushtali) was the eye of the Great Spirit. Perhaps reflecting the cosmology of the ancient peoples of Meso-America, the Choctaws believed that the Sun was a sentient being with the power of life and death. Its great eye continually watched them, and as long as it did so, they would flourish. According to ancient traditions, the ally of the Sun on earth was the sacred fire, and the Choctaws believed that any wrongdoing on their part would be reported to the great Sun by its earthly representative. Spiritual power, especially the ability to generate or sustain life, was placed at the center of the Choctaw cosmology. The Sun, *hushtahli,* was tremendously important—it had the power of life and death. Choctaws believed that the Sun was a sentient being; as long as the sun looked down on the people, all could be well. If the Sun turned away his eye, calamity and chaos would result. Choctaw warriors appealed to the Sun for success in warfare. The Sun led them down the bright path to victory and enabled them to return home safely.[4]

Because of these beliefs, in ancient times, sacred fires were laid with reverence, often in the shape of a spiral, so that a circular path of burning resulted. Choctaw women incorporated a circle and cross motif into their arts and décor to represent the power of the Sun and his little brother, Fire. This symbol continues to be used today.

POWER

Among the Choctaw people, power differs from the definition of a measure of the ability to control others. In a native context, power refers to the spiritual power of a person. All people possess inherent spiritual power, which can be accessed in times of need. In everyday life, both women and men have special and unique areas of spiritual power. Since women created life through giving birth, they are and have always been esteemed for their innate spiritual power. Native gender roles have always recognized the vital roles women play as mothers to the nation, and therefore, Choctaws highly esteemed women and did not view them as inferior in any way to men. The creation of life was the most important ability of the powerful, and since women gave birth and raised corn and other crops, their power was self-evident from birth.

Men could tap into power too, but theirs was of a different nature. In ancient times, during preparations for warfare, men transformed themselves from their day-to-day roles of uncle, brother, husband, father, and defender/provider to an altered state in which they tapped into their spiritual power and became dangerous warriors. When they returned from a raid, they had to go through a ceremonial return to their community roles, ridding themselves of their war-like powers in order to return to their daily roles within the village.

Choctaws have always believed that male and female spiritual powers were complimentary and that both are essential to the well-being and continuity of the community. Unlike societies organized by patriarchy, in Choctaw society women always had true equality with men. They controlled major economic resources and were consulted in all political matters, including war.

Choctaw clans were matrilineal—every Choctaw was descended from a single female ancestor, and all Choctaws took their clan identity from their mother's lineage. Children belonged to the clan, and therefore, in ancient times, when Choctaws divorced, the children always stayed with the mother. The houses, crops, and fields were the property of the women and clans, and men simply held their own tools and personal belongings as their own. This kinship system resulted in women and children always having the means to subsist themselves. Contrasting this kinship system with patriarchal systems like those practiced in Europe and 19th-century America, women and children were never homeless, never subjected to oppression based on their sex, had real economic power, and had an esteemed place in their society. They were never dependent on the goodwill or charity of men, which resulted in no orphans, no workhouses for the poor, no begging, and greatly reduced levels of oppression and coercion in individual human relations.

Modern Choctaw people today often continue to esteem women for their roles in the creation and nurturing of life and for their strength in the modern family. Although the ancient clan system is no longer functional, women still often form the glue that holds families together and, in many Choctaw families, elder women keep extended families connected. In the blended world of modern Choctaws, women still hold a special place and have a unique role. Women were highly regarded and viewed as powerful and vital members of Choctaw society. Unlike their treatment in European (and later American) patriarchal systems, men did not dominate women, and women were not subordinate to the control of wealth and resources by men. In 18th-century England, for example, a woman whose husband died often was forced to go with her children to a workhouse or poorhouse if she had no brother, father, or uncle who would take her in and support her and her children. Within Choctaw society, everyone was a member of a clan—a large extended family, who were all descended from one common female ancestor. If one's husband died, a woman and children were unaffected economically. Women "owned" all the houses and fields, so widows and children did not become homeless as they often did in Western European societies. The clans shared out produce from the fields and a woman's brothers and uncles furnished game for her and her family.

MOTHER EARTH

Native people and Choctaws traditionally understood the world as a living being—their Mother. As a sentient being, Mother Earth could not be owned.

The Great Spirit gave all creatures and beings a place on the earth; it belonged to all. No one could own a portion of the earth, just as no one can own a specific portion of the air one breathes. In the Choctaw worldview, all the beings and creatures of the earth were interrelated—brothers and sisters—and they were all interdependent on each other. If one group of beings suffered a drought or famine, all the other parts of the earth would suffer too, because each one was dependent on the other. In some cases, Choctaw believed that the spirits of other kinds of beings or creatures could retaliate if mankind imposed on them, or, for example, if the proper gratitude and respect were not expressed when taking the life of an animal for food. Modern American beliefs in private property and the idea that man has dominion over all animals and lesser creatures lead to a different kind of society.

The idea of private property was completely alien to indigenous societies of North America. Native Americans viewed the land as belonging to everyone equally. One clan or family group or even individual could use the land that belonged to the tribe, but they could not buy or sell it, and it was not exempt from the communal worldview. The people using the land could not neglect their obligations to other creatures that were connected to this land, and they could not exploit or abuse the land or anything on it. Choctaws shared a huge territory that encompassed much of southern and central Mississippi, western Alabama, and parts of Louisiana. They guarded their hunting grounds and territory from the intrusion of other tribes. However, within the Choctaw Nation, any person, family, or clan could use any portion of the land for farming or stock raising, and Choctaw law said that no one else could encroach upon them.

No one ever starved while others ate. There were no poor houses, no huge differences between the rich and the poor, and no hoarding or greed. During traditional times prior to the introduction of alcohol by Europeans, visitors reported that among the Choctaws and other Native American peoples, there were no thieves, no liars, and violence in the homes and villages was almost unknown.

MODERN CHOCTAW RELIGIOUS BELIEFS

Today there are an array of religious beliefs among the Choctaws, including traditional native beliefs, syncretic beliefs, and Christianity. Choctaw people are spread out across the world and influenced by Western or American beliefs. Many Choctaws have adopted Christianity and have replaced many of the ancient Choctaw beliefs with Christian tenets. Others have selectively adopted some Christian beliefs and blended them with traditional Choctaw ones. Still others continue to hold fast to the traditional Choctaw

spiritual beliefs in a modernized form. Contemporary American society invades Choctaw homes through radio, television, and film, and the popular culture teaches Choctaw children values that do not necessarily conform to those of Choctaw culture. Materialism and its displays of power, fame, and success based primarily on wealth directly contradict traditional Choctaw ideals of sharing, harmony, and balance. Choctaw elders are concerned about the erosion of Choctaw values through the enormously seductive power of materialism.

CHOCTAW CHURCHES AND CHRISTIANITY

In the early 1800s, the United States sent Christian missionaries to the Choctaw Nation to provide education and to try to convert the Choctaw to Christianity. The missionaries met with few successes among the Choctaws themselves, but found many converts among the African American slaves owned by a small number of Choctaws who were of mixed white and Choctaw heritage. Many of these so-called mixed-bloods sought to adopt white ways of living and promoted Christianity among the Choctaws. The vast number of Choctaw people, however, maintained their traditional beliefs throughout the 19th century.

The Choctaws who joined Christian denominations during the 1800s built small churches in their rural communities. Many of these churches still exist and are still primarily attended by Choctaw people. These churches have services and singing in the Choctaw language. Cyrus Kingsbury, a 19th-century Presbyterian missionary to the Choctaws, translated Christian hymns into Choctaw with the help of Choctaw devotees like Allen Wright, a well-known Choctaw minister.

Gospel singing is popular among the Choctaws. A large number of Choctaws in Oklahoma attend Southern Baptist churches, and quite a few go to the Presbyterian churches. Tiny Indian churches dot the rural landscape in Oklahoma. Their congregations are small in number, but their spirituality and fervor is undeniable. The Angie Smith Memorial United Methodist Indian Church in Oklahoma City holds an annual Gospel singing program, in addition to services conducted in Choctaw. Other Choctaw churches are tucked away in tiny communities in rural areas.

The Mississippi Choctaw United Methodist Church in Philadelphia, Mississippi, draws members from the main Choctaw reservation community. In addition, the Mount Zion Missionary Baptist Church, Holy Rosary Indian Mission Church, and the Baptist Indian Center, among others, hold services for Christian believers among the Mississippi Choctaw people.

Notes

1. John R. Swanton, *Source Material for the Social and Ceremonial Life of the Choctaw Indians* (Birmingham, AL: Birmingham Public Library, 1993), 198.

2. Charles Hudson, *The Southeastern Indians* (Knoxville, TN: University of Tennessee Press, 1976), 139.

3. *Holy Bible,* King James Version, Genesis 1:26.

4. Swanton, *Source Material,* 196.

4

Social Customs, Gender Roles, Family Life, and Children

THE SOCIAL AND FAMILY TRADITIONS of the Choctaws have gradually changed in response to American colonialism, forced assimilation, and internal adaptations that allowed the people to retain their identity while meeting new circumstances and the challenges of living in a world not of their own making. The persistence of a distinct Choctaw identity demonstrates the adaptability that has allowed the Choctaw people to survive where many others have perished. Recognizing the great value of traditional Choctaw beliefs and way of life, Choctaws today have selectively incorporated some of the values of U.S. society, while retaining their unique identity as a people.

TRADITIONAL CHOCTAW KINSHIP

In order to appreciate contemporary Choctaw ways of living, one must understand the traditions of the past that were developed over thousands of years of living. Choctaws kinship was based on the ancestral lineage of the female. This system of kinship created a society that had equality between males and females, a division of labor that valued women's work, shared governing between men and women, and extended families that provided complete economic security for women and children. The most important aspect of Choctaw life prior to the 20th century was personal relationships and kinship.

Matrilineal Kinship

From ancient times, Choctaws were born into the clan of their mother, which gave them their identity and a well-defined place in Choctaw society. A clan is defined as a group of people who all are descended from a single ancestor. Matrilineal clans are made up of people who are all descended from a single female ancestor, through the female line. In other words, they reckon their ancestors only through their mother, her mother, her mother, etc., all the way back to a single female. Each clan of the Choctaws was based on descent from a single common ancestor. Clans were the smallest unit of family that historical Choctaws recognized as important. Nuclear families—father and mother, plus their children—were not regarded as important as they are in modern American society.

A whole world of ready-made relationships greeted the Choctaw baby at birth. All his or her maternal relatives were members of his or her clan and were considered close relatives. Unlike modern-day America's nuclear family, which consists only of the parents and children, each Choctaw was closely related to all his or her maternal relatives—no matter how distant. For example, a second or third cousin—if related through one's mother—was considered as close a relative as a brother or sister. In historical times, if a Choctaw traveled to another town in which they knew no one, he or she could go to the Clan Mother of his or her clan and be assured a hearty welcome and treatment not only as an honored guest but also as a lost brother or sister.[1]

Distant relatives—those people not of one's mother's clan—were even spoken to using a more formal mode of speech. In the Choctaw matrilineal kinship system, one's father was not a member of one's clan, so he was not a close relation. Although he made his home with his wife and children, their home was not considered to be his. If his wife divorced him, he went home to live with one of his sisters or another matrilineal female relation.[2] His mother and sisters would always welcome him home to their house. Since Choctaws were forbidden to marry a person from their own clan, husbands and wives were never of the same clan. Therefore, they were not close relatives.

The role and responsibilities of father as it is defined in traditional American society were not performed by the biological father in Choctaw society. The eldest matrilineal uncle of a child (mother's brother) took on the role of father. In all important decisions about a child, the mother and her brother would consult with each other and make the decision. Maternal uncles undertook much of the training of the sister's children, especially in teaching boys the skills needed as a hunter and warrior.[3] In this way, each family was intermeshed in relationships that were complex and overlapping.[4]

Because Choctaw society had a clan system instead of being based on a nuclear family, if a child's mother died, there were aunts, a grandmother, and a grandmother's sisters to take her place. This system surrounded each child in a supportive and loving web of relations for their entire life. There were no gangs historically in Choctaw society, because each person belonged to a supportive, large family.

In societies where kinship is matrilineal, women often seem to have a particularly strong position within the web of relations that makes up the society. Choctaw women discharged important responsibilities and were not just family leaders, but also participated in the political and economic decisions of the tribe. The matrilineal clan system, led by matriarchs, inculcated Choctaws in the proper roles of women—they were important leaders recognized as vital to the community. To the Choctaws, strong female participation and leadership was simply a part of life. This contrasts starkly with the patriarchal societies of Europe and the United States, in which women were devalued and treated as dependents. In 19th-century America, legally, like a child, a woman belonged to her husband, and she had sharply limited social, economic, and civil rights. Choctaw women, by contrast, had great responsibility, were recognized and relied upon as leaders, controlled important economic activities of the community, and had a voice in all the functions of the tribe. Choctaw men recognized the importance and equality of women and believed this was normal and natural. In fact, this system of equality was pervasive throughout the indigenous tribes of North America. When eastern Native Americans first conducted meetings with European leaders, they asked, "Where are your women?" and they were stunned that Europeans did not include women in important political and economic decision-making.[5]

Women and children found great security in the matrilineal clan system and were protected from adversity when fathers or husbands died. The matrilineal clans owned the fields and crops, and all the children belonged to the clan, not to the nuclear family. If a father or husband died, unlike in European societies where this situation would be an absolute calamity for the wife and children, little changed for the Choctaw family, because brothers, matrilineal uncles, and sons took the place of fathers in Choctaw society. The clans also assigned young, single men to hunt for widows or others who had no immediate family member to provide for them, so no one starved if others ate. Hunters typically brought their kills to clan leaders upon returning from the hunt, and the clan leaders divided up the meat so that all could have a portion. Houses belonged to the women, so if a husband died, their shelter did not change. They simply continued in the security of their clan relations.[6]

Prior to the 20th century, it was a crime to marry someone who was of one's own clan—it was considered incest and was harshly punished. One could only marry someone from outside one's clan. Anthropologists call this exogamy. These restrictions were much more limiting than in modern U.S. society. Since one's maternal second, third, and fourth cousins were part of one's clan, they were not candidates for marriage. However, this broad, inclusive way of reckoning kinship meant that individuals were born into a huge family that gave one a sense of belonging and stability that is often lacking in today's society.

The clan relations of Choctaw and other native societies' beliefs are often misunderstood by nonnative scholars, who sometimes assume that the individual was unimportant in such a close-knit tribal community. However, although different groups of people—the clan, other clans, the village, the tribe—were tightly interwoven throughout the nation, the individual had great freedom and value. This individualism differed tremendously from the concept in modern American society, however. Within Choctaw Nation, from birth, a person grew up without a preoccupation with self. They did not conceptualize their personal identity as separate from that of the clan and nation. However, each person had a very highly developed sense of self as a part of, and inextricably linked to, the clan and nation. Still, as an individual, he or she had the duty and responsibility to act as an individual contributor to the clan and tribal nation. They believed, for instance, that an individual person could bring calamity and ruin on the nation if that individual personally disregarded the mores and proper rituals necessary for the maintenance of balance and harmony. A hunter who killed without giving thanks to the spirit of the game could bring terrible consequences down on the whole nation.[7]

Likewise, a warrior had great responsibility to prepare himself individually for war and to listen to his dreams and read the signs. If he failed to do this, he would be failing in his responsibility to the raiding party and in his duty to his comrades. If a warrior had a dream with a negative message about the raid to take place, the individual warrior would share it with the others, and each one would individually decide whether or not to go on with the plans. However, every individual was accountable to himself and made the decision to go ahead or cancel the plans individually. This form of individual freedom and latitude derived from communal responsibilities and concern differs almost completely from modern American society's emphasis on the individual. The traditional Choctaw style of self-reliant individual responsibility to the group inculcated a high degree of accountability to the society.

Choctaw kinship relationships formed the model for their thinking about the world and everything in it. The tribe was formed of people who were all relatives—close or distant, they were still related. People outside the clans were definitely outsiders and were not related in the web of kinship. Inside this web, people were governed by clan law, which protected each one from violence, coercion, and incest. There was a complete system of law that governed the tribe which was enforced by the clan elders. Councils of clans met regularly to discuss different issues and concerns and to consult one another, to convey cautions, and to report transgressions. The law proscribed murder, rape, manslaughter, and stealing and provided punishments for these as well as for bad social behavior and disregard of spiritual beliefs. Within the tribe, every person was protected against transgression, and punishment was swift and sure. Crime within the nation was almost nonexistent until alcohol became a problem in the 19th century.

In addition to defining oneself and one's kinship relations, Choctaw identity also defined to whom one was *not* related. In the world of Choctaw tribal beliefs, someone outside the world of kinship relations was a nonentity, a potential enemy, a person unprotected by kinship law. If a person who was captured in a raid was not adopted into a clan, he or she had no standing or identity within the nation and could be subjected to torture or even death by virtue of existing outside the clan system that ordered relationships between Choctaws.

Outsiders, Strangers, and the Enemy

People who were not relatives were outsiders, strangers, or the enemy, because they did not exist within the Choctaw kinship system. Choctaws, like others in their time, took captives of enemies occasionally. Choctaws usually adopted captives into the tribe. Male adults were usually not taken captive, because they could not be assimilated into the tribal structure. They were viewed as warriors to the death and were, therefore, unadoptable. Women and children, including young adolescent boys, were integrated into the nation, augmenting the population and replacing people who were lost or killed by other tribes or the U.S. military. A ritual adoption took place in which the old identity or blood was symbolically washed from the person, and once purified, the captive would become just like a native-born Choctaw.

Because everyone outside the clan system of the Choctaw Nation was considered to be a nonentity or enemy, when Choctaw leaders formed alliances or friendships with other tribes, a mechanism for making them a relative came into common usage. "Fictive" or fictional kinship relationships were devised and adopted, so that relationships could be formed outside the tribe. Often, this took the shape of elder brother or maternal uncle. This system was common across much of Native America and was understood by everyone. Once a fictional kinship position was established, both parties would adopt the traditional responsibilities of that relationship. This was very common in historical times. It brought strangers and outsiders into the position of a relative within one's clan and provided a way for Choctaw people to interact with outsiders.

When Europeans began their invasions and colonization of North America, the Choctaws and most other indigenous nations tried to employ their usual establishment of fictive kinship relations with them, but Europeans did not understand what the native leaders were doing; nor did they understand the obligations and reciprocity inherent in these relations. For example, Europeans and later Euro-Americans thought they were establishing their superiority and position of authority over Native Americans by referring to the Choctaws as "children" and themselves as the "father" or the king or U.S. president as the "Great Father." The Choctaws would have seen this not so much as a power relationship in which one was dominant and the other was dependent, as they would have seen this as a relationship between rather distant relatives, like their own way of seeing a biological father and his children.

GENDER ROLES

In the days when the matrilineal clan system formed the center of Choctaw society, women and men were viewed as complimentary, essential components of society. Both were essential to the survival of the people and nation, and, unlike the American patriarchal society, women were held in high esteem. As explored in Chapter 3, each gender was understood to be able to tap into the world of spiritual power to draw on incredible resources that resulted in achievements beyond the grasp of ordinary beings. Women could create life—bearing and rearing children were vital powers necessary to the survival of the nation. In addition, women used this same area of spiritual power to raise crops—thus, they "gave birth" to the seeds, nurtured and protected the plants as they grew, then harvested and processed the food necessary to the people.

Men, of course, tapped into great spiritual power as hunters and warriors, transforming themselves from their ordinary, day-to-day roles within the clans to a raised level of spiritual strength and heightened skills of hearing, seeing, and thinking. This spiritual power allowed them to be great hunters, and to protect the people from all enemies.

Spiritual power was highly respected and a central concept in Choctaw life. Along with the special power that could be accessed by men and women, other individuals had unique roles. Rainmakers tapped into an otherwise inaccessible realm of power from which they gained the ability to call rain. Medicine men and women and healers called upon special gifts and knowledge that came from spiritual power. (Other spirits and beliefs are discussed in Chapter 3.)

A Choctaw village in Louisiana bayou country during harvest. (NGS Image Collection/ The Art Archive at Art Resource, New York)

Women planted and nurtured the crops, bore and raised children, gathered roots, herbs, nuts, and berries, made clothes and footwear, prepared food, and cooked meals. They cared for the members of their extended family, participated in clan life, and maintained and taught the way of life and beliefs of the Choctaw people. Their work was respected and valued, and their spiritual power was viewed as more powerful than that of males. With the matrilineal kinship identity form used by Choctaw people and the balanced view of the sexes, Choctaw women were and are considered self-reliant, independent, strong leaders, and often continue to be the central figure in Choctaw families. The traditions that recognized women as vital, essential leaders, and members of Choctaw society has changed little over the centuries, in spite of the decline of the clan system in today's Choctaw communities. Women hold leadership roles throughout the communities and are expected to be independent. Although the dominant society's treatment of women is somewhat improved over its subjugation of women in the past, Choctaw women have always been strong leaders appreciated for their vital role in preserving families, traditions, and kinship relations.

Today, Choctaw women often work outside the home, in the greater American economy. They also form the center of many families and extended families, where the matriarch or respected female elder is the core around which the rest of the extended family revolves. Choctaw women serve in elected leadership roles in the Choctaw Nation of Oklahoma and in the Mississippi Band of Choctaw Indians. They continue to pass on the oral traditions of the Choctaw people, transmitting values and beliefs based on the traditions of the past.

Choctaw men also are involved in a myriad of work, play, and other activities in modern-day America. Families today are clearly more influenced by the nuclear family than they were in the past, but far more often, Choctaw families include more distant relatives. Family relations are robust and complex, and maternal relatives still maintain an important position in many extended Choctaw families. It is not unusual for especially maternal relations to live with a sister's family. Men continue to hunt in many rural communities, and it is not uncommon for families to enjoy meat from wild game as the foundation of special meals. The traditions of war continue to find expression among Choctaw men, who, like many other native men, serve in large numbers in the U.S. Armed Forces.

Contemporary Choctaw Families

Choctaw families today reflect a wide variety of adaptation to U.S. society. Although matrilineal clan relationships have been all but forgotten, women continue to hold a place of esteem and importance that is a reflection of traditional Choctaw ways. While many Choctaws have adopted the Christian system of patriarchy, others still maintain the equality of men and women. A mother or grandmother is often the recognized leader of a family group, reflecting ancient Choctaw traditions.

Unfortunately, in some Choctaw families, dysfunction, strife, and domestic violence have been the result of diminishing traditional values. In many Native American communities, a breakdown of tribal traditional beliefs where women are valued as equal and essential contributors to all aspects of life has led to dysfunctional families in which women and children live in fear for their physical and mental well-being.

With the assimilation of many Choctaws to Christianity and its norms of patriarchy, the traditional system of Choctaw matrilineal clans has waned. Most Choctaws have adapted the dominant society's patrilineal kinship structure, while maintaining closer extended family relationships and a stronger role for females, especially mothers and grandmothers than is found in non-Native American families.

Choctaw men and women today take their identities from the nuclear family. Their surname is usually taken from the father, as is the custom in U.S. society. However, many families are still led by women—matriarchs who are accorded authority and recognition that is a holdover from the traditional Choctaw matrilineal clan system. Today one may still see many extended families headed by matriarchs, although contemporary Choctaws may not call them "Clan Mother."

Many Choctaw families continue to define themselves more broadly than the nuclear families of U.S. society. Nieces and nephews, cousins, aunts and uncles are all considered very close relatives and often reside with relatives other than those in their nuclear family. These families reflect the clans of olden times, providing stability and redundant relations to children and the elderly and enriching the lives of Choctaw people. The individualism and resulting loneliness that can be pervasive in the dominant society are missing in many Choctaw families because of the extended kinship system that still prevails. Both men and women have been forced to assimilate the roles of U.S. society through the economic system that pervades modern life. Men and women must hold jobs outside the home in order to earn money, but they often struggle to make ends meet. Many Choctaw families live in poverty; the rates of poverty for Choctaws in rural Oklahoma and Mississippi greatly exceed those of the dominant society, and employment opportunities that provide more than minimum wage or that offer benefits such as health insurance are few and far between.

Traditional Child Rearing

Traditional child-rearing techniques used by Choctaw society in past times resulted in adults who held themselves accountable to the group—the clan or town or nation. The values of the society were inculcated without harsh discipline inflicted by adults as was common in European and white American families during the 19th century. Children were not spanked, and the idea of coercing obedience to the parent was unheard of among Choctaws and other Native Americans. Instead, children learned by example and were taught that accountability to the group and becoming a person of value to the group were the most important attributes for success as adults. If a small child misbehaved, older children were expected to steer them away from undesirable behavior through example. If a child's behavior required adult intervention, it almost always took the form of shaming; quiet admonition, not yelling, often delivered indirectly. For example, if the offending child was playing with older children, an adult might reprimand the older child for the behavior of the younger, with both children present, in order to deliver the message that the behavior was unacceptable and that younger children should learn to behave by acting like older children. The responsibility the younger child would feel for causing the older child to get into trouble would be far more effective in curbing unwanted behavior in a society that valued harmonious relations among the group.[8] Choctaw families generally continue these child-rearing practices today, relying to a great extent on nonphysical methods of discipline and encouraging learning by example.

MARRIAGE AND DIVORCE

Choctaw marriage and divorce practices today reflect those of U.S. society. U.S. and state laws govern Choctaw marriages and divorces, and state courts adjudicate disputes in these areas. Today's practices differ enormously from the Choctaw life of the past. Prior to about 1850, the most important consideration in choosing marriage partners was the degree of kinship that existed between them. First, the couple had to be from different moieties. Moieties were two kinship groups that divided the nation into two parts. One was called the *Kashapa Okla* (the Divided People) and the other, the *Okla in Holahta* (the Beloved People). Each moiety was further divided into clans, or *iksa*. The Choctaw clans are listed in Table 4.1:

Since all the members of a particular clan were considered close relatives, they were forbidden to marry one another under the laws of incest. The bride and groom's families would carefully determine if the couple had a kinship relationship that barred their union. If not, they were free to marry.

A woman was never forced to marry anyone she did not choose. When a Choctaw man wanted to begin a relationship with a woman, he sometimes would test her interest by rolling pebbles toward her until he got her attention. If she was interested, she would roll them back. If not, she expressed her disinterest by ignoring them. Sometimes the young man would find some excuse to visit a woman's home, and before leaving, he would place his hat on

Table 4.1
Choctaw Moieties and Clans

Kashapa Okla Moiety	Okla in Holahta Moiety
Kush Iksa	Chufan Iksa
Lawokla	Iskulani
Lulak Iksa	Chito
Linoklusha	Shakchukla

her bed. If interested, the prospective bride would leave his hat there. If not, she would immediately remove the hat and place it elsewhere.

After the couple had each expressed interest in the other, the courtship often began by the prospective groom bringing gifts to the bride's uncle and mother. This gift-giving would be followed by invitations to visit and encouragement and hearty welcomes given by the girl's mother and matrilineal uncle. The marriage ceremony itself was a joyous occasion for both families and their friends. The bride and groom were instructed to stay in their house until their relatives called them out. The families would mark a spot about 200 yards distant with a pole decorated with colorful ribbons. First, the relatives of the bride would bring her out, and she would run down the path to the pole. When she had covered several yards, the relatives of the groom would call him out, and he would chase the bride down the path toward the pole. If she was still willing to be his bride, she would signify this by being caught—but sometimes after giving the groom a lively chase. Her relatives could assist her, and they often helped her get away, or blocked the path of the young man, or tried to hold him back. All in good fun, the man would continue to chase her until he caught her. Both families and their friends would root for their young person, and everyone had a great time.

Once the bride had been caught, the young couple would be taken to a place of honor where a cloth had been laid on the ground and strewn with flower petals. All the girl's relatives would sit around her while her uncle came up to stand behind her. He would hold a basket or cloth above her head, and her relatives would shower her with gifts. But as soon as each gift was tossed into the basket, another relative would snatch it away. This went on until everyone had a gift. Next, a big feast was prepared by the women, often followed by an all-night dance. The couple would usually live with the girl's mother, along with her sisters and their families, and their unmarried brothers.

Divorce was easy. The woman would simply put his belongings outside the door of their house, and he would understand that their marriage was at an end. The woman always kept her children; they belonged to her clan, whereas the father was of a different clan. Men who were divorced went to live with their sister.

Pregnancy and Childbirth

Childbirth was viewed as a natural part of the life of every woman. When a Choctaw woman went into labor, she simply absented herself for a few hours. She would then return to her duties, introducing her family and friends to the newest member of the clan and tribe. Choctaw women rarely had problems in childbirth, and when they did, knowledgeable senior women attended her. It was very rare for a Choctaw woman to use a male physician until well into the 20th century.

After birth, the Choctaw baby was placed in a small portable cradle, called a *unllosi afohka*. Many of these cradles were elaborately decorated, tangibly expressing a mother's love. Babies would stay in these cradles until they could crawl. When the babe reached this age, he or she would be wrapped in a blanket on the mother's back, and she would continue to carry the child everywhere she went.

In ancient times, the Choctaws practiced what today seems a peculiar custom. Shortly after birth, the mother would apply an earth compress or a small bag of sand to mold the head. The forehead from the rising of the nose to the hairline was thus flattened, which was considered beautiful by the Choctaws. After completion, the bridge of the nose would no longer be equidistant between the chin and the hairline.[9] These practices fell out of favor in the early 19th century.

Today's Choctaw women generally have their children in a hospital. In the recent past, some Choctaw women were sterilized without their knowledge or consent. In the 1970s and 1980s, Indian Health Service doctors engaged in such practices, often justifying their actions on racial grounds. These abuses have only recently come to light, and no one has been held accountable for these abuses of power. Over the past two decades, the Indian Health Service has implemented new policies to assure that Indian women are no longer subjected to such practices.[10]

THE ECONOMY

In historical times, the Choctaws had a subsistence economy, which meant they grew their own food, and if they had a surplus, they might trade it for something that they needed. In addition, they hunted, and game was a vital part of their diet. The Choctaws were outstanding farmers. For many years, long before the invasions of the Europeans, the Choctaws always grew a surplus, and their agricultural prowess was second to none. They almost always had a surplus to trade or buy, and frequently supplied needed food to nearby white communities. During the early 19th century, white men who came into the Choctaw Nation and married Choctaw women grew crops for the market. A handful of these men bought slaves and expanded into cotton, just like plantation owners of the United States South. Some of them became very successful financially, and they were also active in Choctaw politics during the late 1820s when Andrew Jackson and the U.S. government forced the Choctaw people from their ancient homelands.

During the 1820s, U.S. policies devastated the Choctaw subsistence economy. White intruders exterminated the game, leaving Choctaw families without an important part of their diet. During these years before the infamous Indian removals, many white squatters invaded Choctaw lands, in anticipation of the election promises of Andrew Jackson, who promised to acquire the homelands of the Choctaws through whatever means necessary. The agricultural practices of the Choctaws were completely disrupted causing many people to lose their crops or to be unable to plant at appropriate times. In the 1830s, with the so-called removals, all the people who were expelled to the western wilderness lost their farms and fields. The Choctaws who remained in what became the state of Mississippi were forced to hide out in the backwoods, unable to plant and grow crops or hunt under threat of discovery and expulsion to the West.

In the West, the Choctaw subsistence economy was reestablished, and by 1840, many fields were planted with crops for home use. A few wealthy intermarried whites continued to use slave labor to grow cotton and other crops, and many were very, very successful until the U.S. Civil War. But the vast majority of Choctaws in the West continued their traditional ways of subsistence, growing enough to feed themselves, but not to sell to the market.

The U.S. Civil War devastated the economy of the Choctaw people in the West in the 1860s. After the war, the U.S. government forced the Choctaw Nation to relinquish half its territory in reparations for joining the Southern Cause during the Civil War. From 1865 to 1880, once again the Choctaws rebuilt their economy, and, in some cases, achieved some modest success. However, during the 1880s, the U.S. government passed the Dawes Act, which marked the beginning of the seizure of the Choctaw Nation's lands in the West that, under the Treaty of Dancing Rabbit Creek, were guaranteed to the Choctaw Nation forever. In 1906, the U.S. government unilaterally dissolved the Choctaw Nation, seizing their lands and redistributing them so that enormous amounts of the land found its way into the hands of white citizens. After that date, the Choctaws of the new state of Oklahoma had no economy separate from that of the rest of the United States. They had no land, no reservation, and no federal relationship. Unfortunately, Choctaw people continued to be excluded from the equality under the law, and racist attitudes among U.S. citizens led to their further impoverishment.

The economy of the Choctaw people remaining in Mississippi, Alabama, and Louisiana generally never recovered after the forced removals of the 19th century, because Choctaw people were not allowed to openly own land, farm, or participate in the mainstream economy. Most Choctaws lived in dire poverty, determined to remain in the lands of their ancestors, but unfairly excluded from the fundamental rights to life and labor enjoyed by U.S.

society. After more than a century of intense and unrelenting oppression, Mississippi Choctaws obtained a reservation, opened formal schools for their children, and the U.S. government opened an Indian hospital. In the 1960s, the Mississippi Choctaws, under the leadership of their tribal chairman Phillip Martin, seized the opportunity of economic development, accomplishing an economic miracle that established businesses and opportunities for the Choctaw people.

CHRISTIANITY

In 1818, some of the first white missionaries came to the Choctaw Nation, supported by a special U.S. program to "civilize" the Choctaw people. In the 19th century, the dominant society believed that only European ideals and way of life were "civilized." To them, the Choctaws were savages who had no religion and whose way of life was simply wrong. Of course, the Choctaws and other Native Americans knew their belief systems were not savage, but racist ideals of the dominant society were forced on them.

Christian ideology, including its foundation on patriarchy, was brought by missionaries, and endorsed by traders, U.S. Indian agents, and others who came into contact with Choctaws. Missionaries opened small schools on Choctaw lands where they adamantly insisted on proselytizing their religious beliefs alongside, and woven into, the educational process. Children were subjected to method of teaching and discipline to which they were not accustomed, and if they did not conform, they were expelled. Very few Choctaw converts resulted from the first few decades of Christian religious instruction, and Choctaw leaders repeatedly protested the harsh discipline and preaching of Christianity that their children had to endure in order to learn to read or speak English.

Choctaws appreciated education and sought it for their children. Viewing the threat of losing their lands, Choctaw leaders believed that the children should learn to read and write the English language in order to better protect the Choctaw Nation from Americans seeking to expand into their territories. Unfortunately, the U.S. government would not provide it without religious indoctrination. In the 1830s, under President Andrew Jackson, the U.S. government forced the Choctaw Nation off their homelands and into permanent exile. This horrific process resulted in the destruction of many of the ways of life and beliefs of the Choctaw people. Thousands of elders died on the Trail of Tears and shortly after the arrival of Choctaws in the West, and hundreds of elders refused to leave Mississippi, staying behind in hiding. The clans and other traditional beliefs, ceremonies, and rituals never recovered from this devastation. In the region that is now called Oklahoma, Choctaws tried to reform their settlements and re-create their old institutions of three distinct districts. However, the number of deaths, illness, and anomie rendered many of their efforts futile. The clans slowly faded, leaving an enduring respect for women as strong individuals who are valued contributors to Choctaw life as its legacy.

During the latter part of the 19th century, Christianity was adopted by many Choctaws, especially those who were indoctrinated at the Choctaw boarding schools that were run by Christian denominations. These beliefs began to erode the respected position of Choctaw women, as patriarchal ideals replaced the traditional belief systems of the Choctaws. Under 19th-century Christian beliefs, women were subservient to men. They were not to speak in church, nor were they allowed to assert their natural abilities as leaders. Other aspects of Euro-American social and cultural beliefs seeped into Choctaw culture, including ideas that forced women into subservient positions in the economy and families. Christian preachers taught that the role of men was, in part, to dominate wives and children. Extended families based on matrilineal kinship were, according to most missionaries, the work of the devil. In setting up women over men, as missionaries saw it, Choctaw women and their family relations directly challenged the family life sanctioned by God and had to be replaced by the "civilized" family life composed of a nuclear family, with the undisputed head of the family being the father or husband.[11]

Over the 19th century and into the 20th, women's roles and overall gender relations within the Choctaw societies were devastated by the destruction of the traditional Choctaw beliefs in spiritual power, matrilineal clans, communal ownership of land, and the high esteem in which Choctaw men held Choctaw women. With the idea of patriarchy and the adopted practice of Christianity by many Choctaws, women's lives and roles in the Choctaw Nation were changed forever.

SOCIAL CHANGE IN THE 20TH CENTURY

During the 19th and early 20th centuries, many of the ceremonies and dances diminished in importance as Choctaws struggled under the oppression of American colonialism. Mississippi Choctaws remained to themselves as much as possible, and continued to speak the Choctaw language and maintain many of the traditional ways. In part because mainstream society did not allow their participation in education, politics, and the white economy, Mississippi Choctaws were less affected by the intrusion of these beliefs and worldview, and thus retained not only their language but also much of the traditional Choctaw worldview. In Mississippi, Choctaws slowly assimilated the dominant white society's beliefs and ways of life, which began to affect the lives of most of the Choctaw people. The concept of "progress" paired with the intrusion of the idea that mainstream ways were superior to Choctaw ways, produced a growing number of Choctaws that internalized the dominant society's way of life. The influence of these ideals and concepts led to increasing acceptance of white values and beliefs, which seriously eroded the traditional worldview of Choctaw people. Two of the most serious adverse results of assimilation were that women became devalued through the demise of the matrilineal clans that formed the basis of Choctaw life, and the inculcation of the idea of private enterprise and emphasis on individual accumulation of wealth.

These resulted in a vacuum in the rule of law and its enforcement by the clans, which led to social chaos and lawlessness. In the second half of the 19th century, the Choctaw Nation in Indian Territory was invaded by whites who fled from society or the law, and who were not subject to Choctaw law enforcement or jurisdiction. A state of lawlessness became the norm in the Choctaw Nation, and the United States seized upon this problem, which was caused by the United States , to move to organize Indian Territory into a U.S. territory, which would lead to statehood.[12] The treaties by which the Choctaws and other nations were forced to move into exile in Indian Territory in the 1830s had a clause that stated that they would never be forced to become a part of a U.S. territory or state. Unfortunately, when the United States abandoned its treaty promises in the late 19th century, native nations were dissolved by the United States and incorporated into a U.S. territory and then the state of Oklahoma against their wills.

The chaos created by the massive influx of intruders gave the United States an excuse to call for the dissolution of the Choctaw Nation and the forced division of Choctaw lands and sale as private property, resulting in the loss of 90 percent of the Choctaw land base. The remaining 10 percent was owned privately by nuclear families and over the 20th century became almost valueless as a result of multiple overlapping title claims.

As a result of these policies, Choctaw lives changed drastically. The cohesion of the people disintegrated. The clans no longer were effective; their major central role in the lives of Choctaw people was wiped out. Patriarchy grew in importance and expanded in effect. Women's roles as equal partners in the society lessened significantly as consensus and communal decision-making were replaced by white forms of hierarchical and authoritarian rule. Instead of consensus and joint decisions on important issues before the nation, Choctaw leaders increasingly used external force through the Choctaw Lighthorse—a police force created to protect the private property of white men married to Choctaw women. As more Choctaws accepted white ways of accumulation of property and individual self-interest as more important than the welfare of the community, systems of force that promoted inequality and a hierarchy of power expanded to coerce traditional Choctaws to comply with these fundamental social changes.

Patriarchy increasingly replaced the balanced foundation of gender equality that was part of the fundamental framework for social, political, and economic systems in the Choctaw Nation, forcing women into secondary roles and diminishing their importance and influence to reflect that of the dominant white society. By the time the United States forcibly extinguished the existence of the tribes and declared their lands to be the state of Oklahoma, the oppression of women and their economic, political, and social subjugation had become the norm in many Choctaw communities. However, the old ways continued to be practiced in modified ways. Women continued to be very influential in Choctaw homes, and echoes of the old ways of equality between the sexes were not easily diminished.

Throughout the 20th century, Choctaw people in Oklahoma unevenly maintained and practiced traditional ways. Those in rural areas heavily populated by Choctaws continued to hold ball plays, stomp dances, and other community gatherings, while many urban Choctaws, especially those of mixed heritage, tried to blend into the white society that controlled all access to jobs and could limit Choctaw access to education and other opportunities enjoyed by the white society.

After more than two centuries of oppression, many Choctaws began to awaken to the destruction of their unique society in the 1960s and 1970s. The civil rights era of these years produced great social movements demanding equality for oppressed minority groups in America. Red Power united disenchanted youth in expressing racial and ethnic pride, and led to revitalization movements throughout Native American communities across the nation. Pride in Choctaw identity revived many of the traditional ways, leading the way home for many urban Choctaws who had been scattered across the nation in the search for economic security and a life without poverty for their children. Each decade since the 1960s has marked the increasing revival of the Choctaw language, community gatherings, political and social identity, and a reawakening of aspects of the unique Choctaw worldview. The tribal government of the Choctaw Nation of Oklahoma has increasingly asserted self-government and a huge push for the recognition of native sovereignty in its relations with the U.S. government.

The Nation opened casinos, bingo halls, convenience stores, and highway travel stops to increase the wealth of the nation in order to deliver social services controlled by the Choctaw people. Hospitals, schools, and community and senior centers offer medical care, educational opportunities, and social and community functions to the people throughout the 10 and one-half counties of the former Choctaw Nation landmass. Land acquisition has also been an important goal of the nation, and gradual accumulation of a common land base is beginning to show important results.

Every year, at the traditional time of the Green Corn Ceremony, the Choctaw Nation of Oklahoma holds a national festival on Labor Day weekend. Attended by thousands of Choctaws from across the United States, and non-Choctaw guests, the festival features a Choctaw princess contest, history lessons and storytelling, Choctaw gospel and hymn singing, ceremonies, sale of Choctaw arts and crafts, entertainment, and food. In addition, the gathering reinforces identity and belonging and is the place for hundreds of extended family reunions and renewals of old friendships. Stickball, the Native American forerunner of lacrosse, is a highlight of the festival. Young boys and girls get to watch and try their hand at the game, making converts of many. As in old times, the excitement caused by the Little Brother of War is embraced by young and old alike.

Each spring, Choctaws join together for a commemoration of the terrible times of the forced dispossessions of the 1830s. A short stretch of the Trail Where We Cried is walked by hundreds of Choctaws, many of whom experience a solemn spiritual connection through this ceremonial remembrance of their ancestors' travails. By joining together in this communal recognition,

The modern game of stickball is enjoyed by many Choctaws and other southeastern native peoples. (Choctaw Nation of Oklahoma)

Choctaws reinforce traditional beliefs that the past is always with us and that it is an important part of who we are and from where we come.

The maintenance of these important events among the Choctaws is evidence of the determination of the Choctaw people to educate its citizens and the general public about Choctaw affairs, the history of the Choctaw people, retention of the language and traditions, and the hospitality and generosity that are traditional values of the Choctaw people.

Notes

1. Charles Hudson, *The Southeastern Indians* (Knoxville, TN: University of Tennessee Press, 1975), 189, 192.

2. Ibid., 199.

3. Ibid., 187.

4. Ibid., 201.

5. Ibid., 268–69 and Devon A. Mihesuah, *Indigenous American Women, Decolonization, Empowerment, Activism* (Lincoln, NE: University of Nebraska Press, 2003), 43.

6. Hudson, *The Southeastern Indians,* 201.

7. Ibid., 156–57.

8. H. B. Cushman, *History of the Choctaw, Chickasaw, and Natchez Indians* (Greenville, TX: Headlight Printing House, 1899), 295–96.

9. John Swanton, *Source Material for the Social and Ceremonial Life of the Choctaw Indians,* Smithsonian Institution Bureau of American Ethnology Bulletin 103 (Birmingham: Birmingham Public Library Press, 1993), 118.

10. Jane Lawrence, "The Indian Health Service and the Sterilization of Native American Women," *American Indian Quarterly* 24, no. 3 (Summer 2000): 400–19.

11. Mihesuah, *Indigenous American Women,* 49.

12. Devon A. Mihesuah, *Choctaw Crime and Punishment, 1884–1907* (Norman, OK: University of Oklahoma Press, 2009), 19–20, 27–29 and Angie Debo, *The Rise and Fall of the Choctaw Republic* (Norman, OK: University of Oklahoma Press, 1972), 91.

5

Choctaw Oral Traditions

THE CHOCTAWS, LIKE many other great societies around the world, did not use the written word to convey history, beliefs, values, and traditions from one generation to the next. Instead, storytellers and designated elders mesmerized Choctaw adults and children in the evenings, when everyone gathered around the fire to hear wonderful stories that educated, enlightened, conveyed morals and beliefs, and entertained. In many places today, Choctaws still gather on porches and in family rooms to listen to the stories, many of which are hundreds of years old. Hog stories, *shuka anumpa*, create laughter and fun times, while serious lessons from the Trail Where We Cried and other solemn events instruct the young people in the history of the nation, using this painless method of education in the form of stories that are easily absorbed and remembered.

At least two origin stories have been passed down the centuries, and are still told today in many Choctaw families. The first, which is found in Chapter 1, describes how the Choctaw people migrated from a distant home in the West, traveling for years following the direction indicated each morning by the sacred pole. When they arrived at Nanih Waiya, the sacred Mother Mound, the sacred pole remained erect, and the Choctaw people realized they had arrived at their new home.

The other origin tradition commonly heard in Choctaw homes relates how the Choctaw people and other great southern nations emerged from the sacred Mother Mound from deep inside the earth. One day in the mists of the ancient past, a passageway opened from the peak of Nanih Waiya, the great

Mother Mound, which led deep into the darkest regions of the earth. After a time, the Muskogee people emerged from the passageway, wet from their long journey from the center of the earth. They lay on the sides of the Mother Mound until they were rested and dry, and then they rose up and began their travels to the East. Soon after they left, the Cherokee people began to emerge from the top of the Mother Mound. After they had sunned themselves on the sides of Nanih Waiya, they too rose and followed their eldest leader, who followed the trail of the Muskogees toward the East. One evening the Muskogees camped and smoked the sacred tobacco, and somehow the surrounding woods caught fire and burned, erasing the trail left for the Cherokees to follow. When the Cherokee leaders reached the burned area, they lost the path taken by the Muskogees and turned north, traveling many suns until they reached a beautiful region in which to make their homes. After the Cherokees had departed, the Chickasaws soon emerged into the warm sun on the mound of Nanih Waiya. After they dried themselves and rested, they found the trail taken by the Cherokees, and followed them to the North. When they reached the Cherokee camps, they founded their own nearby. Last, the Choctaws came forth from the Mother Mound. They too dried themselves and rested, and when they descended from the slopes of the mound, they beheld a beautiful, verdant landscape, and they decided to make their homes in the shadow of Nanih Waiya. For untold centuries, the Choctaw people revered their homelands, generation after generation living and dying within bow shot of their Mother.[1]

Choctaw oral traditions continue to be told among families and kinship groups by elders at Choctaw gatherings. Several of these traditions are included here.

OKA FALAMA OR THE RETURNED WATERS

Many of the peoples of the earth have oral stories about a great flood, which have been passed down through the generations. Recorded by missionaries to the Choctaws in 1818, it bears striking resemblances to the Great Flood story related in the Hebrew Bible. A few tantalizing differences from the old Bible story are found throughout the Choctaw narrative.

In ancient times, after mankind had existed for generations, human beings became so corrupt and wicked that *Aba* (the Great Spirit) became angry and decided to wipe out the human race. He sent a prophet to warn the people, but despite his urgent message, people everywhere simply ignored him, continuing in their evil ways. After many months, autumn arrived, and dark clouds rose from the earth to the sky. For weeks on end, the sun disappeared behind thick clouds both day and night. No break was seen in the clouds, which grew thicker and thicker with each passing day. Finally, the earth was wrapped in a blanket of darkness, and all the people and animals became terribly afraid. Despite their fear, the people continued their shameful activities, becoming used to awakening in darkness. Before long, great echoes of rolling thunder reverberated throughout the earth, with huge crashing noises becoming incessant. Several days passed, with many of the people so fearful that they hid themselves and covered their ears. Trembling in the complete darkness, surrounded by constant thundering, the people began to believe that the sun would never shine again. They began to sing their death songs and waited to die. The Choctaws revered the sun, and its representative on earth, fire, and the fear that the sun would stop coming out was very profound and terrifying to the Choctaw people.

Soon a new sound was heard—rain began to fall, increasing in volume until the skies seemed to be simply turning into water. Soon a great rumbling was felt through the earth; the rain suddenly parted, and in the distance, all could see a great light, growing larger every minute. But it was not a light after all; it was the gleam and reflection off gigantic waves that shook the earth as they rolled closer to the Choctaw lands. Wave after wave billowed into the sky, destroying everything in their path as they sped over the earth. Soon the giant waters reached Choctaw Nation, killing all the animals and people, leaving the earth a desolate wasteland. Everyone on earth was killed, except the prophet, who had tried to warn the people to change their ways. The prophet made a raft of sassafras logs and floated high on the waters, as fish swam around him, and the dead bodies of mankind and animals bobbed up and down everywhere he could look.

A long time passed, and finally one day a black bird passed overhead, flying in great circles in the sky. The prophet called out to him for help, but the bird only squawked and cawed and then flew away. A few more days passed, and another bird hovered over the raft—this time a bird colored in shades of blue, with red eyes and a red beak. The prophet called out to it, asking if there was dry land anywhere, and in reply, the bird let out a mournful cry and then flew away in the direction of the setting sun. Just as the bird went out of sight, a strong wind came up and blew the prophet's raft in the same direction. All night long, the raft flowed swiftly, driven by the unflagging wind. All through the night, the prophet watched the sky, as the clouds began to part and move away, for the first time in months. When dawn came, the prophet woke up to find a beautiful, clear blue sky, and the sun shining, bringing warmth and happiness in equal measures. Peering off into the distance, the prophet sighted land—an island appeared enshrouded in early morning mists. All day he traveled, drawing closer and closer to the beautiful island, until just before dusk, he reached its lovely shores.

Exhausted by months of worry, the prophet made a little camp on the beach, and slept the deep sleep enhanced by his relief and glad heart. When the sun rose the next morning, the prophet woke up and with renewed enthusiasm, and he left the beach to explore the rest of the island. He found it populated by many different varieties of animals, except the mammoth, which had disappeared from the earth. Birds sang and flitted through the lush trees and shrubs, and flowers bloomed gaily in the meadows. Toward noon, the prophet discovered the very black bird that had ignored him days before on the raft, which had deserted him to his fate. He believed this bird to be cruel, and so he named him *Fulushto,* the raven, who forever after was a bad omen to the Choctaw people. But to the prophet's delight, he also spied the blue colored bird, who led him to the island and safety. With great joy, he called him *Puchi Yushubah,* lost pigeon. After many months, the great waters receded, and soon thereafter, *Puchi Yushubah* became a beautiful young woman, and the prophet and she fell in love and married, and they peopled the world.[2]

A Choctaw woman, 1834. (Smithsonian American Art Museum, Washington, D.C./Art Resource, New York)

OHOYO OSH CHISBA OR THE UNKNOWN WOMAN

One of the most important oral traditions of the Choctaw people is a story about how corn was brought to the Choctaw people. Corn was the most important food of Choctaws and thousands of other native people of the Americas. Thought to have first been grown somewhere in modern day Mexico or Central America, corn today feeds massive numbers of people throughout the world. This story also illustrates the importance of women in traditional Choctaw society, and the high esteem in which they were held. Acknowledged as beings of great spiritual power, women create life. Women's power was inherent at birth—unlike men's power, which had to be sought through ceremony and prayer to the Creator. In this story, the Choctaw people receive the greatest gift of all, through a woman.

In the swamps around the Alabama River, alligators silently drift like logs through the water. Bird chatter and call overhead, while otters splash and beavers retrieve branches, constructing elaborate dams and nests where they nurture and teach their young. One night in the distant past, two hunters camped on a rise in the swampland, roasting a crow over their campfire. It was the only food they had had for days, and, despite their gnawing hunger, it was poor fare indeed. The hunters were young and strong Choctaw men, who had been desperately seeking game needed by their hungry families and kin. After eating the tough, stringy crow meat, each curled up in his blanket, and tried to ignore his hunger pangs and fell to sleep. Just as they were drifting off to sleep, they heard a low moan, soft and melodious as a dove. A few minutes passed, then it came again, louder this time, but from a distance, a sound like none they had ever heard before. Both of the hunters rose and peered into the darkness surrounding them. The full moon emerged from behind a cloud, and they could suddenly make out the distant river bank and the huge trees that lined it, with moss hanging down from their great branches, nearly touching the water. Suddenly, they saw a beautiful young woman emerge from the trees a few yards down stream. The moon reflected the gossamer cloth of her robe, and her black hair shone round her lovely face. A wreath of fragrant flowers crowned her head. She beckoned to them, and as they approached, a strange light surrounded her, giving her a supernatural appearance. The hunters thought her to be the Great Spirit, and the floral wreathe that she wore represented the spirits of the dead.

Obeying her gesture, both hunters approached, offering their assistance in any way possible. She told them she was hungry, so one of them ran back to the camp and brought her the remains of the hawk. She accepted it with thanks, and ate a small portion. Then she said that she would always remember their generosity and when she returned to her home, she would tell her father *Shilup Chitoh Osh,* the Great Spirit of the Choctaws, of their kindness. She told them she must leave, but before she could go, she made them promise to meet her at the same place when the next midsummer moon came out. Bidding them an affectionate goodbye, she was borne away on a gentle breeze, disappearing as mysteriously as she came. For a few minutes the hunters stood there in disbelief, and then they slowly made their way back to camp, expressing wonder at their experience, and agreeing to keep silent about the beautiful apparition and their promise to return. At dawn the next day, they left their camp in the woods and returned home to their village.

The following summer they kept careful watch and when the midsummer moon began to rise, they set out for the camp near the river in the woods. Once there, they went down to the river to the little rise where the past winter the lady had appeared to them, approaching it with great trepidation. When they reached the exact spot where she had stood, no one was to be seen. For a few minutes, they talked softly, wondering what to do next, when they recalled that the lady had not said that she would be there, but to look where she had stood. In that spot, the hunters saw strange plants growing, plants they had never seen before. Approaching them, they realized that the plants grew nearly six feet high, and held large, cylindrical pods almost in offering to the men. One of the hunters peeled back the outer layers of the pod, and saw gleaming rows of multicolored kernels. They tasted the kernels and looked at each other in amazement. Within a few days, the hunters had returned home, bringing the pods to the clan mothers, who followed them to the spot by the river where the plants grew. The clan mothers pronounced the new plant to be *tunchi* and immediately took the best kernels to save for planting the following spring. Each and every year thereafter, the wondrous plant provided food for the people, and every year they prospered. This was how the world was given the gift of corn.[3]

CHAHTAH OSH HOCHIFOH KEYU OR THE NAMELESS CHOCTAW

This story tells of the joys and sorrows of love. Two young Choctaws fill the roles of star-crossed lovers, somewhat reminiscent of the story of *Romeo and Juliet.* Despite the similarities, the Choctaw story introduces their beliefs that wolves are special creatures very close to men. Traditional Choctaw people believed that wolves and all other creatures had a human-like consciousness, with the same feelings and ideas as people. They viewed all of nature as filled with sentient beings or spirits who brought messages or sometimes assistance to human beings.

Years ago, a fine young man, the only son of a great war leader, lived in the village of *Aiasha* (habitation). He was known for his fine character, good looks, and bravery. All the elders believed he would become a great warrior, but he had not yet succeeded in proving his courage by slaying an enemy, taking a captive, or striking the fallen body of dead enemy, which was considered by the Choctaws to be very brave. All native warriors tried to protect their fallen brothers so that their remains were treated with dignity.

Choctaw boys were given a name in childhood only when they had performed a courageous and memorable feat. But somehow, this young warrior had never so distinguished himself, despite the high hopes of all who knew him. So, since he had earned no name through some extraordinary action, he was known as *Chahtah Osh Hochifo Keyu* (the Nameless Choctaw). In the same little Choctaw village lived a young woman renowned for her beauty, who fell in love with Chahtah Osh Hochifo Keyo, as he did with her. They wanted to marry as soon as they could, but first Chahtah had to gain a name through bravery in war.

The following summer, the enemy attacked a hunting party, killing one Choctaw hunter. The others returned to the village to sound the alarm, and for three days the warriors prepared for war through ceremony and dance. The last night before the war party left, Chahtah spent part of the evening with his true love. Chahtah and his lover sat on a hill that overlooked the campsite far below, where over 400 warriors danced, rending the quiet evening with their cries and yells. The following dawn, they left for the long trip west to attack their enemy, the Osage, at the head of the Arkansas River. Once they reached their enemy's country, the sun had set, and they happened upon a large, dry cave where they decided to spend the night.

It was very late, so the warriors decided to sleep, and while they did so, two scouts went out to reconnoiter the area, one to the east, and one—Chahtah—to the west. Later that night, a lone Osage hunter came up to the opening of the cave, thinking to spend the night in the shelter that he knew well. Ever alert, the Osage discovered the tracks of his tribes' bitter enemies, the Choctaws. Silently he stole away, running swiftly back to his village. Joined by a large war party, the Osage returned to the cave before dawn, and piled dried tree limbs and brush across the opening of the cave, setting it on fire. The Choctaw warriors had no way to escape, and they all died, down to the last man. The Osage returned to their village to celebrate their victory, while, in the meantime, one of the two Choctaw scouts returned to the cave and found everyone had been killed by the enemy. He assumed the other scout, Chahtah, was also dead, so he immediately started out for home. A few days later, he entered the village, and related the sad news to everyone. It was assumed that Chahtah had also been discovered and killed, and this news was especially hard for his beloved to hear. She immediately began to waste away, and within a few short weeks, she was laid in a grave on the very spot where she and Chahtah had spent the evening the night before the war party left.

Although Chahtah had been spotted by the enemy, and was vigorously pursued for several days and nights, he eventually escaped, but not without injury. Running for his life, he scrambled down a ledge, fell, and broke his ankle. He hid in an old hollowed-out log off the trail in a dense and rugged wood. Several days went by, and his pursuers finally gave up. When he emerged from his hiding place, Chahtah realized that he had traveled many miles with the enemy hot in pursuit, and now he did not know where he was. For several days, heavy rains soaked the area, blotting out the sun. When the sky finally cleared, Chahtah took his bearings and started for home. His progress was very slow and painful, and he could only travel a few miles each day. Hunger was his constant companion, since he could not move well to hunt. Then one day, when he was very weak and in despair, he lay resting in a lovely glade deep in the woods. He had drifted into a sleep-like state, when a small rustling sound alerted him. He opened his eyes, and there, not far away, was a spotted deer, frozen in fear. Chahtah quickly picked up his bow and shot the deer with an arrow, piercing its heart. He couldn't believe his good fortune. After reserving a small portion to sate his hunger, Chahtah offered the remaining meat as a sacrifice to the Great Spirit. His ankle wound was not healing well, and infection set in. Chahtah drifted in and out of consciousness, laying there in the quiet glade. When the sun set, he woke up and made a small campfire; its light and heat were comforting. Suddenly, he heard a rustling of the thickets surrounding his camp as a great snow-white wolf emerged from the brush, and calmly walked up to Chahtah, crouched down and began licking his wound. Then the beautiful animal looked up, and asked, "Friend, where did you come from and why are you here in this wilderness?"

In his illness, Chahtah could not tell if the wolf was an illusion or was real. He reached out and stroked the huge wolf's head, feeling the warmth of a living animal and the reality of the beast's fur. Chahtah spoke with him, telling the wolf of his travails, how he was followed by the enemy, and how he hurt his ankle. For several days, the wolf stayed with Chahtah, filling his water pouch with fresh water from a nearby stream, and bringing back fresh-killed game for his nourishment. Chahtah's ankle quickly began to heal, and his strength and determination returned. Soon, he was able to walk again, and he bid his great furry friend goodbye, and set out for home once again. The rest of his journey passed without incident, and finally, after months of weary and difficult travel, Chahtah came home.

When he entered the village, he found a great cry going on, which was the ceremony marking the one-year anniversary of the death of a Choctaw. No one recognized him at first, he was so changed. However, when he began singing his songs, his relatives immediately knew him, and they told him of the tragic death of his beloved, who thought he had died. They related how she had pined away for him and had died of a broken heart. Chahtah's grief was boundless. He withdrew from everyone, and went off to a quiet spot outside the village to mourn his beloved. So great was his sorry that he too died of a broken heart, and the villagers placed his scaffold next to that of his beloved. Every year at the rise of the midsummer moon, a lone wolf is heard outside the village, howling all night long, in remembrance of the Nameless Choctaw and his beloved.[4]

THE MAN AND THE TURKEY

Shuka anumpa (hog stories) are humorous stories told just for fun. They are not designed or meant to be teaching tools, and usually carry no moral instruction or serious comment about anything. As such, they expect nothing from the audience, other than an appreciation of a bit of humor.

In old times, Choctaw mothers and their brothers approved or disapproved the marriage of young people. Grooms were expected to be proven warriors and successful hunters, and to have earned a reputation and name for these endeavors. Nonetheless, young men who had not yet proven themselves would occasionally try to win the favor of a young woman despite their lack of proven track record.

One day, long ago, a certain young man fell in love with a beautiful young woman. Unfortunately, he had no reputation and had not won a name in combat. Neither had he success at hunting. But he really wanted to marry this girl, and was determined to obtain the permission of her family. So after several weeks of hunting with no success, he arose at dawn the next morning and was out on the hunt before dawn. He almost stumbled over a gaggle of wild turkeys, and he tripped and fell while they scattered in panic. As he fell, his loaded gun went off, and, lo and behold, when he picked himself up, he found that his gun had slain a turkey. He hefted his prize, and started back to the village, where he walked around for quite a while, showing off his great catch. He passed the house of his beloved, and saw the impressed look of her mother as he walked by. Suddenly, he was struck with a great idea! That evening, he slipped out of the village and returned the turkey to the place he had shot him. The next morning, he walked out of the village, carrying his gun, making sure that many people saw him go. A few hours later, he returned to the village, carrying his prize turkey. And again, shortly after dark, he returned the turkey to the woods and returned to sleep in the village. Each morning, his beloved's mother saw him leave the village and later in the day, return with a turkey, and after a few days of this, she told her brother, "This guy's a really good hunter. Every day for a week he had brought home a turkey." That evening, the mother and her brother waited for the young hunter to return, so that they could give him permission to marry his beloved. After awhile, they saw him returning to the village, and as he drew closer, they could see that he was again carrying a turkey. But to their surprise, as he came up to them, they saw the flies and smelled the stink of the decomposing turkey, which by now was quite distinct. At once they realized the trick he had played on them, and they chased him round and round the village until they could chase no more.[5]

WHATYOUSAY

This story related by a Choctaw woman named Gladys Willis in 1996 reflects the humorous misunderstandings that sometimes occurred when people tried to communicate across cultures and languages.

A Choctaw man named Ashman met up with a white man one day, as he was traveling down a wooded path somewhere in Mississippi.

The Choctaw asked the white man, "What's your name?" in Choctaw, "Katah chihohchifo?"

To which the white man replied, "What you say?"

Then Ashman asked him "Where are you from?" in Choctaw, "Katima ish minti?"

Once again, the white man asked, "What you say?"

Ashman walked on, and when he reached home, he related the strange story to his family of the white man he met on the trail, whose came from the town of "Whatyousay," which was also his name![6]

SKATE'NE

For centuries, Choctaws have passed on stories about what are commonly known as the supernatural. These tales include stories of little people, ghostly lights, gigantic snake-like creatures that live in rivers and streams, creatures that are neither animal nor human, ghosts, spirits, witches, and goblins. Many of these stories are taken somewhat seriously, while others are used more for entertainment, just as a scary movie may be used today.

A long time ago, it was a beautiful summer day, late in the afternoon. The heat of the sun was almost violent, but children were out playing throughout the neighborhood, defying the heat that kept their elders inside. Down the path to the house, an old, old woman shuffled along, coming toward the children. As soon as they saw her, they panicked and ran back toward the house. The old woman called out to them, "Do not be afraid, for I am your great-great-great grandmother and neither you nor your mother have ever seen me. Go in the house and tell your mother I have come."

They soon returned and spread out a quilt on the ground for the old lady to sit, and brought her food and drink. As they sat there, she casually asked the children where their father lay when he went to sleep at night. They told her, and then they talked of many other things.

That night, the old woman crept into the house and entered the room where the children's father lay asleep. Taking a great shiny knife from under her apron, she sprang onto the sleeping figure and cut off his head. She placed his head in a basket, and covered his body with the blanket, and then slipped out the door into the night.

The next morning, the man's wife thought it was strange that her husband lay abed late, since he usually rose before dawn to go hunting. She went up to his sleeping figure and called his name, but he didn't stir. Then she pulled the cover back, and saw that he had no head! She screamed and ran out of the house to the neighbors' to get help.

In the meantime, the old woman walked down the road, out of the village and onto the path through the woods. After awhile, she met a bear, who stopped and asked her, "What do you have in that basket, Old Woman?" She quickly replied, "Nothing that you should see, for it will cause you to go blind. It is full of poison and is very, very bad." At that, the bear went on his way.

The day passed and still the woman kept walking on the path through the woods. Suddenly, she heard a growl so she stopped, and out of the underbrush sauntered two wildcats. "What do you have in that basket, Old Woman?" asked one. She told him it was poison and that if he looked upon it, he would go blind. "Oh, stop your blathering and hand it over!" he snarled, as he grabbed the basket out of her hand. He looked in the basket, and when he saw a man's bloody head he threw it down and ran off into the woods. His friend caught up with him and they talked over their discovery, and knew that the old woman had been the person who had prowled around at night, killing animals and people in the village.

They decided to kill the old woman before she murdered anyone else, so they returned to the path and intercepted her once again. One wildcat stayed to guard her and the other went back into the woods to look for a club. While he was gone, the old woman said to the wildcat who was guarding her, "Your friend knows that if he kills me, he will have good luck forever. So you should not wait for him. Go and find a club and you will be the one who has good luck." Hearing this, the wildcat thought, "I should be the one who gets the reward—I stopped the old woman first and I deserve to have good luck forever." He left the old woman and went into the woods nearby to look for a club. Great luck! He had only gone a few feet when he found the ideal weapon, a thick branch that would do the job nicely. He returned to the path, quick as he could, but the old woman was gone. She had turned herself into *skate'ne* (an owl) and had flown away before he got back. The old woman was not a human being at all. She was a witch and could change her shape at will.[7]

Na Losa Falaya

The *na losa falaya* have been the center of frightening tales for centuries. They demonstrate the malevolent forces that exist in the world, who can tap into infinite and magical powers. The strange and frightening *na losa falaya* resemble human beings, but are not human. They are about the size of a man, but their face is ugly and wrinkled, their eyes are tiny holes, and their ears are long and pointy. They don't live near people, but are usually hidden away deep in swamps or the backwoods where people seldom venture.

When a hunter has been out hunting all day, and the shadows grow long just before sunset, sometimes the *na losa falaya* will sneak up behind him and suddenly cry out in a voice that is human. Startled by the loud noise, the hunter will quickly turn to face the sound, and seeing the *na losa falaya,* many simply lose consciousness, sinking to the ground unaware. The *na losa falaya* then approaches the unconscious human and sticks a thorn into his hand or foot, which bewitches the hunter and gives him the power of evil doing. When the hunter awakens, he is alone and unhurt, and returns to his village with a strange tale that, he thinks, ends well.

After awhile, however, the thorn will do its work, and, without explanation or reason, the hunter will begin to take a new path of evil. No one can help him unless a medicine man or woman finds the thorn and removes it, performing ceremonies to expel the evil introduced into the man's body and spirit. The *na losa falaya,* when they are young, are able to remove their viscera (intestines) at nightfall that then makes them so light that they can float over marshes and swamps as small lights, and are frequently seen by human beings.[8]

Kowi Anuksaha

Small children of three or four years of age often wander away from camp and go into the woods. Usually all ends well, with the child found by his mother or older siblings, and brought back safely into camp. But every once in a while, the *kowi anuksaha* finds the little child before his family does.

The *kowi anuksaha* stands only two or three feet tall, but is shaped like a human being. He is actually a spirit, and not a living creature at all. He lives under rocks in rough areas of the backwoods, usually fairly close to human beings, who often are completely unaware of these neighbors. When a little child wonders from the camp, the *kowi anuksaha* may be watching, waiting for the young one to be just out of sight of the camp. He grabs the hand of the child and leads it back to his dwelling place under the rocks, where he and three other *kowi anuksaha* have gathered. These three others are white-haired and look like very old, very small human beings. When the child enters the dwelling, the first of these beings offers the child a knife; the second, a bouquet of herbs, all of which are poisonous. The third offers a bunch of good herbs that are used to make good medicine.

The choice made by the child determines his future. If he accepts the knife, he becomes a bad person and could even end up as a murderer. If he chooses the poisonous herbs, he will be a poisonous influence on all he meets, and will never be known to help kin or friend. But if he accepts the good herbs, he will have chosen the life of a good medicine man and strong leader of his people, and will use good medicine to help one and all. His family and friends will benefit greatly from knowing him, and he will be honored as a person of generosity and courage. When the child chooses the good herbs, the *kowi anuksaha* keep him with them for months or years, and teach him all the secrets of healing and good medicine. When the child returns to his people, he never tells where he has been or what he has learned. He only uses his knowledge when he becomes a grown man, and all his clan will benefit from his wisdom.[9]

Aside from the supernatural, hog tales, and historical legends, Choctaw storytellers also relate personal stories. Passed down from generation to generation, they remain alive and current in the minds of the listener, thus preserving the immediacy of the past and reinforcing the Choctaw's traditional views of time and space. Many traditional Choctaw people understand that the past is always with us, that one can reach out and embrace the past, because it is always near. The dispossessions and exiles that began in the 1830s are still a vivid memory unforgotten by many Choctaw families. The second great betrayal by the United States occurred at the end of the 19th century, with the Dawes Act of 1887, and subsequent legislation revoked the solemn word of the United States, and broke the treaties that promised that the Choctaw lands in the West would never become a part of any U.S. state or territory. In addition, the patent, or land title, held by the Choctaw Nation was ignored, and the United States seized the Choctaw lands and opened them to white settlement as part of the state of Oklahoma. These events are still in the minds and hearts of many Choctaws, and will never be forgotten, as long as the traditions are passed from generation to generation as they have been for millennia.

Choctaw Grady John was interviewed by author Tom Mould, and in 1998, he related this story, passed down in his family from the 1830s:

Removal

Eighteen thirty. President Jackson, he removed a lot of them to Oklahoma. Lot of Choctaw living in Macon coming this way. You know, Macon, in that area?

You know Dancing Rabbit Creek? They thought that was a peace treaty, signed. But Choctaw signed it to go to Oklahoma. They tricked them.

Choctaw used to be one of the largest tribes in the United States. Anybody ever told you that? We were the largest tribe.

That's when the removal to Oklahoma. All of them didn't make it. Dehydrated. A lot of them just couldn't go. Died. They buried them along—from Greenwood to Little Rock on to Oklahoma.

If archaeologists looked for it, they could kind find the Choctaw burial grounds somewhere—not grounds, but they just covered it up.

They moved from there. Half just made it.

OK, they had the land. All of them had land when you got there. But you know what happened? OK. A lot of Caucasian people made whiskey; went up and drank with them. They got drunk and they made them sign. And they lost it. Because he didn't know, he was drunk. He signed the paper. And the law say, "Here it is. You done signed it."[10]

Another family story tells of the return of many Choctaws from the land of exile in the 1830s and 1840s, back to their homelands in Mississippi and Alabama. Coming or going, the Choctaws were always shorted by the United States, who was aiding the fleecing of the Choctaws by its white citizens. In a story recorded by Tom Mould in 1997, Jake York related the experience of his father's great-grandfather, who was named Solomon York. York traveled to the western Choctaw lands (in what is today Oklahoma), with his grandfather, Scott York. Scott did not stay in the West, but returned to his homelands—he "snuck back," as Jake York said.

After many years, Solomon York, living in the West, had prospered, and had some land and a place on it. Many Choctaws lost almost everything when the United States seized the western lands, breaking the treaty promises that were the "supreme law of the land."[11] The United States allowed Choctaw families to reserve 160 acres of land, and after each head of household had received that, the entire land remaining was sold to whites. The children of these families, and certainly their descendants, had claims to no land, and most of these Choctaws became landless as adults. Had the United

States been true to its treaty promises, all these people would have had part of the communal land holdings of the Choctaw Nation.

Solomon York's estate, like many others, was sold off and the proceeds were divided among his living descendants. York related that all his family members living at the time received checks from the sale of Solomon's land and house. York says, "And they all got a check for, eventually some got a dollar and twenty-five cents, some got a dollar fifteen, and some got ninety-five cents. I think he [Scott] got something like a dollar. But my aunt's the one that showed me. She saved hers. It was a ninety-five cents check." Thus, the members of the Choctaw Nation, who had once owned most of the states of Mississippi and Alabama, now had been reduced to nothing but a check for a few cents and the dissolution of their tribe by the U.S. government.[12]

LAND SWINDLING

The Choctaw people weren't simply the victims of an oppressive colonial government. Individual citizens of the United States were given advantages under the law to obtain Choctaw land through all kinds of dishonest means and chicanery. The same storyteller, Jake York, related another example of how whites got the Choctaw's land, in an interview recorded by Tom Mould in 1997:

They got swindled out. See, they didn't understand the written part. Like even if they get groceries, and if you don't pay for it, you'll give up your property or land but they would put their "X" there when they get groceries. And that's how they got swindled out of their land.

My dad used to tell me about that all the time, how they got all these lands from the different people, property owners [native people]. That's how they were swindled out. There was lot of different ways they'd swindle them out. Like even liquor. They would get them drunk and they said, "Put your 'X' over here." They would make it like it was something else, they'd be purchasing a cow or something. It would wind up like it was their land that they were putting up.[13]

GRANDFATHER'S LAND

Thousands of Choctaws lost their lands through fraud and dishonest practices in the first quarter of the 20th century. Many Choctaw people who spoke little English and could not read made easy targets for white men. In this brief story, Inez Henry recalls how her grandfather lost his land.

Inez Henry's grandfather was among the thousands of Choctaws cheated out of their land. In 1986, she told Tom Mould that her father had owned 40 acres. Later in his life, he got sick. She said, "So then a white man had already drawn up the papers wanting the land, but as long as grandfather knew what was going on, he would not sign his name." After awhile, her grandfather became so ill that he was drifting in and out of consciousness. She said, "So when he laid there unconscious, two white men came. . . . They put a writing pen in his hand and, holding his hand, had signed his name. When he died, Mama wanted to stay but the white man got mad. Mama also got mad. When they both got mad at each other, the white man got an end of a hoe and beat her with it, and so Mama moved out."[14]

DISPOSSESSIONS AND DEATH

Other Choctaw families have passed stories of the great Dispossession and March into Exile. One Choctaw woman related a poignant account of her great-great-great grandmother, Sukey, who was forcibly dispossessed from her snug cabin and cleared fields and marched 500 miles to the wilderness in 1832. She lost everything and arrived in the West with nothing but the clothes on her back—no home, no tools, no money, and two of her children died on the trail west. But then, this was the experience of some 60,000 southern native people. This terrible era is called "Indian Removal" in U.S. history textbooks.

One day in the late summer of 1832, without warning, the U.S. soldiers ordered everyone to leave their homes, their crops, all their possessions, and their animals, and gather at a camp for the forced march to the West. The staging camp was about five miles from the small cabin where Sukey lived with her three children and husband, Thomas LeFlore. LeFlore was a captain over many men, and he was away when the order came down. Sukey gathered up her children and walked to the camp late in the afternoon.

Dozens of Choctaws were already there, the men quietly chatting, and the women tending children, many with tears streaming silently down their faces. Sukey found a vacant area and sat down to wait. One of the captains said he would send a runner to try to find Captain LeFlore and let him know where Sukey and the children were. The U.S. lieutenant announced that they would depart at dawn, and the soldiers would rouse the camp before first light. No one slept that night. The camp, along with the entire nation, was in deepest mourning. The women set up the mourning cry, keening all night, while the warriors silently turned their faces toward the woods, in stoic dignity.

The next morning, the soldiers came and ordered them to assemble for the march. They lined up by kinship groups. Many of the women and children were barefoot and wore only thin summer clothing. By the time they had been on the road for a few days, many began to suffer. Cholera had broken out in many of the white towns they were forced to pass through, until finally, one morning the first Choctaw died from the terrible disease. The days rapidly grew shorter, and the nights closed in early as the fall weather turned chilly and rainy. The Choctaws had no extra clothing or blankets with them, since the army forced them to leave so suddenly. The soldiers did not have blankets and other supplies the Choctaws had been promised. When the weather became really bad, the Choctaws found out that their U.S. guards also had purchased no tents, so all the people—men, women, children, and the elderly and sick—all had to camp in the open, in the chill rains and howling wind. Many got sick, and Choctaw people began to die. They suffered enormously as cold autumn rains descended day after day.

But the soldiers would not allow the people to stop. On and on they walked, with only a few wagons for the infirm and the sick. Many of the old people simply could not walk on, and the soldiers ordered them abandoned by the side of the road. One night they camped in a great forest, surrounded by huge oaks whose leafless limbs swayed with the coming storm. The winds picked up and began to howl through the trees, as the people crouched below. Sukey held the baby, while her two other children huddled with their cousins a few feet away. Suddenly, the rain began, and great crashes of thunder rent the air. The sky lit up with enormous displays of lightening that brightened the entire camp momentarily. Many of the children grew afraid, and some began to cry. Sukey could not see her two eldest children through the rain.

Suddenly, an enormous crashing sound rent the air, and Sukey looked up to see a huge tree limb come crashing down onto the huddled group of Choctaws below. It landed with a great thud that shook the land, and Sukey was horrified to see that the limb had landed just where her older children had been moments before the crash. Handing her baby to her sister, Sukey and many other men and women hurried over to the huge limb, trying to reach the children underneath, some of whom could be heard crying out for help. Soon the men organized themselves to lift the great branch and free the children beneath. They heaved in unison, but the great limb did not move. Again and again they tried to raise it, but each time they failed. Sukey and the other women had in the meantime cleared some of the small branches away and held the hand of her eldest, even though no other part of the child was visible. Her hand grew cold, and Sukey knew she was gone. Little Woman, her middle child, lay trapped from the waist down under a huge branch. Her pelvis was crushed under the tree limb, and no one could free her, so Sukey held her as close as she could, while Little Woman slowly died. In the morning she was gone, and the soldiers brought up the horses and moved the great branch off the children trapped beneath. More than 15 Choctaws perished that night, 14 children killed by the falling limb, and one elder, who, in great distress, simply gave up the struggle to survive.

Sukey and many of the other women of the tribe tried to insist that they be allowed to remain to give the funeral rites to the deceased, and to conduct the ceremonies for the dead. However, the American soldier in charge refused them this comfort, stating that their "savage" customs would not be tolerated. Instead, he had his men dig holes in the ground for those who perished, and insisted that the Choctaw people move on down the Trail Where We Cried. Sukey arrived in the wilderness of the place of permanent exile, where, within a few dozen years, the U.S. government would once again confiscate the land of the Choctaw people. Shortly after their arrival, her youngest child took sick, and died in her arms from the whooping cough. Now childless, Sukey was eventually reunited with her husband, Thomas. She lived to be more than 100 years old, and died just before the United States again betrayed the Choctaw people by seizing their lands and creating the state of Oklahoma.[15]

THE CHOCTAW LANGUAGE

The Choctaw language is one of several North American indigenous languages in the Muskogean language family. Other languages still spoken today within this family are Chickasaw, Alabama, Creek-Seminole, Koasati, and Mikasuki. The homelands of all of these indigenous nations were originally in close proximity in what are now the southeastern states of Mississippi, Alabama, Georgia, Florida, and parts of South Carolina and Tennessee.

There are approximately 11,000 fluent Choctaw speakers today, most of whom reside in southeastern Oklahoma. Another large group of Choctaws in Mississippi keep their language alive, speaking it in their homes, and teaching it to their children. Choctaw is the 89th most commonly spoken language out of the 322 languages that are spoken in the United States. In Neshoba County, Mississippi, more than 1 in 10 people speak the Choctaw language.[16]

Compared to some other Native American languages, Choctaw is not a very difficult language for native English speakers to learn. There are only 21 letters in the Choctaw alphabet and most of the letters are spoken like they are in English, with only a few exceptions. This similarity helps learners who are native English speakers learn to speak Choctaw more easily. Counting from 1 to 10, Choctaw speakers say "acafa, tuklo, tukcina, usta, tahlapi, hamali, untuklo, untucina, cakali, pokoli." Some common words and phrases in Choctaw are listed in Table 5.1.

The Choctaw people in the 17th and 18th centuries were renowned orators. Speaking in public was an art form with the Choctaws and each chief had a special assistant who was his speaker. In traditional times, the entire nation would occasionally assemble for a national council. The three district chiefs would send out runners to all the towns announcing the upcoming

Table 5.1
Common Words and Phrases in Choctaw

English	Choctaw
Hello	Halito
How are you?	Chim achukma?
Yes	A
No	Keyu
Where?	Katommah
What is your name?	Nanta chi-hochifo?
Who?	Kata
What?	Nanta
Why?	Katimah

assembly, carrying a bundle of sticks that corresponded to the number of days before the day of the meeting. Each morning the runner would throw away one stick, and when he reached the chief he was sent to invite, he would hand him the bundle. Each chief would likewise discard one stick for each day as he traveled to the assembly. Hopefully, all the people would thereby arrive at the national assembly by the designated day. National assemblies were also accompanied by feasts and ball plays and had a great festive air. The place at which the actual meeting would take place was called the council square, which was usually 60 feet long and 40 feet wide. After all were assembled, the chiefs and captains would share a pipe. The speaker would then arise and give a speech, telling one and all why the meeting was called and the subjects under review. He would lay out the position of each of the chiefs and would give their reasoning for their view. The speaker was an influential and respected man whose position was only inferior to that of the chief.

Debate would go on until every man had his say. No one interrupted another, and everything was done according to a solemn formality. The speaker would then give a big talk, in which he summarized the discussion and debate, explaining the positions taken by all, and their reasoning for their point of view. He would speak slowly, pausing after each sentence, at which time the entire assembly of chiefs and headmen would murmur "Aah!" or "Yes," if they approved what he stated.[17]

CHOCTAW STORYTELLERS TODAY

Today, as in the past, Choctaw storytellers continue the wonderful tradition of transmission of Choctaw culture, values, beliefs, and worldview down through the generations, from elders to children. Sitting on the porch on a pleasant summer evening in Oklahoma or Mississippi, the day's heat winding down with the gentle breeze, Choctaw people share their lore and wisdom through words. Many Choctaws still believe that words have a life of their own; once they leave the mouth of the speaker, they are imbued with the spirit of the thought and meaning, with unpredictable results. For this reason, most Choctaw people don't mindlessly speak. They consider their words carefully and speak with deliberation, especially in settings such as the classroom. Because words have such enormous impact and potential for doing good or causing harm, Choctaw speakers and storytellers speak carefully and have great respect for the power of the spoken word.

In many Choctaw families today, storytelling remains the main conduit for continuing knowledge of the Choctaw past. Storytelling conveys the Choctaw perspective of history. For example, in some families, the history of the Choctaw dispossessions is recounted and remembered through the eyes of the Choctaws who walked the Trail Where We Cried, forced out of their ancient homelands in Mississippi to travel by foot to the land that is now the state of Oklahoma. Other Choctaw families continue to convey personal stories of evading the American officials who rounded up the Choctaw people in the 19th century to force them out of their homelands. Their ancestors were the heroic survivors who today are the Mississippi Band of Choctaws. Through these stories, Choctaw people see the policies of the United States from a different perspective often not discussed. Choctaw storytellers today include Timmy Tingle, Greg Rodgers, Stella Dyer Long, and Presley Byington, among others. They take their stories to the public, including nonnative audiences, and have entertained people, while providing a look into the world of the Choctaw people. Beloved elders, aunties, grandparents, unknown to the outside world, continue storytelling traditions within Choctaw families everywhere.

LITERATURE

Modern Choctaw authors include both academic and popular writers. Choctaw historian Devon Mihesuah had written many books and articles on Native Americans and the Choctaws. Included in this extraordinary body of work are *Indigenous American Women: Decolonization, Empowerment, Activism,* which is a noted work on U.S. colonialism and its impact on the native peoples of North America. *Cultivating the Rosebuds: The Education of Women at the Cherokee Female Seminary, 1851–1909* illuminates the forced assimilation of Native American youth through an astute analysis of the everyday lives of young women in a boarding school in Indian Territory. Her most recent works include *Choctaw Crime and Punishment: 1884–1907,* a historical tour de force of a neglected but crucial time period in the history of Indian Territory as the Dawes Act works to destroy the Choctaw and other indigenous nations, and a moving collaboration between Mihesuah and her father-in-law titled *First to Fight.* This biography of a modern Comanche offers startling insights into the lives of modern indigenous people, edited with the subtle skill and nuanced interpretation of Devon Abbott Mihesuah. Professor Mihesuah is an enrolled member of the Choctaw Nation of Oklahoma and is professor of history and Cora Lee Beers Price Teaching Professor in International Cultural Understanding at the University of Kansas. In addition to her many books and articles, she is an internationally renowned indigenous scholar, activist, and speaker.

Other Choctaw scholars include Greyson Noley, an Indian education specialist and chair of the Department of Educational Leadership at the University of Oklahoma, and Michelene E. Pesantubbee, who is on the faculty at the University of Iowa in Religious Studies and American Indian and Native Studies. Professor Pesantubbee's book, *Choctaw Women in a Changing World: The Clash of Cultures in the Colonial Southwest,* analyzes the historical role of women in traditional Choctaw society and how the forces of colonization changed and altered their role. Dr. Noley has worked in the field of indigenous education for decades and has served as historian to the Cherokee Nation of Oklahoma and worked with hundreds of teachers and students in his long career.

Another well-known Choctaw scholar is LeAnne Howe, who is an award-winning Choctaw fiction writer, playwright, and poet whose first work, *Shell Shakers* (San Francisco, CA: Aunt Lute Books, 2001), won the American Book Award. She has continued to produce quality fiction, including *Evidence of Red* (Great Wilbraham: Salt Publishing, 2005) and *Miko Kings: An Indian Baseball Story* (San Francisco, CA: Aunt Lute Books, 2007). LeAnne is a professor at the University of Illinois at Urbana-Champagne, where she teaches American Indian Studies and English.

Notes

1. Oral traditions heard at the Mississippi Band of Choctaws Annual Fair in July 2002 and from Charlie Jones in 1996, notes in possession of the author; and John R. Swanton, *Source Material for the Social and Ceremonial Life of the Choctaw Indians,* Smithsonian Institution Bureau of American Ethnology Bulletin 103, Reprinted with an introduction by Virginia Pounds Brown, (Birmingham, AL: Birmingham Public Library Press, 1993), 31–36.

2. H. B. Cushman, *History of the Choctaw, Chickasaw, and Natchez Indians* (Greenville, TX: Headlight Printing House, 1899), 222–24.

3. Ibid., 214–16.

4. Ibid., 217–22.

5. *Choctaw Tales,* Collected and annotated by Tom Mould (Jackson, MS: University Press of Mississippi, 2004), 184–85.

6. Ibid., 180.

7. Based on "Skate'ne" (unknown), recorded by David I. Bushnell, 1909, in Mould, *Choctaw Tales,* 99–101.

8. Based on Pisatuntema (Emma), "Na Losa Falaya," 1910, in Mould, *Choctaw Tales,* 113–14.

9. Ahojeobe (Emil John), "Kowi Anuksaha," 1909, in Mould, *Choctaw Tales,* 131–32.

10. John Grady, "Removal," 1998, in Mould, *Choctaw Tales,* 154–55.

11. Clause 2 of Article VI of the Constitution of the United States declares that "all treaties made, or which shall be made, under the authority of the United States, shall be the supreme law of the land."

12. Jake York, "Sneaking Back from Oklahoma," in Mould, *Choctaw Tales,* 155–56.

13. Jake York, "Land Swindling," in Mould, *Choctaw Tales,* 156.

14. Inez Henry, "Grandfather's Land," in Mould, *Choctaw Tales,* 156.

15. Interviews with Genevieve Kirkpatrick, Ruth Fowler Dodd, Irwin T. Dodd, Annie Haney, and Charlie Jones, notes in possession of the author.

16. http://www.usefoundation.org/userdata/file/Research/Languages/choctaw.pdf.

17. Swanton, *Source Material,* 97.

6

Choctaw Cuisine and Agriculture

TRADITIONAL AGRICULTURE

FOR THOUSANDS OF YEARS, Choctaws have been recognized as master farmers, producing more than enough to feed themselves and having a surplus to sell or trade.[1] Agriculture was, perhaps, the most important sector of their economy, which also included hunting; fishing; trapping; gathering of roots, berries, nuts, and other wild plants and herbs; and trade. From ancient times, the Choctaws burned their fields to enhance the soil and to clear trees and underbrush from new fields. Their agricultural methods were thousands of years old, tried and true techniques that rarely failed.

Choctaw women's spiritual powers enabled them to be the givers and nurturers of life, so it followed that planting and raising plants would be one of the most important parts of women's daily lives. Women planted the crops, sang to them as they did to children, tended them, harvested them, and prepared the food for cooking and storage. Men and older boys cleared fields and occasionally assisted in the work, but women "owned" the fields and worked them together.

Men and older boys cleared new fields by girdling the trees and burning off the underbrush and saplings. Choctaw women then took over, breaking up clods, removing stones, and making the small hills in which the seeds would be planted. Corn, beans, and squash, called the three sisters, were interplanted in each hill. Corn seeds were planted first, in the top of the small hill—three or four seeds per hill. Once the corn plants started growing, they were thinned out, leaving the strongest plant to come to maturity. Next, bean seeds were planted in a ring around the top of the hill, and the bean seedlings were trained to use the corn as a trellis, twining up the lower part of the plant. As the bean plants grew up the corn stalk, they reinforced the stalk's strength, helping to stabilize it, and keeping it from blowing over in the wind. The bacteria that grow on the roots of bean plants absorb nitrogen from the air and convert it to a form that corn plants need to grow well. Squash seeds were planted lower on the hill, to shade the soil and reduce weed growth. These three plants, cultivated by almost all Native Americans, complimented each other, increasing the plant yields attainted by native women farmers.

In addition to corn, beans, and squash, Choctaw women planted watermelon, pumpkins, peppers, sunflowers, little barley, peas, potatoes, sweet potatoes, cabbage, leeks, onions, and garlic. Every day the women went out to hoe and weed and sing to the growing plants, bringing the children with them to shoo away birds and pick insect pests. In the absence of trees, they would build an arbor for shelter when the sun became too hot.

Corn was the most important crop of the Choctaws. Modern plant scientists believe that indigenous peoples of what is now called Mexico developed corn from a native grass called "teosinte," which is very different from the corn of today. By the time of the invasion of Columbus and his men from Italy in 1492, hundreds of strains of corn had been developed by Native plant breeding, of many different colored kernels, different sizes of cobs, and varying yields per plant and with a huge variety of characteristics and adaptations. The development of corn for short-growing seasons progressed over hundreds and hundreds of years, until varieties existed that could be grown as far north as the Great Lakes, an amazing accomplishment that was unmatched anywhere in the world. The domestication and development of corn by indigenous Americans prior to the arrival of Europeans is one of the most important contributions to mankind ever produced. It remains one of the world's major crops and is grown as food for humans and animals.

FAVORITE FOODS AND RECIPES

Corn was and still is of particular importance in Choctaw cuisine. Traditional dishes are often made for family gatherings, celebrations, and other special occasions. *Banaha, tomfulla, walakshi,* and hominy are favorites:

Banaha[2]

(Courtesy of Devon A. Mihesuah. Used with permission.)

2 cups of cornmeal
1½ cups boiling water

Banaha. (Courtesy of Choctaw Nation of Oklahoma)

1 tsp baking soda
1 tsp salt
Corn shucks

Boil corn shucks for 10 minutes. In a large bowl, mix together the water, cornmeal, baking soda, and salt until it is doughy. Roll into longish shape that will fit into the corn shucks. Wrap the shucks around the dough and tie with a shuck string, and then boil in pot of water for 30–40 minutes.

Tomfulla (Holhponi)[3]

(Courtesy of Devon A. Mihesuah. Used with permission.)

3 cups ground corn or cornmeal
• 6 cups water or chicken broth depending on taste preference
(If you use a smaller pot, then use 1 cup of corn and 3 cups of water.)

Place ingredients in cooking pot and boil for 3 hours or until the mixture is soft.

Traditionally, the dish was boiled for hours, sometimes all day. But if you cannot stand in front of a stove that long, then use a crock pot instead. Set on high and cook for 4 hours. You will need to stir it often during the first hour and check periodically to make sure it does not dry out.

Add water or chicken broth when needed.

Optional additional ingredients:

1 cup cooked pinto beans
½ cup green chilies
½ cup diced hickory nuts
½ cup diced turkey breast
½ cup diced onions
½ cup sweet corn (redundant, but it intensifies the corn taste of the entire dish)
• ½ cup sweet peas
Pepper to taste
• Garlic to taste
• Diced or shredded ham
• Old World ingredient

Grape dumplings. (Courtesy of Choctaw Nation of Oklahoma)

Walakshi (Blue Grape Dumplings)

The traditional way to make:
Gather wild grapes in the fall and dry them on the stem for later use.
To cook, boil the grapes and then strain them through a cheesecloth. Set juice aside. Make the dumplings from the *banaha* recipe above, and then drop them into the grape juice and cook until done. The grape juice is absorbed by the dumpling and the remainder of the juice is thickened. *Walakshi* was always furnished by the bride's relatives at weddings, while the bridegroom's relatives furnished the venison.[4]

Choctaw Hunter's Stew[5]

2 lbs deer meat
2 T beef suet
½ tsp salt
½ tsp pepper
6–8 carrots
3 stalks celery
2 lg onions
2 lg potatoes
1 lg can tomatoes
1 lg can whole kernel corn

Cut the meat in bite-size pieces and brown in suet. Add the salt and pepper, then cover with water and bring to a boil. Add the vegetables to the meat, turn down the heat, and simmer until done.

Wild Onions

(Courtesy of Devon A. Mihesuah. Used with permission.)
In this recipe from Choctaw author Devon Mihesuah, she tells us, "Each spring, Choctaws head out to look for the 6- to 12-inch stems of wild onions that feature inch-wide clusters of small white blossoms. Wild onions go into a variety of dishes and you can decide what you like best. I prefer them on top of baked potatoes, with scrambled eggs, and mixed with squash." Here is her recipe:

1 cup chopped wild onions
Cooking spray or 1 T butter, or liquid from meat
1 cup water

Cook the onions in the water until the water is almost gone, then use cooking spray or butter and add desired seasonings (pepper and garlic are what we use). Then either add stirred eggs and cook until done, or add onions to your other dishes.[6]

Wild onion with eggs (Courtesy of Choctaw Nation of Oklahoma)

Everyone loves Indian tacos and Indian fry bread—except for people who are calorie and/or fat conscious. But for those who just like good eating, here are recipes for these well-known powwow treats.

Indian Fry Bread

2 cups flour
1 tsp salt
3 tsp baking powder
1 cup milk

Mix flour, salt, and baking powder together. Add milk and stir to make a stiff dough. Pat down to ½ inch thick on a well-floured board. The dough can be cut into squares, or a small ball can be rolled out into a 7- or 8-inch plate-size patty. Heat oil to 350 degrees in a heavy skillet. Place the patty in the oil carefully and press the patty flat. Cook 3–4 minutes and then flip the patty and cook the other side. When the patty is golden, remove from the pan and drain on a paper towel.

Indian Tacos

The meat filling:

1 lb ground beef
1 pkg taco seasoning mix

1 can Ranch Style beans
2 cups shredded cheddar cheese
2 cups chopped tomatoes
1½ cups chopped onions
Picante sauce

The fry bread:

2 cups self-rising flour
1 cup milk or warm water
1 T cooking oil

Place ground beef in heavy skillet, stir and brown until all beef is crumbled. Drain the meat and place back in the skillet. Add the taco seasoning mix with water as the directions on the package call for. Cook until well done. While the meat is cooking, shred the cheese and lettuce, and chop the tomatoes and onions. Set aside. Put beans in a saucepan to heat. In a heavy skillet, add 1 tablespoon of oil to heat. Mix the flour, milk or water, and oil. Place the dough on a well-oiled piece of waxed paper and knead well. Next, pinch off a piece of dough about the size of an egg. Roll this out to approximately ¼ inch and fry using medium heat. Brown on one side, then turn and brown the other side. Pat with paper towel to absorb excess oil. Place taco on a plate. Spoon a helping of meat mixture on the bread, then add a layer of beans. Add lettuce, tomatoes, and onions to taste. Top all with cheese and picante sauce.

Parched Corn

A favorite snack of some Choctaws is parched corn. Very simple to make, it is filling and nutritious, and is easy to carry.

Dried corn on the cob
1 T canola oil
Salt to taste

Shell the corn kernels off the cob. Heat 1 tablespoon oil in a frying pan on medium heat. Add corn and constantly stir until the kernels turn light brown. Lightly salt to taste.

Choctaw Beer

This homemade beverage was tremendously popular in southeastern Oklahoma during the 1890s. Hundreds of the East European immigrants who worked in the Choctaw Nation mines in the 1890s adopted Choctaw beer as their special beverage of choice. It is still made in parts of southeast Oklahoma, and is still served today at Pete's Place in Krebs, Oklahoma. Composed of barley, hops, fishberries, tobacco, and alcohol, it "had a wallop comparable to the kick of a mule."[7] Variations of Choctaw beer continued to be produced throughout the 20th century.

CHOCTAW AGRICULTURE AND SUBSISTENCE ACTIVITIES TODAY

Choctaw people living in Oklahoma suffer from an acute shortage of land, even though it is an essential resource for Choctaw people. Since most younger families have, at most, one or two acres, they are unable to participate in the market economy. Instead, most plant subsistence crops and are barely scraping by. Extended families and older families are more likely to own larger parcels of land, but often these are still inadequate, and instead, can form a liability to the owner by the archaic rules of public assistance. Anthropologist Sandra Faiman-Silva related the story of one elderly widow who in the 1980s received a reduced amount of $120 per month from public assistance, because by U.S. government guidelines, she was well to do, as the owner of about 160 unproductive acres. Oil leases with major U.S. corporations provided her with an income of two or three dollars per month, but the land, in essence, simply acted as a bar to the receipt of government assistance. These unfortunate policies keep many Choctaw people in extreme poverty. Unlike many others, this woman has maintained the allotment of land from the Dawes era unencumbered, but it has not been to her benefit.[8] Even though this woman carefully preserved her allotment from conmen and profiteers, it was too little land to successfully use in agricultural production for the market.

Faiman-Silva also has documented how nonnative individuals and corporations have "undertaken the common practice of paying delinquent taxes on Choctaw-owned property over several years, intending to purchase the trace at delinquent-tax land sales," allowing these companies to amass enormous tracts of land at hugely discounted prices.[9] The Choctaw property owners were often unaware that any taxes were due on the property, and many times the land was sold completely without their knowledge or notification. Colonial subjugation continues unabated in Choctaw lands. Choctaws, who have become grossly impoverished by some policies, are unable to hire lawyers to protect their meager claims. Faiman-Silva describes a typical case of fraud perpetrated against an elderly Choctaw in the 1970s. The elderly man deeded one acre of land to an intermarried white man for a small amount, so that he and his family could have a place to live. The bill of sale was duly notarized and filed with the proper authorities, but somehow the 1 acre had been changed to 20 acres. The old man and his family were unable to afford the legal battle promised by the swindler, so they were unable to contest this obvious fraud. Other whites have simply moved fences or taken over land belonging to Choctaws, who are too poor to hire attorneys to defend themselves.

An enormous amount of Choctaw land in Oklahoma is now in the hands of two timber corporations, who, for decades, have been engaging in questionable acquisition practices to build up their holdings.[10] Unrelenting conversion of Choctaw land to ownership by these corporations have left the Choctaws surrounded by abundance, while simultaneously excluding them from its benefits. Some Choctaws believe that these giant timber businesses exploit Choctaw people as cheap and temporary labor, offering few, if any, benefits, and providing only temporary work. Since these companies own such vast amounts of land and most employment opportunities in the area are offered through them, people are afraid to offend them, lest they be unable to obtain work. Choctaw laborers have almost no alternatives for employment and are left in an unenviable position of having no employment for wages or submitting to terms that seem to be exploitative.[11]

Springtime in Oklahoma finds many Choctaws gathering pokeweed (*Phytolacca americana*) and wild onions. Fishing and hunting for small game, especially squirrel, provide fresh sources of protein. Mustard greens and beans of all kinds soon begin to yield delicious fresh produce, and wild fruits ripen throughout the summer. Many families pick blackberries, wild strawberries, Muscatine grapes, and huckleberries—enough to eat and reserve for making into jams and jellies.

During spring planting times, many Choctaw people plant large gardens full of corn, beans, tomatoes, squash, potatoes, beans, cucumbers, and onions. In the rather mild climate of southeastern Oklahoma, families often plant second crops of mustard and turnip greens in the early fall, which they harvest until late November, or even December, until the first frost. Wild turkeys and deer are hunted during the fall season, providing delicious venison and turkey throughout the winter months.

HEALING, HERBS, AND CURES NUTRITION, HERBAL KNOWLEDGE, AND WESTERN MEDICINE

Choctaw women were intimately familiar with the plants of the woods and clearings where they lived in what are now the southern states of Mississippi and Alabama. They were also incredibly knowledgeable about the medicinal properties of herbs, bark, roots, and other forms of plant life. Choctaws and other Native people developed the use of willow bark (*miko* hoyanidja), which contains acetylsalicylic acid, which is 'aspirin.' Choctaw healers made an herbal tea from boiling the stems and leaves of the willow tree—the equivalent to taking an Aspirin tablet today. Aspirin is considered to be one of the wonder drugs of modern man, but it was, in fact, used for centuries by Native Americans prior to its discovery by European and Euro-American societies. Many other natural treatments and cures were used. However, in the mid-19th century, bleeding, cupping, and other primitive methods from Euro-American medicinal practices were sometimes incorporated into use by Choctaw doctors, much to the detriment of patients.

Although healers may be found among the Choctaws today, it is also common for Choctaw people to consult Western medical practitioners. Access to physicians, nurses, and modern institutions of medicine has improved tremendously over the past three decades. For example, Choctaws living in the traditional 10 and one-half counties of the old Choctaw Nation in Oklahoma have access to 7 medical clinics and a hospital at Talihina, Oklahoma. Westernized medical care has improved tremendously over the past 20 years, as the national government of the Oklahoma and Mississippi Choctaw peoples took over much of the administration and management of health-care facilities within those regions.

Historically, Choctaw people ate unprocessed foods that were highly nutritious and they were physically active and, almost without exception, physically fit. Tooth decay was rare since people consumed almost no processed sugar.[12] However, during the 20th century, restricted access to hunting areas, poverty, and shrinking territories led to an increasingly sedentary lifestyle. Poverty and fast food often go hand-in-hand with poor nutrition, resulting in an epidemic of obesity and diabetes among Choctaws and other native peoples. Consumption of soft drinks loaded with sugar have led to poor dental health.

Today, Choctaws and other Native Americans sometimes mistakenly believe that foods such as Indian fry bread and Indian tacos are "traditional," when, in fact, these and other high fat, low nutrition foods are recent innovations that use Western methods of cooking and ingredients that are nonindigenous to the Americas. Choctaw historian Devon Mihesuah's excellent book *Recovering Our Ancestors' Gardens: Indigenous Recipes and Guide to Diet and Fitness* presents true traditional ways of eating and shows how Choctaws and other Native Americans can return to more healthy foods and active life ways to attain the fitness of their ancestors. Rejecting modern processed foods and imbalanced unhealthful diets, Mihesuah offers a path to health that would lead to a decreasing incidence of the current manifestations of illness caused by poor diets and sedentary lifestyles.

Choctaws in the late 1800s and early 1900s may have been poor in terms of material wealth, but they enjoyed a rich and varied diet that was conducive to fitness and health. Many of them grew a wide assortment of vegetables, ate wild game, and had very limited processed sugar in their diets. They were lean and fit, and suffered from almost none of the modern ailments that result from fat- and sugar-laden diets and sedentary lifestyles.

Food forms the center of many community and family gatherings, visits of friends and relatives, and celebrations and thanksgiving. Traditionally, when a visitor comes knocking, Choctaw women are often ready with stews, soups, and other foods to welcome and nourish guests. Offering food and eating together forms a wonderful foundation for renewing acquaintances, appreciating friends and relatives, and sharing news. In summer evenings across southeastern Oklahoma, families and friends sit out on porches and end a good meal by telling stories and sharing oral traditions of the past, thus forming a part of the good life of many Choctaw people.

CHOCTAW HERBAL REMEDIES

Choctaw healers are both men and women, and are highly respected and quite successful at treating wounds, snakebites, broken bones, and minor ailments of all sorts. Their knowledge of the plants and herbs of the woods and meadows has always been extraordinary. Over millennia, herbal remedies were developed by Native Americans which were the product of great knowledge, powers of observation, and an indigenous world view, which sees the interconnectedness of all things. Illnesses and treatments were believed to be holistic in nature, involving not only the physical body, but also the spirit world. To be efficacious, a holistic approach was necessary. Unlike modern Western medicine, Native medicine men and women treat the spirit as well as the body. Ceremony was important in all treatments, and even today, many Choctaw healers incorporate these beliefs in their medical practices.

Refuting the Eurocentric stereotype of ignorant 'savages,' Choctaw and other indigenous medicine men and women used their vast knowledge to cure ailments, lessen pain, and to heal cuts, broken bones, and wounds. In the past, snakebites were treated using a method called "dry sucking." The wound was literally sucked by the healer and then an herbal poultice was made and laid on the wound. A pungent root called rattlesnake master was chewed by the victim and used in the poultice. Usually, the patient would quickly recover within a few days. Some healers boiled the leaves and bark of the Eastern Cottonwood Tree (*Populus angulata*) and allowed the steam to saturate the wound.

Poultices and other herbal remedies are still commonly used to treat wounds and cuts today. They reduce swelling and increase the rate of healing.

Ground ivy is pounded and formed into a poultice that is laid upon a wound after the healer cleaned the wound with the resin from a copal tree. The steam from boiling the bark of the Eastern Cottonwood Tree (*Populus angulata*), is allowed to saturate the wound in order to promote healing. Another remedy used for cuts combines the tea made from boiling the roots of *Obolaria virginica,* commonly called Virginia pennywort, and *Liquidambar styraciflua,* or the sweetgum tree, and creating a poultice that is applied directly to the wound. Perhaps the best-known poultice, however, is a combination of sugar, soot, and spider webs, which also stops bleeding.[13]

Other common complaints are successfully treated using herbal remedies. For example, for intestinal disturbances, an herbal tea is made from persimmons dried by the sun and mixed with a special type of bread. Severe colds are treated with a tea made of the boiled leaves of whiteleaf mountain mint (*Pycnanthemum albescens*) or *shinuktelele.* The patient drinks the tea while it is steaming hot, inducing a sweat that is believed to provide relief from symptoms such as a stuffy head. Many people swear by this recipe. Chewing the bark of the common buttonbush, or *notem pisa* (*Cephalanthus occidentalis*), has long been used as an effective remedy for toothache. When the bark is boiled in water, the resulting tea can be used to bathe sore eyes.

One of the popular flowers used in many gardens today, the purple cornflower *(Echinacea purpurea),* has been used by Choctaws for hundreds of years as a treatment for coughs and sore throats. Dandelions, the scourge of modern gardeners, has always been used by Choctaws for medicinal purposes, and combined with chicory, it makes a good substitute for coffee.

For severe cuts, the roots of *Obolaria virginica* (Virginia pennywort) are boiled in water and the resulting liquid is combined with the liquid derived from boiling the roots from the sweetgum tree (*Liquidambar styraciflua*).

Many other herbal medicines have been used by the Choctaw people from time immemorial. These treatments are the result of expert knowledge of herbs, thousands of years of development and careful observation, and a holistic worldview. Many Western pharmaceutical companies and physicians have belatedly realized the enormous potential and value of the vast body of knowledge of human healing and treatments developed by Native Americans.

CHOCTAW TRADITIONAL HEALERS

Among the most prominent 20th-century Oklahoma healers was Billy Washington who lived in Ardmore, Oklahoma. Like other *alikchi,* Washington received his training from spirit beings, called *kowi anuksahas,* who were small, furry beings who looked human. Choctaws of the time believed that *kowi anuksahas* taught them how to do medicine, and assisted them through-out their life in finding and using medicinal plants. These old Choctaw heal-ers were greatly admired and highly esteemed within Choctaw communities. Their healing powers were undoubted by the Choctaws, although they were persecuted by members of the dominant society.[14]

Today, Choctaw traditional healers continue to offer their services in rural areas, but they are known only to Choctaw communities and are consulted on an informal basis. Their knowledge of the plants and herbs of the woods and meadows and their medicinal properties are extraordinary. Even modern pharmaceutical companies have in recent years recognized the value of this traditional knowledge.

Choctaw healers and medicine men and women treated all sorts of ail-ments with herbal remedies. During the 19th century, they came into occa-sional contact with white medical practitioners, who introduced the medical beliefs of the dominant society, such as cupping and bleeding. One doctor, Gideon Lincecum, lived and worked in Mississippi near the Choctaw people, and had many as friends and acquaintances. He and his medical brethren struggled to treat their patients in a terrible cholera epidemic in 1833, with little success. Losing dozens of patients, Lincecum grew disillusioned with Western medicine, asserting that the medical practices of the day did more harm than good. "I felt tired of killing people," he said, "and concluded to quit the man killing practice."[15] He then turned to one of the great Choctaw healers, Alikchi Chito, who taught him some of the herbal medicine prac-ticed by the Choctaws. Lincecum began using these remedies in his practice, and, calling himself a "botanic doctor," found great success with Choctaw healing methods and herbal remedies.

Choctaw herbal remedies have proven to be highly efficacious and many people still use them today. Although most Choctaws visit physicians and use hospitals and clinics regularly, some of these old remedies continue to be used for relief from colds and minor aches and pains.

Notes

1. H. B. Cushman, *History of the Choctaw, Chickasaw, and Natchez Indians* (Greenville, TX: Headlight Printing House, 1899), 194.

2. Devon Abbott Mihesuah, *Recovering Our Ancestors' Gardens: Indigenous Recipes and Guide to Diet and Fitness* (Lincoln, NE: University of Nebraska Press, 2005), 152.

3. Ibid., 138.

4. Peter J. Hudson, "Choctaw Indian Dishes," *Chronicles of Oklahoma* 17, no. 3 (September, 1939): 334.

5. "Recipes: Choctaw Hunter's Stew," *Choctaw Nation of Oklahoma*, http://www.choctawnation.com/culture-heritage/choctaw-traditions/food/.

6. Mihesuah, *Recovering Our Ancestors' Gardens,* 145.

7. Steven L. Sewell, "Choctaw Beer: Tonic or Devil's Brew?," *Journal of Cultural Geography* 23, no. 2 (2006): 105.

8. Sandra Faiman-Silva, *Choctaws at the Crossroads: The Political Economy of Class and Culture in the Oklahoma Timber Region* (Lincoln, NE: University of Nebraska Press, 2000), 130–31.

9. Ibid., 132.

10. Ibid., 134.

11. Ibid., 146–47, 149, 150.

12. Mihesuah, *Recovering Our Ancestors' Gardens,* 48.

13. "Traditional Choctaw Medicine," *Choctaw Nation of Oklahoma,* http://www.choctawnation.com/culture-heritage/choctaw-traditions/choctaw-medicine/.

14. Victoria Lindsay Levine, "Music Revitalization among the Choctaw," *American Music* 11, no. 4 (Winter 1993): 394.

15. Greg O'Brien, "Gideon Lincecum (1793–1874): Mississippi Pioneer and Man of Many Talents," *Mississippi History Now,* http://mshistory.k12.ms.us/articles/82/gideon-lincecum-1793-1874-mississippi-pioneer-and-man-of-many-talents.

7

Choctaw Arts, Ceremonies, and Festivals

ORAL AND WRITTEN COMMUNICATION

BECAUSE CHOCTAW SOCIETY was an oral society and did not have a system of writing until the 1800s, oration, song, and other oral expression held a very special and important place. Oral traditions formed not only a source of entertainment, but were also passed on by elders to the next generation, to educate them in the beliefs and values of Choctaw society. Storytelling developed into an art form, as did public speaking. Historically, when Choctaws met in a village, their *mingo* or chief did not address the people; instead, his speaker would convey his words to the people. Speakers were men who were exceptional orators, who could fascinate listeners with their verbal skills. In meetings in which important decisions were made by consensus, the speaking and persuasive skills of the speaker guided the people toward a decision desired by the *mingo*. They often spoke for hours and were renowned for their power of persuasion. At important meetings of the whole tribe or village, the people would gather and sit with their own clan.[1]

Order and courtesy reigned over the assemblies of the Choctaw. Only one person spoke at a time, and a speaker was never interrupted. In the great national meetings, the speaker would recount the history of the Choctaw Nation: what issues and challenges they had met as a nation and overcome, short biographies of prominent leaders and heroes, their successes in war and their defeats, the nation's remembrances of days of adversity and prosperity, and contemporary challenges and possible solutions. In order of their age, beginning with the eldest, several people would speak, sometimes for hours.[2]

Issues that called for decisions by the assembled people were debated and discussed by all, with the goal of arriving at a decision that had unanimous support. After everyone had expressed themselves, with all searching for compromise and unanimity, a vote would be taken. For a few minutes there would be silence and meditation, during which time no sound was heard. People whose point of view did not prevail and who could find no acceptable unanimous compromise would withdraw from the assembly, in the interest of the vast majority finding unanimity. But never did the Choctaws force decisions upon one another. The stereotype of a dictatorial chief is just that—a stereotype invented by whites who imagined that native societies were authoritarian, like their own. In fact, individuals were not bound by "majority rule," as people are in modern American society. Choctaw democracy was much more free. Choctaw society tried every possible compromise and accommodation in order to gain consensus among people, so that decisions would be unanimous.

The oral traditions, passed from generation to generation, changed very little over the years, and many examples of the power of memory of the tradition givers and storytellers confirm their great ability to use the oral word accurately over time. They cultivated their memory in ways that a modern literate society does not do, and often the skepticism of oral transmissions made over centuries is doubted because scholars apply their own society's deficient memory and reliance on the written word to judge oral societies, whose oral abilities were much more highly developed, especially compared to literate societies.[3]

Choctaws today generally continue the traditional patterns of measured speech, listening courtesy, and do not consider it necessary to fill silence with small talk or jabbering. Historically, Choctaws and other southern native people were amazed at the constant talking of Europeans and Euro-Americans. A French official once noticed that a group of warriors watched them with a slight smile of amusement on their faces. Asking one what they found to be funny, one of the warriors told him that, "If we smile when we see you talking together, it is because you remind us of a flock of cackling geese."[4] Most Choctaws speak when they have something to say and are comfortable with silence.

Choctaw oral patterns continue from time immemorial, while written communications in Choctaw only began in the 1820s, when American missionary Cyrus Byington, Choctaw Allen Wright, and others first began writing in Choctaw. Using the Latin alphabet, they devised a writing system that incorporated the unique intonations and sounds of Choctaw. Within a few years, Byington produced a dictionary that is still used today. Most of the other writings were translations of Christian theology: the Bible, hymnals, and sermons used to proselytize the Choctaws. The writing system immediately began to be used by other Choctaws in letters and other documents. Before long, the Choctaws in what became the state of Oklahoma established newspapers that were written in both Choctaw and English.

The official newspaper of the Choctaw Nation of Oklahoma is the *Bishinik*, which began publication in the late 1970s and is sent out monthly to the enrolled members of the nation. *Bishinik* includes news stories, articles of cultural and historical interest, announcements, accounts of events, obituaries, wedding and birth notices, and much more. It is printed in the English language. The Mississippi Band publishes *Choctaw Community News* each month, which, like the Oklahoma newspaper, contains a wide variety of information of interest to tribal members.

MUSIC AND DANCE

As long as there have been Choctaws, they have made and enjoyed music and have used dance in ceremonies and for social interaction. In historical times, Europeans reported that Choctaws loved to sing, and that they had a wide array of songs.[5] Their healers sang and prayed before treating their patient, and war songs were sung to prepare for action against their enemies and in victorious celebrations of victories.[6]

Choctaws expressed many emotions through song—funeral lamentations, songs to encourage ball players, songs of triumph, songs that were prayers, songs of exhortation, and songs seeking guidance or help from the world of spirits. Choctaws sang their death songs when they endured torture and death by the enemy.[7] They were renowned among other tribes for their dances and songs. In fact, even though in past times when the Creeks (Muskogees) were their enemy, they still borrowed many Choctaw songs and dances and incorporated them into their society.[8]

Among many Choctaws, gospel singing is very popular, and is often conducted in the Choctaw language. Christian churches throughout Oklahoma and Mississippi communities conduct hymn singing in the Choctaw language, and special musical presentations are given by Choctaw Christian and gospel singers. Every year at the Choctaw annual fairs in Oklahoma and Mississippi, gospel sings are held. These are very popular events, and, occasionally, go on well into the night.

The Choctaws have a rich and varied history of dance. Choctaw dances continue to be popular and are part of the programs at every Choctaw cultural event. Choctaw dances are meant for participation, not performance. The dances include both women and men, who wear traditional Choctaw clothing. Many of the ancient historical dances include the war dance (*Hoyopa-hihla*), scalp dance (*Hakshup-hihla*), the ball play dance (*Tolih-hihla*), the Green Corn dance (*Tanshusi-hihla*), the eagle dance, and the buffalo dance, but they are not usually performed today. The fast war dance (*Panshka Hetha Pathki*) and social and animal dances make up the bulk of the dances performed today.

The Mississippi Choctaw divide the dances into three types: social, war, and animal dances. In a striking departure from other Native American tribes, women have always participated in the Choctaw war dances. The most popular dances today are those that mimic animals, like the winding and sinuous line of the snake dance, or the quick darting movements of the raccoon dance.

Social dances are very popular among all ages of Choctaws. Oklahoma Choctaws revived the stealing partners, wedding dance, and friendship dance in the 1970s, in addition to animal dances such as the raccoon dance, quail dance, turtle dance, and the snake dance. In Oklahoma, the Choctaws who had undergone the forced removals from their homelands in Mississippi lost much of their culture and traditional beliefs through forced assimilation. By 1937, many of the dances and songs were stamped out—Christian churches in Oklahoma taught that dancing was sinful.

However, in the 1970s, various Choctaw revitalization movements sprung up, and these included a desire to revive the traditional music and dances. One of the influential cultural revivalists was Oklahoma Choctaw minister Gene Wilson and his Comanche wife Alicia, who made a trip to visit the Choctaw Fair held by the Mississippi Band of Choctaws in 1970. At the fair, Rev. Wilson was inspired by the living culture of the Mississippi Choctaws, especially as manifested in the traditional dances. On his return to Oklahoma, he formed a children's dance group called the Okla Humma Chahta Hiltha. Over the years, the group traveled back and forth to Mississippi, each time learning new dances and chants and improving their technique. Back in Oklahoma, the group was invited to many schools and performed publicly on many occasions. Soon, other groups formed, and schools and churches participated.[9]

In Ardmore, Oklahoma area, another revitalization formed in the 1970s, led by Buster Ned and a group of Choctaw/Chickasaw elders. They founded the Choctaw–Chickasaw Heritage Committee, with the stated purpose preserving the songs and dances of the Choctaws and Chickasaws. Ned's maternal uncle, Adam Sampson, served as the group's songleader. A cultural treasure in himself, Mr. Sampson remembered 90 Choctaw songs and had participated in the dances in his youth before this part of the Choctaw heritage was halted.[10]

Choctaw dances are not simply for pleasure, but are also a vital expression of Choctaw identity and pride. In addition, the dances and music express a spiritual dimension—they represent the resolution of conflict and a renewed sense of harmony and balance in the world. Historically, dances were held as part of a complex ceremony lasting four days and four nights. The ceremony began with ritual purification, dances, and prayer, lasting the entire night before the ball play, which is described in more detail below. In the evening after the ball play, dances would begin. The ball play was the symbol of "symbolic destruction and recreation of the cosmos," while the following dances resolved the conflicts inherent in the games.[11]

This important resolution of conflict allowed the Choctaws to regaining and restoring harmony and balance in the world. The music and movement of each dance incorporates important cosmic symbols of the Choctaw worldview: the number four, the circle, and the four sacred directions. The number four is sacred among the Choctaws, and is imbued with cosmic symbolism representing the sacred four directions. In addition, the number four symbolized all the known forces in the world.[12] The circle symbolized the unending identity and belonging of the Choctaw people, and their belief in the cyclical nature of life. The circle also clearly symbolizes Choctaw beliefs in the community, the equality of each person and creature, and the unbreakable strength of communal life. The four sacred directions, with an emphasis on east and west, reflect the daily renewal of life and the unbroken cycle of life.

The dances traditionally began in the evening and lasted all night, ending with the rising of the sun, which signified the survival of the Choctaws as a people. Renewal and revival were constant themes in Choctaw cosmology and the dances and music of the Choctaw people reflected these important beliefs. Nowadays, the dances follow a potluck supper and seldom continue all night. But regardless of the duration of these events, Choctaw people today still derive many benefits from them and they remain an important part of Choctaw culture.

The singing, or chanting, that accompanies Choctaw dances is of a style called call and response. The call is sung by a male songleader, and the response is given by the dancers in unison, with the women and men singing the same melody. The dances of the Oklahoma Choctaws were divided into four types: war dances, jump dances, drunk dances, and walk dances. Among the Ardmore Choctaw, the snake dance always came last and was believed to summarize and complete the ritual aspects of the dance event.[13]

DANCING IN THE CHOCTAW PAST

An early European observer of the Choctaws wrote that they had many feasts and dances always were given. Some dances were in honor of animals, including dances named for turkeys, bison, bear, and alligator. In the alligator dance, they made masks of the head of the alligator and the animals that he eats, and the people wearing the masks would imitate the actions of each animal, engaging in hilarious antics.[14]

Preparation for the dances began in the early afternoon, when the people donned their favorite clothes, and applied paint. Many of them wore a belt made of 40 or so bells, which were made of pot metal and were as big as a fist. They had small and large bells that people carried to make noise, in addition to rattles of all kinds. Most social dances lasted all night.[15]

The famous American artist George Catlin was enormously impressed by the young men who danced the eagle dance when he visited the Choctaw in the early 1800s. He described how 12 or 16 young men would prepare themselves by painting their mostly naked bodies white with clay, while each held an eagle's tail in his hand. Each one wore an eagle feather. They would dance around spears stuck in the ground, four men at a time. These four would have simultaneously jumped up from a sitting position on the ground, where they all sat in rows of four. When a foursome became fatigued, the next row of four would jump up together and take their place. Catlin reported that each of the dancers' position was squatted down close to the ground, and they moved around the spears with great athleticism and remarkable agility, in imitation of the movements of the great bird.[16]

Historically, there were many more dances than are danced today. The Green Corn Ceremony and other important sacred events were marked by particular or special dances. Nowadays, though, the war dance is the only surviving form of ceremonial dance. The historical dances and music of the Choctaw past continue to resonate with Choctaws today. Although many aspects of the dances and music have been adapted to fit the needs of modern Choctaws, there remains a marked continuity with past practices that reflect a deep, unique Choctaw identity.

MUSICAL INSTRUMENTS

Choctaws have traditionally used drums and striking sticks in accompaniment to their music and dance. Striking sticks have traditionally been used to accompany certain Choctaw dances. They are made of a specific variety of hickory wood and are about 14 inches long, flat on one or two sides.[17] The singer, or chanter, strikes the sticks in rhythm to certain songs. Striking sticks, called staves by musicologists, are not found widely among Native American tribes. About the only other tribes that use or used striking sticks were the Iroquois nations. Some people believe that the Choctaws used the claves during the 19th century, because the use of drums was proscribed due to white fears of slave uprisings among African Americans of the Old South.[18]

Drums are still used today by Oklahoma Choctaw dancers. Unlike the drums used in powwows, Choctaw dances are accompanied by a single drum, usually carried by the songleader or chanter. The dancers of the Ardmore Choctaw–Chickasaw Heritage Committee use a Native American style drum that is commonly seen in Pan-Indian settings, such as powwows. During the revitalization of Choctaw dance and music that occurred in Oklahoma beginning in the 1970s, one of the major groups of this revival decided to forego use of the striking sticks of the Mississippi dancers. The type of hickory needed to make the sticks was difficult to obtain and so they decided to use a double-headed hand drum.

Presley Byington shown making a traditional Choctaw flute. (Courtesy of Choctaw Nation of Oklahoma)

Choctaw dances in Mississippi are accompanied by striking sticks. Drums were occasionally used in the past, but have fallen out of favor in recent decades. However, Choctaw dancers still enter performance arenas to the beat of a drum, and also exit to its accompaniment. Ball players also enter the field of play accompanied by drums. These drums are a modified version of an 18th-century snare drum. The Mississippi Choctaws make their drums from sourwood, black gum, or tupelo gum. Strips of hickory are fitted around the exterior of the drum, and rawhide is stretched over the ends. Snares made of lead are attached to the bottom of the drum, which make a distinctive sound when the drum is struck.[19] The style of the Mississippi Choctaw drum harkens back to the French and Indian War of colonial times, when a European gave them his snare drum. For the past two centuries, Mississippi Choctaw drum makers have used this pattern to make new drums for dances and stickball games.

Handmade drums are prized possessions among the Mississippi Choctaw, and seldom will one be sold to an outsider. In fact, each year at the annual fair, one of the prominent pieces of each community's display is often a drum. In past years, Choctaw competed in drumming contests, where each community backed a candidate.

Cane flutes (or whistles) and bells were often used by Choctaws in historical times, although they are rare today. The flutes, or whistles, were used by medicine men the night before a stickball game, and during the game, to give spiritual power to the players. Whistles were considered to be medicine objects; that is, their proper use could summon spiritual power. As sacred objects were sentient, they were handled with great care.[20] Male dancers sometimes wear sleigh bells or other small bells. Buster Ned, of the Sixtown Dancers of Oklahoma, used to shake a bell to keep time to chants during the dance, while many of the Sixtown Dancers tied bells around one ankle. In the distant past, Choctaw male dancers wore strings of bells tied below each knee.[21]

BALL PLAY

Ball play is an important part of the lives of many Choctaws. It has a long and amazing history. From time immemorial, Choctaws have referred to ball play as the Little Brother of War, demonstrating that it demands many of the same skills as warfare, without, of course, the lethal aspects. Still, it requires strength, athleticism, coordination, and speed.

Choctaws have always been the most enthusiastic players of the ball game called *ishtaboli.* It was much more than a game in Choctaw culture. Each team represented a community, as it does today. Rivalries developed over years, and competition was fierce. Entire communities helped young men

Choctaw Indian men and boys play a game that is the forerunner of lacrosse in the 1840s near Fort Gibson, Oklahoma. (Courtesy of the Library of Congress)

prepare themselves for the games—giving them choice pieces of meat, cheering on their conditioning activities, and advising them on strategy. Every person in the community would be involved. Betting reflected the great importance of the ball plays. Some people bet everything they owned, even shedding the clothes off their back in the excitement of the contest.

As the date for the play drew near, players underwent training. Foot races provided both competition and conditioning. Practice games were played every day. Most players observed restrictions such as eating only animals considered to be brave, fast, and strong. Rabbits were not eaten since they are timid, and easily confused. Hot food was eaten at tepid temperatures to insure no debilitating effect taxed the body. Relations with women were unthinkable for seven days prior to a game. The player's ball sticks were repeatedly checked.

The night before a game, a ball play dance began, often continuing all night. In the old days, opponents might try to use spiritual power to hex their rivals. In 1889, a visitor to the Cherokees reported that the night before a big game, a stone was set up with black beads representing the opposite team placed under it. All evening while singing and dancing the ball game songs, women of the community would step on the stone, hoping to weaken the opposite team with the weight of the women from their opponent's community. On other occasions, if an opposing team found out where their opponents were going to hold their dances the evening before the game, they might sprinkle the ground with a potion made from the hamstrings of rabbits, contaminating the rival team with rabbit-like timidity and confusion.[22]

Historically, ball play was used to settle differences and conflicts among the southeastern peoples, and often averted war between nations. However, on one occasion, the attempt to settle competing claims to territory between the Creeks (Muskogees) and the Choctaws ended in disaster. Sometime around 1790, the Creeks and Choctaws decided to hold a ball play to settle a dispute over possession of a beaver pond on Noxubee River. At that time, beaver pelts were highly prized items in the fur trade, and this pond had many beaver that both Choctaw and Creek hunters sought. To avert war, the two nations agreed to let a ball game decide possession, and a date was set and terms agreed to by both nations. For two whole months, both sides prepared. They picked their best players, who trained daily. Finally, the big day arrived. More than 10,000 Choctaws and Creeks camped out near the ball grounds, placing bets and wagers, and calling out challenges to the opponent. The medicine men from both teams performed ceremonies calling on spiritual power to strengthen the men on their team, and invoking the attention and interest of the spirits. Finally, after all bets were laid and proper ceremonies finished, the medicine men threw out the ball, and the game was on. Advantage seesawed back and forth, now in favor of the Choctaws, then the Creeks, then back to the Choctaws. Fans believed it was the closest match in memory, with each player exerting himself to the highest level, knowing how high the stakes were.[23]

Victory, at last, was declared—the Creeks won, and they immediately began celebrating, shouting and singing their victory over the humiliated Choctaw players. Finally, a disappointed Choctaw player, tired of the exultations of the Creeks, made an insulting remark to one of their players, who then threw a petticoat on the Choctaw, a great insult sure to lead to a fight. Players ran to retrieve their weapons, and a general fight broke out, with knives, axes, guns, and bows and arrows, and even sticks being used. The fight began at dusk, continued all night, until two hours after sunrise the next morning. Finally, the chiefs of the two nations arrived on the scene and put an immediate stop to the fighting.[24]

The shaken warriors tended to their wounded for the rest of the day, while the women dressed the bodies of the dead. Over the next two days, the dead were buried or put up on scaffolds, their valuables placed beside them for the journey to the land of the dead. A great council was called for the third day, where the leaders of the two nations all expressed regret that the game had led to this wild storm of passion and violence. They agreed to reconcile, and smoked the pipe of peace before departing for home.

The casualties were staggering—more than 500 men were killed and many more died from their wounds. The Choctaw and Creeks had fought several wars in the past, but the casualties from the fight at Beaver Pond exceeded those of past wars. The disaster and waste of life that occurred that day remained in the memories of Choctaws and Creeks for decades, its memory laden with terror and despair. For years, Choctaws and Creeks made pilgrimages back to the site of the conflict to mourn the needless deaths. Forty-two years later, when the United States dispossessed the Choctaws, they were still performing this annual remembrance of the terrible disaster at Beaver Pond.

After this disaster, the Creeks relinquished all claims to Beaver Pond. But soon after, the beaver deserted it; in response, it was said, to the dishonor of the great fight after the ball game. The Choctaws never again hunted at Beaver Pond, and everyone avoided it. Years later, in the 1820s, white missionaries built a school at Beaver Pond, unaware of the tragic history. Almost none of the Choctaws would send their children to the school, which mystified the missionaries, who eventually abandoned the site.[25]

An American visitor to the Choctaws in the 1830s described how the dance the night before the ball game began. He related how the ball players danced to the chants of the women and the accompaniment of a snare drum. They danced for more than 15 minutes, striking their ball sticks (*kabocca*) together and singing at the top of their lungs. The women of each side formed two lines between the players, also dancing and singing, appealing to the Creator to bring victory to their side, and exhorting the players to excel.

These dances continued all night long, every 30 minutes, and everyone continued to participate. At nine o'clock the next morning, the players, who had been up all night, rushed onto the field and, at the sound of a gun, began play. On this day, there were some 600 or 700 players on the field at one time, all trying to keep the opposition from scoring. Wild feats of athleticism, along with tripping, shoving, and fisticuffs were used to delay the progress of the enemy. Fights broke out sporadically, and none of the other players interfered. All weapons were left off the field, and no one was allowed to retrieve one. There were so many men playing, that great clouds of dust arose as dozens of men desperately tried to capture the ball (*towa*), but it became lost in the legs and dust clouds, and was rarely seen until it was hit out of the pack.

The women and other men were screaming on the sidelines, cheering or exhorting their side to do better. Hundreds of bets were laid, and the excitement reached fever pitch. Each time the ball passed between the sticks of one side, a point was scored, and this continued until a score of 100 was reached by the victor. On this day, the ball play ended peacefully. Losers were expected to keep their disappointment to themselves. It was considered unmanly to show anger at the loss.[26]

Long ago, players only wore breech clouts. They were all barefoot, as moccasins were not allowed. Women spent months creating beautiful beaded belts that the players wore around their waist. In addition, Choctaw men would create a mane out of horsehair dyed a bright color, and a tail of horsehair or quills. Many of the players wore paint and some had medicine bags around their waist.[27]

Choctaw craftsmen make all the sticks and balls by hand. The *kabocca* are made of hickory. One end is slightly bent, and a pouch or pocket is formed using strips of hide at one end. The ball, or *towa,* is formed from a small piece of wood or a round stone. Cloth is wrapped in several layers over the stone, and then strips of deer hide or leather are woven over the cloth.

Modern ball games are certainly less violent, but they are still raucous, rough competitions. Today, stickball is still hugely popular among the Mississippi Choctaws, and is being revived among the Oklahoma Choctaws. At the Annual Mississippi Choctaw Fair, between 8 and 10 teams will vie for the championship. The deciding game is played at the end of the fair, and fans pack the high-school stadium. Stickball is included as a sport in the State Games of Mississippi held annually, with Mississippi Choctaw rules applying. At the University of Oklahoma, the Society of Native American Gentlemen (Sigma Nu Alpha Gamma fraternity) holds an annual stickball competition. Oklahoma State University, the Chickasaw Nation of Oklahoma, and the Cherokees in Oklahoma and North Carolina all have various levels of stickball play on a regular basis.[28]

Choctaw stickball was the forerunner of the modern game of La Crosse, which has been adopted by nonnative teams and has become a major collegiate sport. In 2001, a professional league was established, and in 2010, teams representing 29 countries competed in the Men's World Championship Games in Manchester, England. The United States defeated Canada in the finals.

BASKETRY

Choctaw basket-making is an ancient art that continues, in altered form, today. River cane was used to make all kinds of household items, including mats, some measuring five feet by six feet. In addition to these mats used for flooring, they wove mats for bedding, to cover the walls and ceiling of their houses, and to wrap the bodies of the deceased. Large burden baskets with flared tops were commonly seen in use by women.

They made small and large baskets with handles for carrying, and sieves and fanners that they used to process hominy meal. Different shapes and sizes were developed for a whole range of needs, providing baskets for storage, carrying, cooking, gathering, sifting, and winnowing, and even as fish and game traps. Aside from the utilitarian functions, basket weavers wove intricate patterns and designs, and used dyes to create beautiful, aesthetically pleasing designs and colors. Today, Choctaws may weave baskets primarily for the market or for gifts, while older ones fetch hundreds, or even thousands, of dollars from collectors. Made from swamp cane that grows wild along many Mississippi creeks and streams, beautiful baskets take shape under the skilled hands of Choctaw women. There are many styles today, including hampers, egg baskets, and vegetable baskets.

Traditional Choctaw baskets are made from river, or swamp, cane, which grows in abundance along creek banks all over the South. Tall cane is the most desirable, since it requires less work than gathering shorter cane. Each piece of cane yields four or five strips. After cutting the cane, basket weavers dye the strips. Historically, Choctaw women used natural dyes and colors obtained from plants. Berries provided shades of red and purple, while roots, bark, and even flowers yielded a variety of colors for the basket maker's artistic selection. Today, commercial dyes are used almost exclusively.

After dying, the cane strips are woven to form unique shapes and patterns in a wide variety of colors. Typically, dyed and natural strips are alternated to form a pleasing and attractive style. Basket-making is still handed down from generation to generation in Mississippi, and has made a comeback in Oklahoma. Beautiful baskets grace the markets and annual fairs of the Choctaw Nation of Oklahoma and the Mississippi Band of Choctaw Indians.

CONTEMPORARY CHOCTAW ARTISTS

Many Choctaw people have gained national or international recognition for their artistic endeavors in a variety of media, including fine art, basketry, and beadwork. Choctaw artist Valjean McCarty Hessing (1934–2006) gained international renown as one of the most prominent Native American artists of the 20th century. Her work is displayed at the Heard Museum and the Philbrook Museum of Art, and is highly sought by collectors from around the world. Other well-known artists of Choctaw heritage include Norma Howard, Glen Coleman Lester, Cheryl Davis, Judith Durr, Marcus Amerman, Jeffrey Gibson, Kelly Clarkson, Randy Chitto, and sculptor Randy Kemp.

American Indian pipes and stone sculpture are the mediums chosen by Argus Dowdy, whose beautiful work has attracted many serious collectors as well as being highly sought for ceremonial purposes.

Film producer Phil Lucas (1942–2007) won numerous prestigious awards for his documentaries. Lucas explored a wide range of issues in Native America, such as native rights, art, culture, and self-determination. He won an

Emmy for his work on the Turner documentary television series, *The Native Americans* (1994).

CHOCTAW NATIONAL DRESS AND ACCESSORIES

In the past, Choctaw people wore clothing made from deer hides and other natural materials, including turkey feathers. Men wore a breech clout made of deerskin and a belt from which they hung their hunting knife. If the weather was cool, they added a shirt made of skin or turkey feathers that were twisted into a network of cords. During winter, they wore deerskin leggings that were fastened to their belt with loops, while the lower ends of the leggings were tucked into their moccasins. Women also wore clothing made from deerskin. A short skirt alone made up their warm weather dress, while during winter they added a shawl of deerskin or turkey feathers that left their right breast exposed. Occasionally, the inner bark of the mulberry tree was used to make shawls. Both men and women wore moccasins, but they usually went barefoot during summer, especially around the village and home.[29]

Choctaw traditional dress. (Donna L. Akers, Ph.D.)

A beautiful example of a Choctaw crocheted beadwork collar to be worn with traditional dress. (Courtesy of Choctaw Nation of Oklahoma)

In the 18th century, Choctaws made beads out of wood that were the size of acorns. They also liked chinquapin nuts strung in a necklace and sometimes used winter berries or seeds from the red haw to finish their dress. The Choctaw gorgets or brooches incorporated design motifs dating all the way back to Mississippian Complex times, and bones and colored stones sometimes decorated their skirts or shawls. Both men and women wore feathers that reflected their accomplishments and status in the clan.[30]

Sometime in the late 18th or early 19th century, both Choctaw men and women began wearing clothing made from cotton cloth, usually gingham. Some accounts ascribe the style of this dress to French Huguenots with whom the Choctaws came into contact along their western borders near New Orleans. The dresses of other white women living in the region were similar to that worn by the Choctaws, so it is unclear if the traditional dress was adopted from any particular group from the Euro-American society.

Choctaw women continue to wear their national dress, or *chahta hoyo illifoka,* only on special occasions. It consists of a one piece dress with a long, slightly gathered, full skirt that reaches to the ankles or lower led. The bodice has long or three-quarter sleeves with cuffs fitted at the wrist. A long apron is worn over the skirt and it is almost invariably white with elaborate appliqué and sometimes embroidery or rickrack. Choctaws like bright colors; the dress fabric is usually a solid color in red, blue, yellow, or green. The lower edges of both the skirt and the apron have multiple rows of gathers. The bodice has an inset yoke edged with ruffles and embellished with appliqué or rickrack.

The decorative appliqué work is uniquely Choctaw and reflects the skill of the artist. The design is usually a continuing repetitive pattern of diamond shapes that many say represent mountains, while others say it evokes the diamond back rattler and shows a reverence for nature. Half-diamond mo-

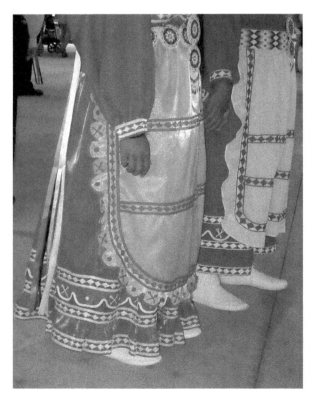

Choctaw traditional dress showing the detailed appliqué used ornamentally. (Donna L. Akers, Ph.D.)

tifs represent Nanih Waiya, the Great Mother Mound, a sacred site of the Choctaw people. Among the Mississippi Choctaws, a series of circles and crosses are popular, representing the stickball play and circular imagery, which symbolized the continuity and belonging of Choctaw communities.

The appliqué work is made from strips of fabric torn (not cut) from cotton cloth. Folding and stitching the appliqué pattern requires skill and patience, and is not lightly undertaken, since many yards of decoration are required for a single dress. The outfits made are highly prized and command hundreds of dollars if custom made.

Choctaw men also wear specially designed clothing to special events and occasions. Although Pan-Indian influences have made inroads with the ubiquitous ribbon shirts found throughout native communities across the United States, Choctaw men still largely favor the appliqué designs that decorate women's dresses and aprons. The traditional wear of Choctaw men since the early 19th century includes a shirt decorated with appliqué worn over jeans or pants. A beaded bandolier embellishes the attire of some Choctaws, and a plain black felt hat is worn, often with a beaded hatband, to complete the outfit. Many men wear a beaded medallion around the neck and some add a feather to their hat.

Women wear an array of jewelry, ribbons, and combs to complete their outfit. A special collar of crocheted beadwork in an open diamond pattern is highly prized and is always worn with the national dress. It is a full collar that goes around the neckline that extends down over the bodice for several inches. A set of beaded jewelry completes the Choctaw woman's dress, including matching earrings, a medallion, and a ribbon lapel pin. Some also wear a beaded belt or sash. A bunch of long, colorful ribbons may be pinned to the back of the dress or hair, hanging almost to the hem of the dress. In old times, these ribbons were only worn by unmarried young women, but today most women wear the ribbons, enjoying the way they sway in dancing.

Many Choctaw women in Mississippi wear a comb (*issep isht elpi*) that is reminiscent of the combs worn in the past that were made of silver. The combs today measure 2 inches wide and about 11 inches long and can be made from any metallic material. Some are even made from a cutout taken from a plastic liter bottle. They have teeth on one edge that slide into the hair, holding the comb in place. The comb is worn with the two open ends toward the front of the head, while the main curve of the comb circles the back. At the turn of the 20th century, these combs were made from a celluloid collar that was worn with the dress shirts of white men. Sometimes, a second comb is worn in front of the first, farther forward on the head to frame the face. These silver or metallic combs contrast beautifully with the dark hair of Choctaw women.

Choctaw beadwork and appliqué continue to incorporate traditional Choctaw motifs that invoke ancient Choctaw beliefs and worldview. The men's shoulder band provides Choctaw artists with a large area for their creative designs, but other designs are found in beadwork jewelry, hair combs, and appliqué. One of the most commonly used designs is the circle and cross. The circle is an almost universal native design that symbolizes the continuing cycle of life and represents the tribe and community. The circle also is a physical manifestation of the absolute individual equality of each person in the Choctaw Nation. People always sat in a circle to indicate that each was equal and that there were no hierarchies of power or privilege among the Choctaws.

The cross represents the sacred fire and is imagined by the laying of four logs, lined up with the four sacred directions. The diamondback rattler, common in much of the American south, appears in the diamond design depicted in beadwork, and also often found on the decorative appliquéd edges of women and girl's dresses. Historically, traditional Choctaws held all other creatures in equality to man, and so the diamond also calls up the respect for all the creatures of the earth in Choctaw cosmology.

Another common Choctaw motif is the coiled snake design, also called the reverse spiral. This is an ancient Mississippian design that comes from the Southeastern Ceremonial Complex, or Southern Cult, of the period from 1250 to 1650 CE. Many artifacts from this regional civilization, which was the forerunner of the Choctaws and other southeastern indigenous nations, bear this design motif. Scholars believe that the coiled snake in artwork represents the Great Serpent, which was a mythological figure common to the Mississippian civilizations, including the Choctaw. The Great Serpent, *Sinti Iapitta,* was a giant snake with a head like a panther or, in other oral traditions, a huge snake whose head had two horns. In both beliefs, the Great Serpent was a water monster with great power. The Great Serpent design is found throughout the eastern United States and was used to decorate pottery and textiles, and is still commonly used today in Choctaw beadwork.

CELEBRATIONS AND OBSERVANCES

In past times, the Choctaw people held an annual Green Corn Ceremony in the late summer, which was an important ritual where they washed themselves clean of the past year, purified themselves, and renewed their spiritual and physical world. Today's Choctaw people continue this annual event in a modern form that incorporates aspects of traditional ways in combination with contemporary realities.

Every year, the Choctaw Nation of Oklahoma holds a five-day Labor Day Festival and powwow at the Choctaw capitol grounds in Tushka Homma (Tuskahoma), which more than 50,000 people attend from all over Oklahoma and across the nation. Art and crafts vendor offer a variety of hand-crafted native jewelry, artwork, clothing, home décor, and other products. In 2010, the Choctaw Nation opened a new arts and crafts building that will also house tribal offices. During the four-day event, Choctaws and their guests participate in a many activities, go to the carnival rides, visit the museum, camp out, and renew acquaintances. Tournaments in fast-pitch softball, horseshoes, volleyball, dominos, and checkers draw hundreds of competitors, while the intertribal powwow that dazzles one and all with fancy dancers, jingle dancers, and drums from all over Indian country put on an amazing show. One of the main highlights of the event is the princess contest, a pageant in which Miss Choctaw Nation, Junior Miss Choctaw Nation, and Little Miss Choctaw Nation are selected to represent the Choctaw people. Terrapin races, tours to see the Choctaw herd of buffalos, cooking demonstrations, storytelling, Choctaw language lessons, and many sports events including stickball round out the varied program. In the evenings, big name country music acts such as Travis Tritt, Vince Gill, and Wynona Judd draw thousands of Choctaws and nonnative Oklahomans.

The Mississippi Band of Choctaws holds a huge Choctaw Indian Fair each year, with arts and crafts, traditional Choctaw dances, and the World Championship Stickball Tournament. The Choctaw Indian Fair is held at the main reservation in Philadelphia, Mississippi, drawing thousands of attendees.

The fair offers storytelling, a princess pageant, and booths displaying beautiful beadwork and baskets crafted by artists from each Choctaw community. Gospel singing is offered, along with demonstrations of rabbit-stick throwing and blowgun demonstrations that draw a lot of attention, and in the evenings, a midway with carnival rides light up the sky.

On August 13, 2009, the Mississippi Choctaw Band held the second annual "Regaining and Embracing Our Mother Mound—Nanih Waiya Celebration" at Nanih Waiya Cave Mound in Winston County, Mississippi. *Nanih Waiya* means "leaning hill" or "place of creation." Since Nanih Waiya Cave Mound is the birthplace of the Choctaw, the mound is a very sacred site, and is of great significance to the Choctaw people. After the 1830 Treaty of Dancing Rabbit Creek, the United States forced the Choctaws to surrender all their ancient homelands, including this sacred mound. The land on which Nanih Waiya sits has been private property for 178 years, until August 8, 2008, when the sacred land was returned to the Choctaw Nation. The Mississippi Band of Choctaw Indians added a production that commemorates this important event in the Choctaw Fair held in 2010 in Philadelphia, Mississippi.

Each May, the Oklahoma Choctaws gather annually to reenact the Trail of Tears, the forced dispossession and exile of the Choctaw nation. Hundreds of Choctaws return to the Choctaw capitol in Tushka Homa to honor those who walked the terrible trail, forced from their homelands into permanent exile in what became the state of Oklahoma. This memorial event not only memorializes the great sacrifice of their ancestors, but also marks the endurance and courage of the Choctaw people. Despite the tremendous difficulties and thousands of deaths on the forced march to the West, the Choctaw people in exile refused to give up or to die off, as the dominant society had predicted. Instead, the Choctaws reestablished their society in the western lands, demonstrating their courage and resiliency as a people who would not be defeated.

Several times in the past few years, guests from Ireland have traveled to Oklahoma to join in this remembrance. Only a few years after the main dispossessions in the 1830s, the Choctaw people took up a collection of money and sent it to Ireland to help the Irish people who were enduring the Potato Famine. The Irish people's suffering was caused by their subjugation by the English, who had appropriated their lands, bringing suffering and death to the Irish people. More than a million Irish men, women, and children starved to death during this famine (1845–1852), and at least another million emigrated to North America. In recognition of this act of compassion and generosity, and in recognition of the suffering of the Choctaw people from similar conditions of oppression, the Irish government sent a delegation to the Trail of Tears commemoration in the 1980s and 1990s, while other Irish private citizens frequently honor the ancestors by participating in this observance.[31]

Choctaw arts and artists have contributed many inspirational works of art to the world, enriching the lives of people while maintaining Choctaw traditions and communicating Choctaw values and worldview. Whether through fine art, sculpture, pipe-making, beadwork, or film, Choctaw artistic endeavors are as old as the Choctaw culture. From time immemorial, Choctaw music, dance, and art have flourished, and all forms of artistic expression continue to be taught to the younger generations—evidence of a strong and dynamic identity and culture.

Notes

1. Angie Debo, *The Rise and Fall of the Choctaw Nation* (Norman, OK: University of Oklahoma Press, 1975), 21.

2. H.B. Cushman, *History of the Choctaw, Chickasaw, and Natchez Indians* (Greenville, TX: Headlight Printing House, 1899), 174, 490–91.

3. Ibid., 206.

4. Ibid., 491.

5. Ibid., 171.

6. John R. Swanton, *Source Material for the Social and Ceremonial Life of the Choctaw Indians,* Smithsonian Institution Bureau of American Ethnology Bulletin 103, Reprinted with an introduction by Virginia Pounds Brown (Birmingham, AL: Birmingham Public Library Press, 1993), 166.

7. Ibid., 162.

8. Michelene Pesantubbee, *Choctaw Women in a Chaotic World* (Albuquerque, NM: New Mexico Press, 2005), 127.

9. Larissa Copeland, "Dancing to Reconnect: Impact of a Choctaw Pastor Still Seen Today," *Biskinik E-News Archive,* October 2010, http://www.choctawnation.com/news-room/biskinik-e-news/2010/10/26/dancing-to-reconnect/.

10. Victoria Lindsay Levine, "Music Revitalization Among the Choctaw," *American Music* 11, no. 4 (Winter 1993): 397.

11. David Nichols, *The Cambridge History of American Music* (Cambridge: Cambridge University Press, 1998), 14.

12. Charles Hudson, *The Southeastern Indians* (Knoxville, TN: University of Tennessee Press, 1975), 134.

13. Levine, "Music Revitalization," 403.

14. Swanton, *Source Material,* 221–22.

15. Ibid., 22.

16. Ibid., 223–24.

17. Ibid.

18. James H. Howard and Victoria Lindsay Levine, *Choctaw Music and Dance* (Norman, OK: University of Oklahoma Press, 1997), 24.

19. "The Choctaw Drum," *Mississippi Band of Choctaw Indians,* http://www.choctaw.org/culture/ihinoshi.html.

20. Francis Densmore, *Choctaw Music,* Bureau of American Ethnology Bulletin 136 (Washington, D.C.: G.P.O., 1943), 117–18.

21. Howard and Levine, *Choctaw Dance and Music,* 28.

22. Hudson, *The Southeastern Indians,* 412.

23. Cushman, *History of the Choctaw,* 190–92.

24. Ibid., 192.

25. Ibid., 193.

26. Hudson, *The Southeastern Indians,* 420.

27. Swanton, *Source Material,* 143.

28. Choctaw Band of Mississippi, "Choctaw Game of Stickball," *62nd Annual Choctaw Indian Fair,* July 13–16, 2011, http://www.choctawindianfair.com/stickballHistory.html.

29. John R. Swanton, "Aboriginal Culture of the Southeast," *42nd Annual Report of the Bureau of American Ethnology* (Washington, D.C.: G.P.O., 1928), 681–83 and

Reuben Thwaites, "Early Western Travels (an Account by an Anonymous Writer who Visited New Orleans in 1799)," in Fortescue Cuming, *Sketches of a Tour to the Western Country,* Vol. IV (Cleveland, OH: A. H. Clark, 1904), 365–66.

30. John R. Swanton, *Source Material,* 44, 102 and "Aboriginal Culture of the Southeast," 685.

31. Debo, *The Rise and Fall,* 59.

8

Contemporary Issues

MANY OF THE ISSUES that the Choctaws face today have their roots in the U.S. Indian policies that supported the system of American colonialism. These issues affect the everyday lives of Choctaw people and will strongly impact their future ability to maintain their identity as a people while living in the midst of American society. The Choctaw Nation of Oklahoma represents the portion of the Choctaw people who were dispossessed from their ancient Mississippi homelands and forced to what is now called Oklahoma on the Trail Where We Cried. The Mississippi Band of Choctaw Indians are the descendants of the Choctaw people who successfully resisted the 19th-century dispossessions and remained on the homelands. The Choctaws of Oklahoma experienced a century of events and oppression that differed from that of the Mississippi Choctaws. The most traumatic being the second dispossession in 1906, when the U.S. government allotted their lands in severalty, sold the surplus above the small amount allotted to each Choctaw family, and unilaterally dissolved the Choctaw government and society.

The resulting state of landlessness has greatly affected the Choctaws of Oklahoma and their quest to assert sovereignty and self-determination. Without a territory or reservation, the Oklahoma Choctaws are a nation without land. This has led directly to the loss of language, culture, and traditions, and isolated Choctaw families from one another. In addition, their landlessness tends to impair the nature of their sovereignty.

The Mississippi Choctaws, on the other hand, have reservation lands where strong communities maintain their identity within the greater Choctaw society. The Mississippi Choctaws suffered from extreme marginalization and race-based isolation after whites took over their lands and forced them into the swamps and backwoods in the 1830s. During the entire 19th century and many years of the 20th, the Mississippi Choctaws were unrecognized by the state, held outside the civil and legal protection of the law, relegated to share cropping on lands they formerly owned, and barred from education. Although the historical experiences of the two major groups of Choctaw people differed greatly, both resulted in historical trauma and a variety of social, legal, and political problems. The major issues faced by the Choctaw people include sovereignty and self-determination and a range of social and economic issues. The struggle over sovereignty is of major importance to the survival of the Choctaw people as a distinct people.

SOVEREIGNTY

Sovereignty is the most important issue facing the Choctaw people today. It affects the very definition of who they are as a people, and their right to self-determination. Sovereignty is defined as supreme, independent authority over a territory and its people. It is the power to choose the way they will live now and in the future, and their right to be a community.

Native sovereignty, despite its recognition in dozens of treaties with the United States, was diminished in U.S. law by the Supreme Court rulings of the Marshall court. In 1823, the court ruled that native nations' claims to their lands were limited to rights as occupants only—that the United States owned all land. Secondly, in 1831, in *Cherokee Nation v Georgia*, Chief Justice John Marshall ruled that native nations did not have the sovereignty of foreign nations, but had a diminished and limited sovereignty and were, instead, something Marshall created, "domestic dependent nations." Using arcane and racist assumptions common in Euro-American ideology of the time, Marshall's ruling greatly diminished the sovereignty of native nations within U.S. law, restricting native sovereignty to matters that do not impinge on the interests of the United States.

The rulings by the Marshall court, in conjunction with the dishonest nature of the treaty system, led to the dispossession of hundreds of Native American nations across the lands now called the United States. The Choctaws were dispossessed beginning in the 1830s, as discussed in Chapter 1. They were forced through the treaty process to yield their Mississippi homelands to the United States in exchange for land in what became the state of Oklahoma. In 1906, the Oklahoma Choctaw lands were again taken by the United States and after a few acres were reserved for each Choctaw family, the entire remainder was sold to the highest bidder, leaving the Choctaw Nation landless. The United States then unilaterally dissolved the Choctaw Nation, and the people were expected to be absorbed into the dominant society. The Choctaw Nation, and any idea of sovereignty, disappeared from the legal landscape of the United States. More than 30 years passed in this state of nonexistence, when in 1934, the Choctaws of Oklahoma were allowed by the United States to form another government.

The Choctaws of Mississippi likewise were not acknowledged or allowed to exist within the American legal system. For more than a century, the Choctaws of Mississippi remained a distinct society and struggled against American oppression. The Mississippi Band of Choctaw Indians was finally given federal recognition in 1918 and the United States opened the Choctaw agency at Philadelphia, Mississippi. From that date forward, the Mississippi Choctaw communities were brought within the system of American law, and have consistently asserted their rights to self-determination and sovereignty.

Some Choctaws believed that giving up recognition of their distinct identity as Indian people and their rights to sovereignty and self-determination were not in the best interest of their people. Choctaw chief Harry J. W. Belvin worked for years to convince Oklahoma Choctaws that they should accept termination of the Choctaw Nation, culminating in the passage of a law in 1959 that authorized U.S. officials to do so. Belvin actively promoted termination, but deliberately obscured the impact it would have on Choctaw people. He never used the word "termination," instead telling unsuspecting tribal members that they would receive large sums of money with the passage of "Belvin's law." The year before termination was to take effect in 1970, tribal activists spread the word of Belvin's deception and stopped the implementation of termination. For years, Belvin had maintained a stranglehold on the office of principal chief and used his power to advocate complete assimilation into the dominant society. Choctaw traditions, language, and ceremonial practices were portrayed as undesirable remnants of a backward past. Through the influence of Harry J. W. Belvin, many Choctaws hid or rejected their identity, quit speaking the language, adopted Christianity, and taught their children to adopt white ways. The culmination of these years of promotion of assimilation by Belvin and others took an enormous toll on Choctaw language and culture among Oklahoma Choctaws. In addition, Belvin's promotion of complete assimilation and termination of the tribal body was the antithesis of self-determination and destroyed any ideas about sovereignty. The Choctaw people rejected Belvin in 1971, electing a new chief who worked to restore the Choctaw Nation as a sovereign Indian nation and to reclaim Choctaw culture and traditions.

However, like many native nations today, the U.S. government has limited the sovereignty of tribal governments to purely internal tribal matters. In recent decades, the United States has allowed tribal governments to develop programs and control funding from the U.S. government in compliance with a form of limited sovereignty that is controlled by the U.S. government. The Choctaw Nation of Oklahoma and the Mississippi Band of Choctaws receive millions of dollars each year from the federal government for a tribal version of programs. Many of the programs are designed to alleviate poverty and assist the poorest people in the United States, such as Head Start; Women, Infant, and Children (WIC) program; Low Income Home Energy Assistance Program; Food Distribution Program (Commodities); and housing services.

Because of U.S. policies that were designed to obtain native lands and the legal fictions and contrivances developed to sustain these fictions, Choctaw sovereignty, like that of many other native nations, is a significantly diminished sort of sovereignty. The Bureau of Indian Affairs, the Interior Department, and a variety of other U.S. government entities hold the power of ultimate decision-making and the ability to nullify or reject Choctaw governmental decisions. If sovereignty is supreme authority over lands and people, no native tribe has sovereignty in its pure form within the United States. In fact, the 1903 Supreme Court decision, *Lone Wolf v. Hitchcock,* decided that the U.S. Congress could abrogate any agreement or treaty with Indian nations at will, by simply passing a law doing so. Thus, the already limited sovereign rights of indigenous nations in the United States are subject at all times to the will of Congress, and can be changed or withdrawn at any point in time, now or in the future.

Given these problems, the sovereignty of the Choctaw Nation of Oklahoma and the other Choctaw bands in the United States is at all times a gamble. Supreme Court Justice Marshall's rulings on sovereignty and U.S. legal rulings since that time have resulted in a body of law pertaining to Native Americans that is contradictory, confusing, and seemingly irrational. For example, in the U.S. Constitution, it clearly and simply states that "Congress shall have the power to regulate Commerce . . . with the Indian tribes."[1] Native nations must now negotiate agreements and revenue sharing with state governments. Many other aspects of Native American commerce, in addition to environmental concerns, resource management, and sacred sites issues, have become subject to negotiation or laws of the state governments, contrary to the U.S. Constitution.

Many native leaders and legal scholars today believe that the U.S. government has systematically undermined even the diminished sovereignty of Indian nations by forcing them to continually compromise sovereign authority and power. As legal scholar Peter d'Errico clarifies, "the fundamental premise of 'American Indian sovereignty' as defined in federal Indian law, is that it is not sovereignty."[2] Despite these problems, Choctaw tribal government continues to assert and claim sovereign status. For example, in 1997, the Mississippi Band of Choctaw Indians signed an executive accord with the state of Mississippi that was aimed at promoting cooperation between two entities for the provision of services to Mississippi Choctaw people. Clearly concerned about any implied diminution of tribal sovereignty, the Choctaws stated that the agreement "shall not be construed to change, enlarge, diminish, or waive the sovereignty or jurisdiction of either party."[3]

In other actions, the Mississippi Choctaws regularly seize the initiative to assert sovereignty on behalf of the Choctaw people. For example, in 2010, the Choctaw tribal government decided to open a new casino that Mississippi governor Haley Barbour and much of the Republican state legislature fought. They cited health and environmental concerns and claimed that the Choctaws were violating the State Gaming Pact signed in 1992. However, the state attorney general's office reviewed the charge and concluded that there was "no viable legal cause of action" to halt the planned casino. Despite Governor Barbour's protests that the casino would hurt "tortoises, fowl, snakes, and plants" in the area of construction, the Choctaws maintain that the state government's real motive is to protect state-regulated casinos from new competition, all of which enrich the state's coffers. Generally, Indian gaming operations are forced to submit taxes and other earnings to state governments. However, in 1992, the gaming compact that Choctaw chief Phillip Martin negotiated with the state provides for "no state 'oversight,' no provisions for the tribe to contribute to maintaining the roads and bridges that casino traffic would need and no provision for payments of taxes to local governments," according to the *Newton County Appeal*.[4]

The new Bok Homa Casino opened in December 2010, despite the continuing opposition of the majority of state and local political leaders in Mississippi. The Mississippi Band of Choctaw Indians is the fourth largest employer in Mississippi, and this project created over 300 new jobs in a region suffering from high unemployment and a poverty rate exceeding 25 percent. During the midst of the battle with the governor and state politicians, *Miko* (Chief) Beasley Denson issued an open letter on tribal sovereignty stating that:

The history of this country is littered with examples of broken agreements between the Indian tribes and the state and federal governments. As representatives of the government of the Mississippi Band of Choctaw Indians, we stand united in our commitment to exercising our right to pursue economic development through gaming under our compact as we determine to be in the best interest of our Tribe. We have a responsibility to provide for our ten thousand tribal members, which in so doing will also benefit the State of Mississippi and all its citizens.[5]

The Choctaw Nation of Oklahoma also struggles to maintain its sovereignty in the face of many challenges from state and local governments, and continuing onslaught through the federal courts. With some regularity, the state and local governments of Oklahoma ignore the concerns of the Choctaw Nation on an array of issues, including water rights, environmental concerns, and gaming disputes, among others, forcing the Choctaw government to assert its sovereign rights through expensive litigation. For example, in early 2010, Oklahoma City government officials claimed to have purchased the entire rights to the water in Sardis Lake, a man-made reservoir located in southeastern Oklahoma near the town of Clayton. The State of Oklahoma had the lake constructed in 1977 by the Army Corps of Engineers on former Choctaw lands, which consist of 10 and one-half counties that are now part of the state of Oklahoma. While the Choctaw Nation claims the right to participate in the decisions on resources that directly affect Choctaw people, the governments of Oklahoma City and the state completely excluded the Choctaws from having any part in the discussions or decisions on the sale of water rights of Lake Sardis. Oklahoma City, 175 miles from Sardis Lake, sought to obtain a plentiful water supply for the city's residents. It plans to pump the water from Sardis Lake to a site near Oklahoma City and will distribute it as needed to the residents of the largest city in Oklahoma sometime in the future. Meanwhile, the lake will disappear and thousands of southeastern Oklahomans will lose the lake's boating, fishing, and recreational value along with the creation of an enormous eyesore and environmental concerns. Sardis Lake is located in Pushmataha County, one of the poorest counties in the nation. The Choctaw Nation is waiting for completion of an environmental impact report from the Army Corps of Engineers before it files suit in the matter. Thus, Choctaw governments in Oklahoma and Mississippi are forced to pay enormous legal costs to assert their sovereign rights, but have no tax base as do state and local governments to pay to defend themselves from actions that diminish or deny their sovereign rights.

Blood Quantum, Identity, and Colonialism

Blood quantum is a very controversial topic among Choctaws and Native Americans. It is a concept that originated in the racial values of the dominant society and has been imported as a criterion to determine eligibility for tribal membership in many tribes. Many Native Americans believe that its use is contrary to native values and traditions, and is a tool used by the U.S. government to control Native Americans, to limit their rights to access funds, programs, and benefits that were paid for by the enormous cessions of Indian homelands required under U.S. treaties. Each native nation has control over setting the requirements for membership in their tribe, so blood quantum doesn't have to be used as a criterion. Therefore, the decisions about membership criteria are the source of ongoing debate among many Native American communities.

Tribal membership in the Choctaw Nation of Oklahoma and the Mississippi Band of Choctaw is determined by the amount of Choctaw blood one has. The use of blood quantum as a measure of race was originally dictated by the U.S. government, who compiled lists of Indian people during the Dawes era (roughly 1887–1910) based on the racist ideas that prevailed in American society of the time. On these lists, the government agent assigned a blood quantum to each individual according to their Indian ancestry, which varied from 1/8 to full-blood. The agent assigned this amount of blood by asking the person about their ancestry and by the appearance, or phenotype, or the individual. Did they look Indian? Exactly how different from a white person did they appear to be? These subjective judgments were susceptible to every sort of bias.

However, the assignment of blood quantum was very important. In order to receive an allotment of land when the United States seized all the communal land holdings of the tribe, an individual had to be on the Dawes Roll, which was supposed to include every single Choctaw person. Most Choctaws sought enrollment because they would be completely dispossessed without it. Although this acted as an incentive to enroll, U.S. policies regarding the land encouraged people to minimize their blood quantum. The government placed restrictions on the title to the land of people who were half or more Indian, retaining control of the title so that the owner of the land could not sell the property. To avoid these government restrictions, many Choctaws declared themselves to be of less Indian "blood" than they actually were. Today, due to the attempt of many of these original enrollees to minimize their blood quantum, the tribal records of their descendants indicate significantly less blood than they actually are. This disqualifies them for many federal programs designed to assist native people, which have a minimum blood quantum. In addition, many Choctaws—often non-English speakers—were afraid to enroll and did not understand what it meant. Many thousands of Choctaw people today are ineligible for tribal membership because their ancestor did not participate in the Dawes enrollment.

Each tribal nation in the United States sets its own rules of enrollment. Unfortunately, the racial system originally used by the U.S. government, in which blood quantum was used to usually exclude Indians, African Americans, and others from full civil rights in America, continues to be used by many Native American tribes to define who is eligible to enroll as a tribal member. Despite the fact that cultural identity cannot be measured by "blood," and contrary to less racist ideas that knowledge of the language and culture and recognition as a member of a community are far more important than genetics, blood quantum requirements still prevail as the deciding factor in tribal enrollment in most Native American nations.

However, the Choctaw Nation of Oklahoma does not require a minimal blood quantum. To enroll, the applicant must prove direct descent from someone who was enrolled on the original Dawes Roll. As a result of this minimal requirement, the Choctaw Nation of Oklahoma has hundreds of thousands of members, some with only a drop of Choctaw blood. However, the blood quantum of each tribal member is used by the federal government to determine eligibility for many federally funded programs. In some cases, Congressional laws funding these programs require each tribe to allow only persons of at least one-quarter blood quantum to obtain benefits. American Indians are the only group in the United States who have to produce a race card to obtain benefits or to participate in government programs.

The Mississippi Band, unlike the Oklahoma Choctaws, has some of the strictest citizenship rules among Native American nations. Enrollment requires a minimum of one-half Choctaw "blood." Thus, with each successive generation, there are fewer and fewer Choctaws who are eligible for tribal membership. Intermarriage with non-Choctaws dilutes the blood quantum of the children by half, making only the children of at least one person who is full-blood eligible to enroll.

The strict requirements of the Mississippi Choctaws are inspired by a desire to carefully control the potential dilution of the tribe. Unfortunately, it also could lead to the extinction of the tribe over the next few decades. Many young people leave the reservation for education or job opportunities, and many of them marry non-Choctaws. The children from their unions are often ineligible for enrollment, even if they grow up on the reservation among their traditional community. That family's descendants cannot be enrolled members of their tribal community, would be ineligible for benefits from the tribe or the federal government, and would lose their identities as Choctaws. The current blood-quantum requirement for tribal membership has important long-term implications. One of the considerations of many tribes who, like the Mississippi Choctaw, have reservation lands is the concern that if they ever arrive at the point that no Choctaw meets the blood-quantum requirement, their reservation lands will revert to the United States and be declassified as tribal lands.

There are pros and cons to the tribal enrollment approaches used by both the Choctaws of Oklahoma and those of Mississippi. The former have expanded their membership from a few thousand to more than 200,000 over the past century. The federal government bases its support to tribes on the tribal enrollment for some programs and on the number of members living in the service area for others. The high enrollment of members of the Choctaw Nation of Oklahoma has increased its support from the federal government, allowing the Oklahoma Choctaws to offer many services to its citizens. The size of Choctaw Nation enrollment has also led to recognition as the third largest Native American tribe in America, and greater influence and visibility. The downside to this unrestrictive membership system is that many enrolled tribal members are completely assimilated into the dominant culture and many know nothing about Choctaw history, traditions, or culture. Although most of them take great pride in enrollment as tribal members, they may have only a small and tenuous cultural identity as a Choctaw person.

The more restrictive membership rules of the Mississippi Choctaws, in conjunction with their residence on reservation lands, have resulted in a close-knit identity and greater language and cultural preservation than that of Oklahoma Choctaws. Enrolled tribal members know their lineage and have a strong community identity. However, the Mississippi Choctaws will have to address tribal membership requirements in the future, as fewer children are eligible for enrollment and as enrollment shrinks. The dilemma they face will be to weigh their desire to maintain cultural cohesion and physical traits that leads to smaller numbers of members with the dilution of diminished blood requirements that would maintain or increase membership.

The history of the Mississippi Choctaws of terrible racial discrimination at the hands of the dominant society in Mississippi has naturally resulted in a sort of clannishness. To survive a century of persecution by white society, they forged strong communal bonds, and kept to themselves. The amazing success of the Mississippi Choctaws in surviving decades of discrimination and ostracism has resulted in a tight community of strong and resilient people. The high blood-quantum requirements for membership in the Mississippi Band of Choctaw Indians make perfect sense, given their history.

Interestingly, blood quantum or racial identification was never a part of traditional Choctaw culture. Race was a concept created by whites that was unknown in Native American societies. Choctaws, throughout their history in the colonial period, adopted non-Choctaws into their tribe, using a spiritual ritual of cleansing and rebirth that transformed non-Choctaws into full tribal members. Their race did not matter at all, and was never considered by the Choctaw people.

In addition, Choctaws never believed that behavior or abilities were dictated by race. To Choctaws, a person's value and worth were a result of their actions, not some innate racial characteristic. However, these beliefs formed the foundation of American beliefs. From the creation of the U.S. government, race was used to determine the level of human rights one had in American law. Race dictated all opportunities and created different categories used by the United States to discriminate against Indians and African Americans. Thus, it was used by the United States to determine Indian identity for the purpose of making up the Dawes Rolls, and has been used by many Native American nations since that time. The system still used by the U.S. government requires Native Americans to produce a document to prove their identity, based solely on "race," an idea that has been long discredited as a relic of irrational prejudice. No other group of people in the United States is required to produce documentary proof to establish their cultural identity.

LANGUAGE AND CULTURE REVITALIZATION AND PRESERVATION

Over the past two decades, the Choctaws of Oklahoma have conducted an intense revitalization effort to recover and maintain their language, beliefs, and traditions and to teach them to children and young people. The tribal government has created many programs and the Choctaw monthly newspaper carries articles about traditional arts, elder interviews, and history in every issue. But the major thrust to revitalize Choctaw ways has come from tribal members throughout the United States. Groups of Choctaws in California, Alabama, Louisiana, and Tennessee have sought to revive the language. Children and adults use the course offered by the Choctaw national government to learn Choctaw online. They hold meetings and classes on history and Choctaw arts and crafts. Many of these programs have been very successful, and the resurgence of Choctaw art has led to many new artists offering fine work for sale at art shows, powwows, and the annual festivals.

The Choctaw people of Oklahoma had to overcome a history that eroded many of their traditions, language, and culture. Stripped of their entire communal land base in 1906, the Choctaw Nation of Oklahoma had enormous difficulty maintaining cultural cohesion. Without a reservation, each Choctaw family was surrounded by nonnatives and was individually subjected to the dominant culture. Even today, there is no reservation on which Choctaws can interact with each other on a daily basis, restricting community meetings to special occasions often requiring travel to a specific place away from one's home. Social factors like racial prejudice and extremely high rates of poverty also tend to isolate many Choctaw families in Oklahoma.

Without a reservation and schools run by the tribe, most Choctaw children attend Oklahoma public schools. The curriculum offers only limited information on Choctaw history or culture, although the Choctaw government has worked diligently to include cultural studies and language instruction in Oklahoma public schools where a large percentage of the students are Choctaw. In public schools, native children sometimes face ostracism and bullying by nonnative students because of their identity as Indian people. Children and youth experience intense peer pressure to conform to the dominant society and its values, and may reject their identity as a means of protecting themselves and of a desire to belong. As a result of these and other pressures, over time, the knowledge and practice of traditional beliefs, ceremonies, and a common language have waxed and waned.

The lack of a reservation has hampered the language and cultural revitalization efforts of the Choctaw people of Oklahoma. Many customs, practices, ceremonies, and traditions have been lost over the decades. However, in recent years, the tribal government has worked diligently to mitigate these problems by building community centers, working with the public schools to include at least a minimal amount of Choctaw history in their curriculums, creating online language courses, and promoting cultural activities.

The Choctaw language belongs to the Muskogean family of indigenous languages. Six Muskogean languages are spoken today, including Alabama, Creek-Seminole, Koasati, Mikasuki, Chickasaw, and Choctaw. Historically, all these peoples' homelands are located in the Southeast. The number of fluent Choctaw speakers today is estimated at 17,890, although some sources suggest a number closer to 11,000.[6] There are several Choctaw dialects, including the Oklahoma dialect, the Mississippi dialect, and a dialect of Mississippi Choctaw, spoken in south central Oklahoma near Durwood.[7] The Mississippi Choctaw communities have minor differences in the three Choctaw dialects that are spoken among the greater tribe in Mississippi.

Although Choctaws in Oklahoma number over 100,000, there are only approximately 6,000 fluent speakers of the language. In Mississippi, despite only about 10,000 tribal members, there are at least 9,000 fluent speakers of Choctaw. Both the Oklahoma and Mississippi tribes are working diligently to revitalize the language and teach their children through schools and social programs and occasions. The Choctaw Nation of Oklahoma offers online courses through the nation's website that attract more than 2,200 students. Online courses in Choctaw are offered through 52 public schools, 35 high schools, 5 colleges, and 14 Head Start centers in Oklahoma. In Mississippi, thousands of Choctaws speak their language in their homes and schools on a daily basis, and up to 90 percent of tribal members are fluent. The Mississippi Band's school system, run by the Choctaws, encourages retention of the Choctaw language through activities and courses. Knowledge of the language and fluency are a source of pride for all Choctaws, and the preservation and revitalization efforts of both the Mississippian and Oklahoman Choctaws bode well for the future of the Choctaw language.

SOCIAL ISSUES

Choctaw people living in the nation in Oklahoma, the band in Mississippi, and other Choctaw communities—such as those in Alabama, Louisiana, and Tennessee—deal with problems including poverty, high unemployment, domestic violence, and substance abuse. Diabetes is epidemic in many communities and is recognized by the Indian Health Service as one of the most intractable health issues in Indian country.

Historical Trauma

Many of the social issues rampant in Indian country are a direct result of U.S. policies implemented over the 19th and 20th centuries. Although each Choctaw community had differing experiences with the U.S. government and people, a common thread of dispossession, forced exile, racism, and marginalization was inflicted on each group. These experiences have resulted in historical trauma, which is a cumulative emotional and psychological wounding over one's life span that is transmitted across generations. Historical trauma experienced by Choctaws during their dispossession from their homelands, decades of racist policies, and generations who could find no work or support their children simply because of their identity have resulted in social dysfunction, substance abuse, domestic violence, and other problems. Native American scholars have documented the myriad problems suffered by today's Indian people from historical trauma. The Choctaw Nation and Mississippi Band have implemented many programs that seek to address the social issues of its people and communities.

Substance Abuse

Alcoholism has always posed a major problem in the lives of native people, but in recent years, methamphetamine and other drugs have also become a huge concern. Methamphetamine addiction is a huge problem in rural Oklahoma, and has led to high crime rates and inflicted great sorrow on many Choctaw families. Its production in home labs in rural areas and small towns pose a danger to people who live in the vicinity, and to the children who reside with parents who engage in this dangerous and illegal production.

Many programs by Choctaw governments in Oklahoma and Mississippi are addressing the problems caused by addiction. In recent years, the Choctaw Nation of Oklahoma opened *Chi Hullo Li,* a culturally sensitive residential treatment facility for young mothers, which helps them recover from substance abuse, learn parenting skills, and recover their physical and emotional health. Based on a model of healing being implemented in many Native American communities, the program addresses recovery and healing through a cultural and spiritual approach meaningful to native people.

Domestic Violence

Native American women fall victim to domestic violence and sex crimes at rates that are simply shocking: 34 percent of Native American women will be raped in their lifetime, and 64 percent will be assaulted. These rates are three and a half times that of white women. In at least 86 percent of these cases, the perpetrator is nonnative. Some sources assert that these crimes are the result of underlying attitudes of the dominant society toward native people. Although these are national statistics, they apply to Choctaw women as well.[8]

The Choctaw Nation of Oklahoma has created programs to address the high rates of domestic violence and assaults. The national government has created programs to educate and prevent such violence and has counselors available at 4 locations throughout the 10 and one-half county areas served by the tribe.

The Mississippi Choctaw have implemented a one-stop comprehensive program to address the needs of victims of domestic violence within the tribal community. The recipient of several awards, this program has greatly improved the quality and availability of services for victims and their families, including legal services, counseling, and therapy. In addition, the tribal government has passed new legislation that gives law enforcement and the tribal judiciary the tools needed to address and diminish the incidents of domestic violence.

Diabetes and Obesity

Diabetes is a huge problem among Native Americans. According to the Center for Disease Control, Native Americans have much higher rates of diabetes than the general population in Oklahoma, with more than 10 percent of the native people afflicted with this serious disease. The Choctaw governments in Oklahoma and Mississippi have worked very hard to address this terrible illness through prevention, education, and treatment. Diabetes afflicts Native Americans two and one-half times more than among nonnative people. In an eight-year period from 1996 to 2004, there was a 68 percent increase in the number of Native American youth between the ages of 15 and 19 with diabetes.[9] Screenings are held at Choctaw schools in Mississippi, and the *Choctaw Community News* runs recipes and nutritional advice to help Choctaw families make healthy choices. The tribe began the Diabetes Prevention Mile High Club to encourage Choctaws to exercise daily and become more physically fit. The Choctaw Health Department has initiated the Special Diabetes Program Initiative, which has helped hundreds of Choctaws maintain a diabetes-free healthy lifestyle through education and exercise. Last, the Choctaw Nation's Diabetes and Wellness Center in Talihina, Oklahoma, offers comprehensive services, including nutritional counseling and individually designed fitness programs and a state-of-the-art fitness facility.

The Mississippi Band also has several programs to address the epidemic of diabetes among Choctaws. Screening services, education services, and medical treatment are offered to all Choctaws, in addition to nutritional counseling, behavior modification, and medical management for diabetics.

Native Americans are more susceptible to diabetes if they are obese, which is a common condition among the rural poor in Mississippi and Oklahoma. Poor dietary habits combine with sedentary lifestyles to produce very high rates of obesity and diabetes among the Choctaw people. The Choctaw Nation and the Mississippi Band offer many programs to encourage better eating habits, nutritional education, and physical fitness. Despite these efforts, many Choctaws throughout Oklahoma and Mississippi suffer from diabetes, and others, through obesity, are at very high risk for diabetes and other ailments, including heart disease.

Poverty and Unemployment

Many problems among Choctaws are related to poverty. More than one in four Choctaw families live in poverty in Oklahoma. Many Choctaw children grow up in homes where food is scarce and housing is inadequate. The high rates of poverty lead to poor preparation for school, increased rates of illness, depression, and suicide. The poverty level of Native Americans living in rural areas of Oklahoma, as do the Choctaw people, is greater than 40 percent. Many of them live not just in poverty, but in severe poverty, which is defined as having incomes less than three-fourths the poverty level. Only 36 percent of men over the age of 16 had full-time, year round work in one survey of Native Americans in Oklahoma. Other sources have confirmed that the level of underemployment of both male and female Choctaws is endemic.[10]

As with many other native nations, almost the entire territory of the Choctaw people was taken by the United States through forced treaty cessions and confiscation, obscured by a variety of official policies that justified American actions. The result was the impoverishment of Choctaw people, which is irreversible and endemic. Without land, people are unable to subsist themselves. In 1900, the Choctaw Nation of Oklahoma communally owned 7,500,000 acres of land in what is now called Oklahoma. As noted in Chapter 1, the United States decided to end tribal landholding and confiscated millions of square miles of native lands by passing laws that enabled them to do so. After the U.S. government seized Choctaw lands in the first years of the 20th century, the Choctaw Nation was unilaterally dissolved and all its territory was taken. After a century of struggle, the Choctaw Nation of Oklahoma now owns approximately 75,000 acres of land in southeastern Oklahoma, but it is not open for Choctaw people to live on. The Choctaw Nation has programs that assist Choctaws to find housing, but the communal lands are all gone. This has resulted not only in incalculable loss of material wealth, but also in the loss of many traditions, and adversely affected the retention of the Choctaw language and culture.

The loss of land by the Choctaw people living in the region now called Oklahoma contrasts sharply with the acquisition of these same lands by U.S. corporations, who have extracted enormous wealth for their shareholders from the natural resources of former Choctaw lands. Timber companies own vast stretches of the former Choctaw lands. One company holds millions of acres in Oklahoma and other areas of the south, and has developed into a gigantic company generating over six and a half billion dollars in annual revenue. Timber companies operating in Oklahoma clear-cut millions of acres of land in the old Choctaw territory, much of which remains an aesthetic eyesore and which has resulted in environmental degradation.

Aside from the devastating effects on the beauty of the land and the health of the ecosystem, the employment policies of many international extractive industries has contributed to high unemployment and underemployment among Choctaw people. A common practice among these employers has been to hire workers on a temporary or seasonal basis, with no benefits, overtime, job security, or promise of continuing work. Many Choctaw men are able to find work for only a part of the year.

The vast majority of jobs available in the area pay minimum wage and offer no benefits like medical insurance, paid vacation, sick leave, or pensions. As a result, many Choctaw families live in poverty, with little hope of improvements in their financial expectations. Young people move out of the area in order to find good jobs. Others remain in the areas in which their families reside, but their expectations of a career or more than a bare minimal income from work are very low.

The Choctaw Nation of Oklahoma has created many jobs and strives to alleviate the paucity of employment opportunities in southeastern Oklahoma. Its annual economic impact is $822,280,105 from business operations that include 7 casinos, 14 tribal smoke shops, and 13 truck stops. However, the majority of jobs available through Choctaw Nation enterprises are not high-paying positions.[11]

Poverty and high unemployment afflict the Mississippi Band of Choctaws, and, to some extent, the Jena Band of Choctaws and other smaller Choctaw communities living outside Oklahoma and Mississippi. The vast majority of people dwelling in rural areas have little opportunity for high-paid careers, and many live on the edge of poverty. Social services such as housing assistance, food stamps, and the distribution of commodities to families help them to subsist, but despite the programs, many Choctaws suffer from economic hardship as a way of life.

Poverty; high unemployment; underemployment; social problems; concerns about maintaining their language, culture, and traditions; and the ongoing struggle to assert sovereignty and self-determination are issues that are common to all Native American nations in the United States. Many of these problems result from colonization—especially the enormous loss of lands and wealth that has proven so disastrous to Indian people. However, in spite of the many challenges faced by Choctaw people, they tenaciously hold to their unique identity, courageously persisting despite all odds. The great strength of the Choctaw people has been their ability to adapt to new circumstances and conditions, and their survival of the past two centuries of U.S. colonialism provides ample proof that the Choctaw people will continue to successfully meet the ongoing challenges they face.

Notes

1. U.S. Constitution, Article 1, Section 8, Legal Information Institute (LII), Cornell University Law School, http://topics.law.cornell.edu/constitution/articlei.

2. Peter d'Errico, "American Indian Sovereignty: Now You See It, Now You Don't," Inaugural Lecture, American Indian Civics Project, Humboldt State University, Arcata, CA, October 24, 1997, http://www.umass.edu/legal/derrico/nowyouseeit.html.

3. "Executive Accord: Accord between the Executive Branches of the Mississippi Band of Choctaw Indians and the State of Mississippi," *Mississippi Band of Choctaw Indians,* http://www.choctaw.org/government/court/accord.html.

4. Jack Tannehill, "Is It Possible that Barbour Could Lose a Fight?," *Choctaw Community News* XL, no. 9 (September 2010): 6 (originally published in the *Newton Country Appeal*).

5. "Mississippi Sovereignty Showdown," *Indian Gaming* 21, no. 1 (January 2011): 42.

6. James Estes, "Table 1: Indigenous Languages Spoken in the United States (by Language)," *Your Dictionary*, http://www.yourdictionary.com/elr/natlang.html.

7. George Aaron Broadwell, Ph.D., "Choctaw," in *Native Languages of the Southeastern United States*, eds. Heather Hardy and Janine Scancarelli (Lincoln, NE: University of Nebraska Press), 159.

8. *Maze of Injustice: The Failure to Protect Indigenous Women From Sexual Violence in the USA* (New York: Amnesty International Publications, 2007), 2, 4.

9. "Facts at a Glance: Diabetes in American Indians and Alaska Natives," *Indian Health Service*, updated June 2008, http://www.ihs.gov/MedicalPrograms/Diabetes/index.cfm?module=resourcesFactSheets_AIANs08.

10. Calvin L. Beale, "The Ethno-Racial Context of Poverty in Rural and Small Town America, *Poverty and Race* 12, no. 2 (March/April 2003), http://www.prrac.org/full_text.php?text_id=804&item_id=7806&newsletter_id=67&header=Poverty+%2F+Welfare&kc=1.

11. "Oklahoma Indian Nations 2010: Pocket Pictorial Directory," *Oklahoma Indian Affairs Commission*, http://digitalprairie.ok.gov/cdm/compoundobject/collection/stgovpub/id/5215/rec/5

Selected Bibliography

Akers, Donna L. "Removing the Heart of the Choctaw People: Indian Removal from a Native Perspective." *American Indian Culture & Research Journal* 23, no. 3 (1999): 63–77.

Akers, Donna L. *Living in the Land of Death: The Choctaw Nation, 1830–1860.* East Lansing, MI: Michigan State University Press, 2004.

Akers, Donna L. "Removing the Heart of the Choctaw Nation: Indian Removal from a Native Perspective." In *Native Historians Write Back: Decolonizing American Indian History,* edited by Susan A. Miller and James Riding In. Lubbock, TX: Texas Tech University Press, 2011.

Clark, Blue. *Lone Wolf v. Hitchcock: Treaty Rights and Indian Law at the End of the Nineteenth Century.* Lincoln, NE: University of Nebraska Press, 1999.

Cushman, H. B. *History of the Choctaw, Chickasaw, and Natchez Indians.* Greenville, TX: Headlight Printing House, 1899.

Debo, Angie. *The Rise and Fall of the Choctaw Republic,* Second ed. Norman, OK: University of Oklahoma Press, 1989.

Deloria, Vine Jr. *Red Earth, White Lies: Native Americans and the Myth of Scientific Fact.* New York: Scribner, 1995.

DeRosier, Arthur. *Removal of the Choctaw Indians.* Knoxville, TN: University of Tennessee Press, 1970.

Faiman-Silva, Sandra L. *Choctaws at the Crossroads: The Political Economy of Class and Culture in the Oklahoma Timber Region.* Lincoln, NE: University of Nebraska Press, 2000.

Foreman, Grant. *Indian Removal: The Emigration of the Five Civilized Tribes of Indians.* Norman, OK: University of Oklahoma Press, 1976.

Howard, James Henri. *Choctaw Music and Dance.* 1st ed. Norman, OK: University of Oklahoma Press, 1990.

Hudson, Charles M. *The Southeastern Indians.* Knoxville, TN: University of Tennessee Press, 1976.

Levine, Victoria Lindsay. "Musical Revitalization among the Choctaw." *American Music* 11, no. 4 (December 1, 1993): 391–411.

Mihesuah, Devon Abbott. *Indigenous American Women: Decolonization, Empowerment, Activism.* Lincoln, NE: University of Nebraska Press, 2003.

Mihesuah, Devon Abbott. *Recovering Our Ancestors' Gardens: Indigenous Recipes and Guide to Diet and Fitness.* Lincoln, NE: University of Nebraska Press, 2005.

Mihesuah, Devon Abbott. *Choctaw Crime and Punishment, 1884–1907.* Norman, OK: University of Oklahoma Press, 2009.

Mould, Tom. *Choctaw Tales.* Jackson, MS: University Press of Mississippi, 2004.

Pesantubbee, Michelene E. *Choctaw Women in a Chaotic World: The Clash of Cultures in the Colonial Southeast.* Albuquerque, NM: University of New Mexico Press, 2005.

Rogin, Michael Paul. *Fathers and Children: Andrew Jackson and the Subjugation of the American Indian.* New Brunswick: Transaction Publishers, 1995.

Swanton, John Reed. *Source Material for the Social and Ceremonial Life of the Choctaw Indians.* Tuscaloosa, AL: University of Alabama Press, 2001.

Wells, Samuel J., and Roseanna Tubby. *After Removal: The Choctaw in Mississippi.* Jackson, MS: University Press of Mississippi, 1986.

Wilkinson, Charles F. *Blood Struggle.* New York: W.W. Norton, 2005.

Index

Agriculture, 24, 115, 122
Akers, Donna L., 47–49, 142, 144,
    169
Allotment, xxvii, 38, 48, 53–54, 122,
    157
American Civil War, xv, xxvi, 35–37,
    52–53, 85
American Indian Movement, xxviii
American Revolution, xx, xxiv, 12
Amerman, Marcus, 141
Applique, 144–46
Apukshunnubbee, 27
Arts: basketry, 6, 140–41, 147; bead-
    work, 141, 143, 145–48; dance,
    xiii, xiv, 3–5, 7, 65, 83, 87, 89, 99,
    131–39, 141, 147–48
Assimilation, xii, xvii, xx, 44–46, 61,
    73, 80, 88, 112, 132, 153
Atoka Agreement, xxvii
Attala, 58

Ball play, 89–90, 111, 131–33,
    136–40, 145, 147
Banaha, 3, 116–17, 119

Barbour, Haley, 155
Barfoot, Van, 43
Basket-making, 6, 140–41, 147. *See
    also* Baskets
Baskets, 5–6, 83, 103, 140–41, 147.
    See also Basket-making
Battle of Horseshoe Bend, 21
Battle of New Orleans, xxv, 21, 24
Beadwork, 141, 143, 145–48
Beaver Pond, 138–39
Belvin, Harry James Watson, 45,
    153
Benning, TN, 58
Bering Strait, 1–2
Bishinik, 131
Blood quantum, 54, 58, 70, 77,
    156–59
Boarding Schools, xxvii, 40, 56, 87,
    112
Bogue Chitto, 58
Bogue Homa, 58
Bohpoli, 63
Bureau of Indian Affairs, xxvii–xxixx,
    56, 154

Byington, Cyrus, 130
Byington, Presley, 112

Calhoun, John C., 23–24, 26–27
Casinos: Bok Homa, 155; Golden
  Moon, 57–58; Silver Star, 57
Catlin, George, 134
Childbirth, xiii, 83–84
Child-rearing, 34, 63, 68, 70, 73–75,
  77–84, 86–88, 93, 99, 105, 110,
  112, 115, 116, 153, 159, 160–61,
  164. *See also* Boarding Schools
Chitto, Randy, 141
Choctaw: civil war, xxiii, 11; language,
  viii–ix, xi, xiii, xvii, xix, xxvii,
  42–43, 46, 52, 58, 64, 70, 87, 89,
  92, 102, 110, 131, 147, 151, 153,
  158–62, 165–66
Choctaw Apache Community, xv,
  xviii
Choctaw beer, 121–22
Choctaw-Chickasaw Heritage Com-
  mittee, 132
Choctaw code talkers, xxvii, 42–43
Choctaw communities: Attala, 58;
  Benning, TN, 58; Bogue Chitto,
  58; Bogue Homa, 58; Conehatta, 58;
  Crystal Ridge, 58; Malmaison, 58;
  Ocean Springs, 58; Pearl River,
  58; Red Water, 88; Standing Pine,
  58; Tucker, 58
Choctaw Community News, 131
Choctaw Fair, 132, 140, 147–48
Choctaw Housing Authority, 57
Choctaw Lighthorse, 88
Choctaw Nation of Oklahoma, xii, xiv,
  xv, xvii, xix, xxvi–xxix, 33, 35–37,
  40, 42–67, 54, 57, 63, 69, 80, 85,
  88–90, 105, 107, 113, 117–18,
  120–21, 124, 131, 135, 141, 143,
  147, 151–54, 156–66, 169
Cholera, 8, 108, 127
Christianity, xiv, 9, 13, 53, 61, 66, 69,
  70, 80, 86–87, 131–32, 153

Claiborne, John F. H., 52
Clans, xiv, 5, 56, 63, 68, 74–78,
  80–82, 86–88
Clarkson, Kelly, 141
Clifton Choctaw Tribe, xv, xviii
Clothing, 6, 22, 32, 55, 108–9, 132,
  142–47
Code talkers. *See* Choctaw code talkers
Collier, John, xxvii
Colonialism, xviii, 9, 13, 40, 57, 73,
  87, 112, 151, 156, 166
Communal landholding, xvi–xxii,
  xxvii, 35, 38, 44, 53, 69, 87–88, 90,
  107, 133, 157, 160, 165
Communal life, xvii–xxiii, xix,
  xxvii–xxiii, 3, 13, 14, 35, 38,
  44–45, 53–54, 58, 62–63, 66–67,
  69, 70, 75–76, 79, 80, 84, 87–90,
  107, 125, 127, 133, 136–37,
  145–48
Conehatta, 58
Confederacy (Confederate States of
  America), xxvi, 36, 53
Constitution: U.S., 154, 18, 23, 29,
  39, 44; Choctaw, xxix, 45–46,
  54–56
Cooper, Douglas H., 53
Corn, xvi, 2–4, 29, 6–5, 67, 90,
  97–98, 115–19, 121, 123, 132,
  134, 146
Cosmic symbols: number four, 6,
  133–34, 146–47; four sacred directions, 133, 146; circle, 3, 65, 67, 95,
  133, 145–46
Cosmological beliefs: renewal, 65, 90,
  133; purification, 3, 64–66, 77,
  133, 146; Cravat family, John, 13
Crystal Ridge, 58
Cushman, H. B., 169

Dance Groups: Okla Humma Chahta
  Hiltha, 132
Dances: animals, in honor of, 134;
  ball play, 132; bells worn during,

134; buffalo, 132; Green Corn, 132; drums used with, 135; drunk, 133; eagle, 132; fast war, 132; jump, 133; walk, 133; quail, 132; raccoon, 132; sacred paint worn, 134; scalp, 132; singing as accompaniment, 133; snake, 132; stealing partners, 132; striking sticks used, 135; stomp, 89; symbolism of, 133; turtle, 132; war, 132; wedding, 132

Davis, Cheryl, 141

Davis, Jefferson, 53

Dawes Act, xxvii, 38–41, 44–45, 54, 85, 105, 113, 122, 136, 157–58, 160

De Soto, Hernando, xxiii, 6–8, 10

Debo, Angie, 169

Deloria, Vine Jr., 2

Denson, Beasley, 57, 155

Design motifs, 143–46; circle, 65, 67, 133, 145–46; coiled snake, 146; cross, 67, 145–46; diamond shape, 144–46; great Serpent, 146

Diabetes, xiv, 124, 162–64

Discrimination, racism, xii–xiii, xvii, xxviii, 28–29, 34, 159–62

Dispossession, vii, xii, xx, xxv–xxvi, 3–4, 13, 15–16, 23, 28, 30–34, 51, 57, 62–63, 85–86, 90, 105–6, 108, 110, 112, 132, 148, 151–52, 162. *See also* Trail Where We Cried

Divorce, 68, 74, 82–83

Domestic violence, 14, 69, 77, 80, 162–63

Dowdy, Argus, 141

Durant family, Louis, 13

Durr, Judith, 141

Eastern Cottonwood Tree (*Populus angulata*), 125–26

Eaton, John, 16, 31

Echohawk, John, xxix

Enabling Act, xxvii

Faiman-Silva, Sandra, 122, 169

Folsom family, Nathaniel, 13

Food, 2, 4–6, 14, 33, 40, 51, 55, 69, 78–79, 84, 97 115, 116, 124–25, 137, 166

Foreman, Grant, 169

Franklin, Benjamin, 19

French and Indian War, xxiii, 10, 12–13, 136

Fry Bread, 120–21, 124

Gardner, David, 46

Gibson, Jeffrey, 141

Gorgets, 143

Gospel singing, 70, 90, 131, 147

Grape Dumplings, 118–19

Great Serpent, 146

Green Corn Ceremony, 3–5, 64–65, 90, 132, 134, 146

Harkins family, John, 13

Harmony and balance, xiii, 13, 6–6, 70, 76, 133

Harris family, Daniel, 13

Harrison, William Henry, 21

Henry, Patrick, 19

Herbal remedies, 125–27; chicory, 126; common buttonbush, 126; dandelion, 126; Eastern Cotton-wood Tree, 125–26; ground ivy, 126; persimmons, 126; purple corn-flower, 126; sweetgum tree, 126; Virginia pennywort, 126; whiteleaf mountain mint, 126; willow bark, 123

Hessing, Valjean McCarty, 141

Historical trauma, 152, 162

Hog stories, 93, 101, 105

Howard, James Henri, 170

Howard, Norma, 141

Howe, LeAnne, 113

Hudson, Charles M., 170

Indian Education Act of 1972, xxiv
Indian Territory, xii, xv, xviii, xxvi,
    24–25, 33, 35–38, 40, 53–54, 63,
    88, 112–13
Irish Potato Famine, 63, 148

Jackson, Andrew, xi–xii, xxvi, 21–22,
    24–25, 28–32, 51, 84–86, 106
Jefferson, Thomas, 16–19
Jena Band of Choctaw Indians, xv,
    xvii–xviii, 166
John, Grady, xx, 106
Johnson, Lyndon B., xxviii

Kabocca, 139–40
Kemp, Randy, 141
Kennedy, John F., 57
Kingsbury, Cyrus, 31, 70
Kinship system xi, xiv, xix, 63, 68, 73,
    74–82, 87, 94, 108; clans xiv, 3–5,
    14, 31, 56, 63, 65, 68–69, 74–83,
    86–88, 98, 105, 129, 143; exogamy,
    76; matrilineal, xiv, 68, 74–75,
    78–81, 83, 87–88; moieties, 6, 82

Labor Day Festival, 90, 147
Language, viii–ix, xii, xiii, xvii, xix,
    xxvii, 42–43, 46, 52, 58, 64, 70,
    86–87, 89, 91, 102, 110, 131, 147,
    151, 153, 158–62, 165–66
LeFlore, Greenwood, 16, 31
LeFlore, Thomas, 108
LeFlore family, Louis and Michael, 13
Lester, Glen Coleman, 141
Levine, Victoria Lindsay, 170
Lincecum, Gideon, 127
Little people, 63, 102
Lone Wolf v. Hitchcock, 39, 154
Long, Stella Dyer, 112
Louisiana Choctaw Tribe, xv, xviii
Lucas, Phil, 141

Malmaison, 58
Marriage, 13, 76, 82–83, 101, 158

Marshall, John, 52, 154
Martin, Phillip, xvii, 57, 86, 155
Medicine men and women, 78,
    104–5, 123–27, 136, 138
Meriam Report, xxvii, 40
Mihesuah, Devon Abbott, 112–13,
    116–17, 119, 124, 170
Miss Choctaw Nation, 147
Mississippi Band of Choctaw Indians,
    xii–xix, xxvi, xxviii, 27, 29–32,
    34, 38, 43–44, 51–55, 57–58, 70.
    80–81, 85–7, 106, 108, 110, 112,
    123–24, 127, 131–32, 125,
    135–36, 140–41, 145, 147–48,
    151–59, 161, 161–64, 166
Monroe, James, 22–23
Moshulatubbee, 27
Mother Earth, 2, 68
Mould, Tom, 106–7, 170
MOWA Band of Choctaw Indians,
    xv, xix
Music, xiv, 131–35, 147–48, 170
Musical Instruments: bells, 134, 136;
    cane flutes, 135–36; drums, 7,
    134–36, 139, 147; striking sticks,
    134–36
Muskogean languages, xix, 110, 161
Muskogee people (Creeks), 21–23, 29,
    37, 94, 131, 138

Nail family, Henry, 13
Nanih Waiya, xvi, 1–4, 6, 62, 93–94,
    145, 147
National dress, 142, 144–45; bando-
    lier, 145; collar, beaded, 143, 145;
    comb, 145–46; hat, 145; ribbon
    shirt, 145; ribbons, 83, 145
Native American Grave Protection and
    Repatriation Act (NAGPRA), xxix
Ned, Buster, 132, 136
Neshoba County, Mississippi, 55,
    110
Nixon, Richard, xxviii
Noley, Greyson, 113

Obama, Barack, xxix
Obesity, xiv, 124, 163
Ocean Springs, 58
Okla Humma Chahta Hiltha, 132
Oral traditions, xi, xiv, 1–2, 33, 65, 80, 93–94, 97, 125, 129–30, 146
Origin story, xvi, 2, 34, 62, 93

Patriarchy, xiv, 67, 80, 86–89
Pearl River, 58
Perry family, Hardy, 13
Pesantubbee, Michelene E., 113, 170
Pete's Place, 122
Pitchlynn, Peter P., 36–37
Pitchlynn family, John, 13, 18
Pokeweed, 123
Poverty, xvii, xx, xxv, xxviii, 22, 34, 40, 43–45, 52–53, 55–56, 81, 85, 89, 122, 124, 154–55, 161–62, 164–66
Powwows, xiv, 120, 135, 147, 160
Private property system of land ownership, (allotment) xxvii, 13, 23, 38–39, 53–54, 69, 88, 122, 157
Prophetstown, 21
Pushmataha, xxv, 20–21, 24–27
Pushmataha County, 156
Pyle, Gregory, 46

Recipes, xiv, 2, 124, 126, 164, 170; banaha, 116; Choctaw Hunter's Stew, 119; grape dumplings, 118–19; Indian fry bread, 120–21; Indian tacos, 120; parched corn, 121; tomfulla, 117–18; wild onions, 119–20
Red Power Movement, xxviii, 89
Red Water, 88
Revitalization, 45–46, 89, 132, 135, 160–62, 170
Roberts, Hollis, 46
Rodgers, Greg, 112
Rogin, Michael Paul, 170
Roosevelt, Franklin D., xxvii

Sampson, Adam, 132–33
Sardis Lake controversy, 156
Satz, Ronald, 53
Self-determination, xxviii–xix, 89, 141, 151–53, 166
Spirit beings, xiv, 63, 102, 126, 146
Spiritual beliefs, 6, 52, 61–62, 70, 77
Spiritual power, xiii, 67, 78–79, 87, 97, 115, 136–38
Standing Pine, 58
Starvation, 8, 33–34, 55, 64
Stereotypes, vii, 28–29, 125, 130
Stickball, 90, 136, 140, 145, 147
Storytelling, xi, 2, 33, 62–63, 90, 93–94, 101–2, 105, 108, 112, 129, 147
Subsistence, 84–85, 122
Substance abuse, 162–63; alcoholism, xxv, 14, 69, 77, 122; methamphetamine, 162
Swanton, John, 170

Tecumseh, xxv, 20–21
Termination and relocation, xxviii, 44–46, 56–57, 153; Choctaw Nation of Oklahoma Termination Act, xxviii
Tingle, Timmy, 112
Tomfulla, 116–17
Trail of Broken Treaties, xxviii
Trail Where We Cried, xii, 32–34, 63, 90, 93, 110, 112, 151
Treaties: Between the Choctaw and Chickasaw Nations, xxvi; Treaty of Doak's Stand (1820), xxv, 25–27; Treaty of 1825, xxv; Treaty of 1866, xv, xxvi, 85; Treaty of Dancing Rabbit Creek, xxvi, xxix, 16, 31–33, 35, 51, 54, 85, 106, 147; Treaty of Fort Adams, xxiv, 47; Treaty of Fort Confederation, xxiv, 17; Treaty of Fort St. Stephens, xxv, 22; Treaty of Hoe Buckintoopa, xxiv, 18; Treaty of Hopewell, xxiv,

12; Treaty of Mount Dexter, xxiv, 18–19; Treaty of Nogales, xxiv; Treaty of Paris, xxiv; Treaty of San Ildefonso, xxiv, 12

Treaty negotiations: U.S. fraud, duplicity, xvii, xxiv, xxvi, xxvii, 15–17, 18–19, 21, 31–32, 35, 38–39, 51, 54, 85, 88, 106–7, 152, 154, 165

Tuscaloosa, 7

Unemployment, 56, 155, 162, 164–66

Washington, Billy, 126
Washington, George, 19

Wells, Samuel J., 170
Wheeler-Howard Act, xxvii, 56 (Indian Reorganization Act)
White invaders, xxv–xxvi, 2, 7–8, 12, 14, 17, 19, 21, 34–35, 52, 85, 88
Wilkinson, Charles F., 170
Wilson, Gene, 132
Witches, 63, 102
Worldview, xiii, xvii, xix–xx, 61–64, 66, 69, 87–89, 111, 126, 133, 146, 148
Wright, Allen, 70, 130

York, Jake, 106–7
York, Solomon, 106–7

About the Author

DONNA L. AKERS, PH.D., is an enrolled citizen of the Choctaw Nation of Oklahoma, and an associate professor of Native American History and Culture at the University of Nebraska, Lincoln. Dr. Akers's book *Living in the Land of Death: The Choctaw Nation, 1830–1860,* an Oklahoma Book Award finalist, presents a history of the Choctaw people's struggle to survive dispossession after arriving in Indian Territory (Oklahoma) from their ancient homelands in Mississippi. She is currently finishing a book manuscript entitled *Genocide in America: The Destruction of Native Nations and People by the United States Government and Citizens.* One of Dr. Akers's journal articles "Removing the Heart of the Choctaw People: Indian 'Removal' from a Native Perspective" has been reprinted in four different collections and is cited as an example of how Native American oral sources should be used to counter Eurocentric scholarship.

Dr. Akers currently lives in Lincoln, Nebraska, with her two children and two canine friends.